When I consider Alvin Plantinga's monumental contributions in such fields as religious epistemology and the metaphysics of modality, it is hard for me to imagine doing my work as a theologian without those contributions. And when I recall the first time I read his Advice, I remember how challenged I was by it to be a more faithful and more rigorous theologian. So I find these fine essays not only interesting but also very helpful—not only as they echo and celebrate his work but also as they extend and sometimes challenge it.

–**Tom McCall**, Timothy C. and Julie M. Tennent Chair of Theology
Asbury Theological Seminary

Woznicki has put together a fine collection of (nearly) two-dozen clear, crisp, and thoughtful essays—both celebrating and critiquing Alvin Plantinga's advice to Christian philosophers of some forty years ago, while offering insightful and timely advice to Christian philosophers who find themselves navigating the new and challenging environment of the first quarter of the 21st century. Inspirational and edifying.

–**Hud Hudson**, Professor of Philosophy
Western Washington University

This volume offers a rich range of reflections, from scholars at different career stages and across denominational lines. Though I have thought and conversed about this topic for many years, I encountered several fresh and wise reflections that caused me to think anew. This is a wonderful compilation.

–**Tim O'Connor**, Mahlon Powell Professor of Philosophy
Indiana University

Advice to Christian Philosophers
Reflections on the Past and Future of Christian Philosophy

Edited by Christopher Woznicki

HANOVER PRESS

Published by Hanover Press

a division of the London Lyceum Inc.

Printed in the United States of America

©The London Lyceum 2024

All rights reserved. No part of this publication may be reproduced, stored in a retrieval system, or transmitted, in any form or by any means, without the prior permission in writing of The London Lyceum, or as expressly permitted by law, by license, or under terms agreed with the appropriate reproduction rights organization.

Hanover Press publishes material that is consistent with the Nicene and Apostles' Creed and the orthodox Protestant confessional tradition.

Scripture quotations, unless otherwise noted, are from the English Standard Version (ESV).

Email: contact@thelondonlyceum.com

Website: www.thelondonlyceum.com; www.hanoverpress.com

Paperback ISBN: 979-8-9881179-5-7

eBook ISBN: 979-8-9881179-7-1

Editorial: Christopher Woznicki

Cover Design: David Fassett

Typesetting: Jordan L. Steffaniak

Library of Congress Control Number: 2024919314

To Mr. Richards,

who introduced me to philosophy in 12th grade

&

Neil Johnson, Joel Enyart, Dave Cox, and Michael Yearley,

pastors who encouraged or supported my philosophical

endeavors.

HANOVER PRESS ANALYTIC AND SYSTEMATIC THEOLOGY EDITORIAL BOARD

Christopher Woznicki, Senior Editor (Fuller Theological Seminary)
Tim Pickavance, Biola University
J. T. Turner, Anderson University
Joshua Lee Harris, The King's University
Matthew Young, Elon University
Philip Bunn, Covenant College
Joel Chopp, Asbury Theological Seminary
Daniel Houck, Calvary Hill Baptist Church
James Arcadi, All Souls Anglican
Rafael Bello, Oklahoma Baptist University
Jared Oliphint, Central Piedmont Community College
Joseph Dunne, Ivywood Classical Academy, University of Michigan—Dearborn
Christy Thornton, The Summit Church
Michael Preciado, Faith OPC
Mark Dickson, University of Connecticut
Jason Allen, Life Connection Church

Hanover Press *Advice* Series

The Hanover Press *Advice* series of books are edited volumes in service to future Christian academics, intellectuals, and pastors. They include contributions from the very best and brightest Christian thinkers that are broadly committed to orthodox Christianity as exemplified in the Apostles' and Nicene Creed. Hanover Press is especially committed to resourcing Protestants and encouraging confessional Protestant theology and philosophy. However, Hanover Press is firstly committed to resourcing Christians. Therefore, the nature of the *Advice* series is to include a wide range of contributors that hold to various beliefs that are occasionally at odds with orthodox Protestantism. We find this to be stimulating to virtuous thinking that prioritizes the theological virtues of faith, hope, and love.

The advice offered in these works ranges from personal reflections to traditional academic arguments. Every style serves a unique purpose to inspire Christians to pursue virtue and intellectual rigor. Many people who eventually become academics or remain involved in academic work reflect on the road they've traveled and wish they had been given advice along the way. The *Advice* series gives these academics a chance to share this advice for a younger generation. However, no matter one's stage of life, the advice shared will prove stimulating and encouraging.

Jordan L. Steffaniak
Publisher

Contents

Preface — 1

1. Advice to Christian Philosophers — 3
Alvin Plantinga

2. A Lesson from Divine Hiddenness
or, Pave Your Own Way — 25
Charity Anderson

3. Christian Philosophy as a Helping Ministry — 31
Michael W. Austin

4. Advice Well-Taken — 37
William Lane Craig

5. From Justin Martyr to Alvin Plantinga and Back Again:
Advice from the First Christian Philosopher — 43
Edward Feser

6. A Glance Back and a Long Look Forward — 53
Gregory E. Ganssle

7. Advice for Christian Philosophers:
Reflections on the Changes in Landscape — 61
Marina F. Garner

8. The Christian (Public) Philosopher as a Border-Walker — 67
Paul M. Gould

9. Context Collapse, Ideological Capture,
and Winsome Non-Violence — 77
Adam Green

10. On the Moral and Intellectual Habitus
of the Christian Philosopher — 88
Ross D. Inman

11. Plantinga's Manifesto: Sparking a Revolution   97
J. P. Moreland

12. Philosophy as Christian Service   109
Dolores G. Morris

13. Reconstructing Advice to Christian Philosophers   118
Meghan D. Page

14. Al's Advice, Emphasis Shifted   129
Timothy J. Pawl

15. Advice from a Road   140
Tim Pickavance

16. The Makings of a Great Philosopher:
Advice for the Next Generation of Christian Philosophers   148
Joshua Rasmussen

17. Advice to Pentecostal Philosophers Redux:
A More Confessionally Determinate Philosophy   157
Yoon Shin

18. "Advice to Christian Philosophers" Forty Years On   168
Peter van Inwagen

19. Stick to the Point   181
Thomas M. Ward

20. The Acorn and the Tree: Plantinga's "Advice
to Christian Philosophers" (Or, How to Take Your Own Advice)   192
Greg Welty

21. A Plea to Christian Philosophers:
From One Who Cares About Philosophy but is Not One of You   207
Christopher Woznicki

22. Broadening Plantinga's Advice   218
Eric T. Yang

23. Christian Philosophers Facing the Non-Christian World   227
Linda Zagzebski

PREFACE

The word vocation is a rich one, having to address the wholeness of life, the range of relationships and responsibilities. Work, yes, but also families, neighbors, and citizenship, locally and globally—all of this and more is seen as vocation, that to which I am called as a human being, living my life before the face of God. It is never the same word as occupation, just as calling is never the same word as career. Sometimes, by grace, the words and the realities they represent do overlap, even significantly; sometimes in the incompleteness of life in a fallen world, there is not much overlap at all. - Steven Garber[1]

Is philosophy a vocation—a thing to which some are called—or is it merely an occupation—something which a few fortunate people do to occupy their working days? I imagine that there are some who might classify it as a third thing: a hobby that scratches one's intellectual curiosity. Though I'd venture to guess that if you are reading this book, it is likely because you are seeking wisdom for how to carry out this vocation or occupation that you find yourself in. Regardless of whether philosophy is a vocation or an occupation Christians will want to seek out what it looks like to be faithful to God in the midst of it. What faithfulness to God as a philosopher looks like will look different based on a number of factors, for example:

- Her personal history
- Her testimony
- The environment she grew up in
- The sort of institution she finds herself doing philosophy in
- Her relationship to the church

The contributors to this volume reflect the variety of differences listed above, and more. The authors come from diverse backgrounds: male and female, Protestant and Roman Catholic, vocational academics and vocational ministers, those who primarily work on philosophy of religion

---
1. Steven Garber, *Visions of Vocation* (InterVarsity Press, 2014), 11.

and those who do not, philosophers from different parts of the globe, etc. What brings them together, however, is the conviction that being a Christian who is a philosopher comes with certain responsibilities to God and neighbor. Not all of these authors will agree *what* those responsibilities are or *how* we best ought to serve our neighbors. Nevertheless, they agree *that* there are certain qualities and actions that Christian philosophers should embody. They offer—given their own perspectives and histories—advice to Christian philosophers. Some pieces of advice are more technical, while others are more reflective, even devotional in nature. In some ways this reflects the diversity of thought present in the Christian philosophical community.

My hope for this volume is threefold. First, that those who are in the beginning stages of philosophy—as a vocation, an occupation, or part of one's education—will find guidance for how to do philosophy as disciples of Jesus. Second, I hope that those who are in the thick of things as philosophers will find encouragement; whether it's encouragement for how to remain faithful to Jesus as a philosopher or how to rethink their vocation or occupation. Finally, I hope that those who are not philosophers—perhaps pastors, theologians, or interested lay people who've given little thought to philosophy—will grow in their appreciation of how this ancient discipline we call philosophy relates to the Christian life.

Students are often told in their *Intro to Philosophy* class that "philosophy" means "love of wisdom." May you, as the reader, grow as a lover of wisdom. The wisdom that you seek might be found in the words of those who have come before you, e.g. Alvin Plantinga's essay, "Advice to Christian Philosophers." This essay which was published forty years ago not only served as a call to action for a generation of philosophers, it also acts as the main point of interaction for the essays in this book. The wisdom that you seek might come from voices who are slightly ahead of you on this philosophical journey or it might come from your peers. I pray that the one in whom all the treasures of wisdom and knowledge are hidden (Col 2:3) may grant you the wisdom necessary to discern what advice is pertinent to your own station in life.

Christopher Woznicki
August 2024

1

ADVICE TO CHRISTIAN PHILOSOPHERS

Alvin Plantinga

Calvin University

NB: This is a reprinted version of Alvin Plantinga, "Advice to Christian Philosophers," Faith and Philosophy 1 (1984): 253–271. It appears with the permission of The Society of Christian Philosophers. It is reproduced in its original form except for changes to formatting.

1. Introduction

Christianity, these days, and in our part of the world, is on the move. There are many signs pointing in this direction: the growth of Christian schools, of the serious conservative Christian denominations, the furor over prayer in public schools, the creationism/evolution controversy, and others.

There is also powerful evidence for this contention in philosophy. Thirty or thirty-five years ago, the public temper of mainline establishment philosophy in the English speaking world was deeply non-Christian. Few establishment philosophers were Christian; even fewer were willing to admit in public that they were, and still fewer thought of their being Christian as making a real difference to their practice as philosophers. The most popular question of philosophical theology, at that time, was not whether Christianity or theism is *true;* the question, instead, was whether it even *makes sense* to *say* that there is such a person as God. According to the logical positivism then running riot, the sentence "there is such a person as God" literally makes no sense; it is disguised nonsense; it altogether fails to express a thought or a proposition. The central question wasn't whether theism is *true*, it was whether there *is* such a thing as theism—a genuine factual claim that is either true or false—at *all*. But things have changed. There are now many more Christians and many more unabashed Christians in the professional mainstream of American philosophical life. For example, the foundation of the Society for Christian Philosophers, an organization to promote fellowship and exchange of ideas among Christian philosophers, is both an evidence and a consequence of that fact. Founded some six years ago, it is now a thriving organization with regional meetings in every part of the country; its members are deeply involved in American professional philosophical life. So Christianity is on the move, and on the move in philosophy, as well as in other areas of intellectual life.

But even if Christianity is on the move, it has taken only a few brief steps; and it is marching through largely alien territory. For the intellectual culture of our day is for the most part profoundly nontheistic and hence non-Christian—more than that, it is anti-theistic. Most of the so-called human sciences, much of the non-human sciences, most of non-scientific intellectual endeavor and even a good bit of allegedly Christian theology is animated by a spirit wholly foreign to that of Christian theism. I don't have the space here to elaborate and develop this point; but I don't have to, for it is familiar to you all. To return to philosophy: most of the major philosophy departments in America have next to nothing to offer the student intent on coming to see how to be a Christian in philosophy—how to assess and develop the bearing of Christianity on matters of current philosophical concern, and how to think about those philosophical matters of interest to the Christian community. In the typical graduate philosophy department there will be little more, along these lines, than a course in philosophy of religion in which it is suggested that the evidence for the existence of God—the classical theistic proofs, say—is at least counterbalanced by the evidence against the existence of God—the problem of evil, perhaps; and it may then be added that the wisest course, in view of such maxims as Ockham's Razor, is to dispense with the whole idea of God, at least for philosophical purposes.

My aim, in this talk, is to give some advice to philosophers who are Christians. And although my advice is directed specifically to Christian philosophers, it is relevant to all philosophers who believe in God, whether Christian, Jewish or Moslem. I propose to give some advice to the Christian or theistic philosophical community: some advice relevant to the situation in which in fact we find ourselves. "Who are you," you say, "to give the rest of us advice?" That's a good question. I shall deal with it as one properly deals with good questions to which one doesn't know the answer: I shall ignore it. My counsel can be summed up on two connected suggestions, along with a codicil. First, Christian philosophers and Christian intellectuals generally must display more autonomy—more independence of the rest of the philosophical world. Second, Christian philosophers must display more integrity—integrity in the sense of integral wholeness, or oneness, or unity, being all of one piece. Perhaps 'integrality' would be the better word here. And necessary to these two is a third: Christian courage, or boldness, or strength, or perhaps Christian self-confidence. We Christian philosophers must display more faith, more trust in the Lord; we must put on the whole armor of God. Let me explain in a brief and preliminary way what I have in mind; then I shall go on to consider some examples in more detail.

Consider a Christian college student—from Grand Rapids, Michigan, say, or Arkadelphia, Arkansas—who decides philosophy is the subject for her. Naturally enough, she will go to graduate school to learn how to become a philosopher. Perhaps she goes to Princeton, or Berkeley, or Pittsburgh, or Arizona; it doesn't much matter which. There she learns how philosophy is presently practiced. The burning questions of the day are such topics as the new theory of reference; the realism/anti-realism controversy; the problems with probability; Quine's claims about the radical indeterminacy of translation; Rawls on justice; the causal theory of knowledge; Gettier problems; the artificial intelligence model for the understanding of what it is to be a person; the question of the ontological status of unobservable entities in science; whether there is genuine objectivity in science or anywhere else; whether mathematics can be reduced to set theory and whether abstract entities generally—numbers, propositions, properties—can be, as we quaintly say, "dispensed with"; whether possible worlds are abstract or concrete; whether our assertions are best seen as mere moves in a language game or as attempts to state the sober truth about the world; whether the rational egoist can be shown to be irrational, and all the rest. It is then natural for her, after she gets her PhD, to continue to think about and work on these topics. And it is natural, furthermore, for her to work on them in the way she was taught to, thinking about them in the light of the assumptions made by her mentors and in terms of currently accepted ideas as to what a philosopher should start from or take for granted, what requires argument and defense, and what a satisfying philosophical explanation or a proper resolution to a philosophical question is like. She will be uneasy about departing widely from these topics and assumptions, feeling instinctively that any such departures are at best marginally respectable. Philosophy is a social enterprise; and our standards and assumptions—the parameters within which we practice our craft—are set by our mentors and by the great contemporary centers of philosophy.

From one point of view this is natural and proper; from another, however, it is profoundly unsatisfactory. The questions I mentioned are important and interesting. Christian philosophers, however, are the philosophers of the Christian community; and it is part of their task as *Christian* philosophers to serve the Christian community. But the Christian community has its own questions, its own concerns, its own topics for investigation, its own agenda and its own research program. Christian philosophers ought not merely take their inspiration from what's going on at Princeton or Berkeley or Harvard, attractive and scintillating as that may be; for perhaps those questions and topics are not the ones, or not the only ones, they should be thinking about as the philosophers of the Christian community. There are other philosophical topics the Christian community must work at, and other topics the Christian community must work at philosophically. And obviously, Christian philosophers are the ones who must do the philosophical work involved. If they devote their best efforts to the topics fashionable in the non-Christian philosophical world, they will neglect a crucial and central part of their task as Christian philosophers. What is needed here is more independence, more autonomy with respect to the projects and concerns of the non-theistic philosophical world.

But something else is at least as important here. Suppose the student I mentioned above goes to Harvard; she studies with Willard van Orman Quine. She finds herself attracted to Quine's programs and procedures: his radical empiricism, his allegiance to natural science, his inclination towards behaviorism, his uncompromising naturalism, and his taste for desert landscapes and ontological parsimony. It would be wholly natural for her to become totally involved in these projects and programs, to come to think of fruitful and worthwhile philosophy as substantially circumscribed by them. Of course she will note certain tensions between her Christian belief and her way of practicing philosophy; and she may then bend her efforts to putting the two together, to harmonizing them. She may devote her time and energy to seeing how one might understand or reinterpret Christian belief in such a way as to be palatable to the Quinian. One philosopher I know, embarking on just such a project, suggested that Christians should think of God as a *set* (Quine is prepared to countenance sets): the set of all true propositions, perhaps, or the set of right actions, or the union of those sets, or perhaps their Cartesian product. This is understandable; but it is also profoundly misdirected. Quine is a marvelously gifted philosopher: a subtle, original and powerful philosophical force. But his fundamental commitments, his fundamental projects and concerns, are wholly different from those of the Christian community—wholly different and, in- deed, antithetical to them. And the result of attempting to graft Christian thought onto his basic view of the world will be at best an unintegral *pastiche*; at worst it will seriously compromise, or distort, or trivialize the claims of Christian theism. What is needed here is more wholeness, more integrality.

So the Christian philosopher has his own topics and projects to think about; and when he thinks about the topics of current concern in the broader philosophical world, he will think about them in his own way, which may be a *different* way. He may have to reject certain currently fashionable assumptions about the philosophic enterprise—he may have to reject widely accepted assumptions as to what are the proper starting points and procedures for philosophical endeavor. And—and this is crucially important—the Christian philosopher has a perfect right to the point of view and pre-philosophical assumptions he brings to philosophic work; the fact that these are not widely shared outside the Christian or theistic community is interesting but fundamentally irrelevant. I can best explain what I mean by way of example; so I shall descend from the level of lofty generality to specific examples.

2. Theism and Verifiability

First, the dreaded "Verifiability Criterion of Meaning." During the palmy days of logical positivism, some thirty or forty years ago, the positivists claimed that most of the sentences Christians characteristically utter—"God loves us," for example, or "God created the heavens and the earth"—don't even have the grace to be false; they are, said the positivists, literally meaningless. It is not that they express *false* propositions; they don't express any propositions at all. Like that lovely line from *Alice in Wonderland*, "T'was brillig, and the slithy toves did gyre and gymbol in the wabe," they say nothing false, but only because they say nothing at all; they are "cognitively meaningless," to use the positivist's charming phrase. The sorts of things theists and others had been saying for centuries, they said, were now shown to be without sense; we theists had all been the victims, it seems, of a cruel hoax—perpetrated, perhaps, by ambitious priests and foisted upon us by our own credulous natures.

Now if this is true, it is indeed important. How had the positivists come by this startling piece of intelligence? They inferred it from the

Verifiability Criterion of Meaning, which said, roughly, that a sentence is meaningful only if either it is analytic, or its truth or falsehood can be determined by empirical or scientific investigation—by the methods of the empirical sciences. On these grounds not only theism and theology, but most of traditional metaphysics and philosophy and much else besides was declared nonsense, without any literal sense at all. Some positivists conceded that metaphysics and theology, though strictly meaningless, might still have a certain limited value. Carnap, for example, thought they might be a kind of *music*. It isn't known whether he expected theology and metaphysics to supplant Bach and Mozart, or even Wagner; I myself, however, think they could nicely supersede *rock*. Hegel could take the place of The Talking Heads; Immanuel Kant could replace The Beach Boys; and instead of The Grateful Dead we could have, say, Arthur Schopenhauer.

Positivism had a delicious air of being *avant garde* and with-it; and many philosophers found it extremely attractive. Furthermore, many who didn't endorse it nonetheless entertained it with great hospitality as at the least extremely plausible. As a consequence many philosophers—both Christians and non-Christians— saw here a real challenge and an important danger to Christianity: "The main danger to theism today," said J. J. C. Smart in 1955, "comes from people who want to say that 'God exists' and 'God does not exist' are equally absurd." In 1955 *New Essays in Philosophical Theology* appeared, a volume of essays that was to set the tone and topics for philosophy of religion for the next decade or more; and most of this volume was given over to a discussion of the impact of Verificationism on theism. Many philosophically inclined Christians were disturbed and perplexed and felt deeply threatened; could it really be true that linguistic philosophers had somehow discovered that the Christian's most cherished convictions were, in fact, just meaningless? There was a great deal of anxious hand wringing among philosophers, either themselves theists or sympathetic to theism. Some suggested, in the face of positivistic onslaught, that the thing for the Christian community to do was to fold up its tents and silently slink away, admitting that the verifiability criterion was probably true. Others conceded that strictly speaking, theism really *is* nonsense, but is *important* nonsense. Still others suggested that the sentences in question should be reinterpreted in such a way as not to give offense to the positivists; someone seriously suggested, for example, that Christians resolve, henceforth, to use the sentence "God exists" to mean "some men and women have had, and all may have, experiences called 'meeting God'"; he added that when we say "God created the world from nothing" what we should mean is "everything we call 'material' can be used in such a way that it contributes to the well-being of men." In a different context but the same spirit, Rudolph Bultmann embarked upon his program of demythologizing Christianity. Traditional supernaturalistic Christian belief, he said, is "impossible in this age of electric light and the wireless." (One can perhaps imagine an earlier village skeptic taking a similar view of, say, the tallow candle and the printing press, or perhaps the pine torch and the papyrus scroll.)

By now, of course, Verificationism has retreated into the obscurity it so richly deserves; but the moral remains. This hand wringing and those attempts to accommodate the positivist were wholly inappropriate. I realize that hindsight is clearer than foresight and I do not recount this bit of recent intellectual history in order to be critical of my elders or to claim that we are wiser than our fathers: what I want to point out is that we can *learn* something from the whole nasty incident. For Christian philosophers should have adopted a quite different attitude towards positivism and its verifiability criterion. What they should have said to the positivists is: "Your criterion is mistaken: for such statements as 'God loves us' and 'God created the heavens and the earth' are clearly meaningful; so if they aren't verifiable in your sense, then it is false that all and only statements verifiable in that sense are meaningful." What was needed here was less accommodation to current fashion and more Christian self-confidence: Christian theism is true; if Christian theism is true, then the verifiability criterion is false; so the verifiability criterion is false. Of course, if the verificationists had given cogent *arguments* for their criterion, from premises that had some legitimate claim on Christian or theistic thinkers, then perhaps there would have been a problem here for the Christian philosopher; then we would have been obliged either to agree that Christian theism is cognitively meaningless, or else revise or reject those premises. But the Verificationists never gave any cogent arguments; indeed, they seldom gave any arguments at all. Some simply trumpeted this principle as a great discovery, and when challenged, repeated it loudly and slowly; but why should *that* disturb anyone? Others proposed it as a *definition*—a definition of the term "meaningful." Now of course the positivists had a right to use this term in any way they chose; it's a free country. But how could their decision to use that term in a particular way show anything so momentous as that all those who took themselves to be believers in God were wholly deluded? If I propose to use the term 'Democrat' to mean 'unmitigated scoundrel,' would it follow that Democrats everywhere should hang their heads in shame? And my point, to repeat myself, is that Christian philosophers should have displayed more integrity, more independence, less readiness to trim their sails to the prevailing philosophical winds of doctrine, and more Christian self-confidence.

3. Theism and Theory of Knowledge

I can best approach my second example by indirection. Many philosophers have claimed to find a serious problem for theism in the existence of *evil,* or of the amount and kinds of evil we do in fact find. Many who claim to find a problem here for theists have urged the *deductive argument from evil:* they have claimed that the existence of an omnipotent, omniscient, and wholly good God is *logically incompatible* with the presence of evil in the world—a presence conceded and indeed insisted upon by Christian theists. For their part, theists have argued that there is no inconsistency here. I think the present consensus, even among those who urge some form of the argument from evil, is that the deductive form of the argument from evil is unsuccessful.

More recently, philosophers have claimed that the existence of God, while perhaps not actually *inconsistent* with the existence of the amount and kinds of evil we do in fact find, is at any rate *unlikely* or *improbable* with respect to it; that is, the probability of the existence of God with respect to the evil we find, is less than the probability, with respect to that same evidence, that there is no God—no omnipotent, omniscient and wholly good Creator. Hence the existence of God is improbable with respect to what we know. But if theistic belief *is* improbable with respect to what we know, then, so goes the claim, it is irrational or in any event intellectually second rate to accept it.

Now suppose we briefly examine this claim. The objector holds that

1) God is the omnipotent, omniscient and wholly good creator of the world

is improbable or unlikely with respect to

2) There are 10^{13} turps of evil

(where the *turp* is the basic unit of evil).

I've argued elsewhere[1] that enormous difficulties beset the claim that (1) is unlikely or improbable given (2). Call that response "the low road reply." Here I want to pursue what I shall call the *high road* reply. Suppose we stipulate, for purposes of argument, that (1) *is,* in fact, improbable on (2).

---

1. Alvin Plantinga, "The Probabilistic Argument from Evil," *Philosophical Studies* 35 (1979): 1–53.

Let's agree that it is unlikely, given the existence of 10^{13} turps of evil, that the world has been created by a God who is perfect in power, knowledge and goodness. What is supposed to follow from that? How is that to be construed as an objection to theistic belief? How does the objector's argument go from there? It doesn't follow, of course, that theism is false. Nor does it follow that one who accepts both (1) and (2) (and let's add, recognizes that (1) is improbable with respect to (2)) has an irrational system of beliefs or is in any way guilty of noetic impropriety; obviously there might be pairs of propositions A and B, such that we *know* both A and B, despite the fact that A is improbable on B. I might know, for example, both that Feike is a Frisian and 9 out of 10 Frisians can't swim, and also that Feike can swim; then I am obviously within my intellectual rights in accepting both these propositions, even though the latter is improbable with respect to the former. So even if it were a fact that (1) is improbable with respect to (2), that fact, so far, wouldn't be of much consequence. How, therefore, can this objection be developed?

Presumably what the objector means to hold is that (1) is improbable, not just on (2) but on some appropriate body of *total evidence*—perhaps all the evidence the theist has, or perhaps the body of evidence he is rationally obliged to have. The objector must be supposing that the theist has a relevant body of total evidence here, a body of evidence that includes (2); and his claim is that (1) is improbable with respect to this relevant body of total evidence. Suppose we say that T_s is the relevant body of total evidence for a given theist T; and suppose we agree that a belief is rationally acceptable for him only if it is not improbable with respect to T_s. Now what sorts of propositions are to be found in T_s? Perhaps the propositions he *knows* to be true, or perhaps the largest subset of his beliefs that he can rationally accept without evidence from other propositions, or perhaps the propositions he knows *immediately—knows*, but does not know on the basis of other propositions. However exactly we characterize this set T_s, the question I mean to press is this: why can't belief in God be itself a member of T_s? Perhaps for the theist—for many theists, at any rate—belief in God is a member of T_s, in which case it obviously won't be improbable with respect to T_s. Perhaps the theist has a right to *start from* belief in God, taking that proposition to be one of the ones probability with respect to which determines the rational propriety of *other* beliefs he holds. But if so, then the Christian *philosopher* is entirely within his rights in starting from belief in God to his philosophizing. He has a right to take the existence of God for granted and go on from there in his philosophical work—just as other philosophers take for granted the existence of the past, say, or of other persons, or the basic claims of contemporary physics.

And this leads me to my point here. Many Christian philosophers appear to think of themselves qua philosophers as engaged with the atheist and agnostic philosopher in a common search for the correct philosophical position *vis a vis* the question whether there is such a person as God. Of course the Christian philosopher will have his own private conviction on the point; he will believe, of course, that indeed there is such a person as God. But he will think, or be inclined to think, or half inclined to think that as a *philosopher* he has no right to this position unless he is able to show that it follows from, or is probable, or justified with respect to premises accepted by all parties to the discussion—theist, agnostic and atheist alike. Furthermore, he will be half inclined to think he has no right, as a philosopher, to positions that presuppose the existence of God, if he can't show that belief to be justified in this way. What I want to urge is that the Christian philosophical community ought *not* to think of itself as engaged in this common effort to determine the probability or philosophical plausibility of belief in God. The Christian philosopher quite properly *starts from* the existence of God, and presupposes it in philosophical work, whether or not he can show it to be probable or plausible with respect to premises accepted by all philosophers, or most philosophers, or most philosophers at the great contemporary centers of philosophy.

Taking it for granted, for example, that there is such a person as God and that we are indeed within our epistemic rights (are in that sense justified) in believing that there is, the Christian epistemologist might ask what it is that confers justification here: by virtue of what is the theist justified? Perhaps there are several sensible responses. One answer he might give and try to develop is that of John Calvin (and before him, of the Augustinian, Anselmian, Bonaventurian tradition of the middle ages): God, said Calvin, has implanted in humankind a tendency or nisus or disposition to believe in him:

> "There is within the human mind, and indeed by natural instinct, an awareness of divinity." This we take to beyond controversy. To prevent anyone from taking refuge in the pretense of ignorance, God himself has implanted in all men a certain understanding of his divine majesty.... Therefore, since from the beginning of the world there has been no region, no city, in short, no household, that could do without religion, there lies in this a tacit confession of a sense of deity inscribed in the hearts of all.[2]

---

2. John Calvin, *Institutes of the Christian Religion*, trans. Ford Lewis Battles (Philadelphia: Westminister Press, 1960). 1.3.43-44.

Calvin's claim, then, is that God has so created us that we have by nature a strong tendency or inclination or disposition towards belief in him. Although this disposition to believe in God has been in part smothered or suppressed by *sin,* it is nevertheless universally present. And it is triggered or actuated by widely realized conditions:

> Lest anyone, then, be excluded from access to happiness, he not only sowed in men's minds that seed of religion of which we have spoken, but revealed himself and daily disclosed himself in the whole workmanship of the universe. As, a consequence, men cannot open their eyes without being compelled to see him (p. 51).

Like Kant, Calvin is especially impressed in this connection, by the marvelous compages of the starry heavens above:

> Even the common folk and the most untutored, who have been taught only by the aid of the eyes, cannot be unaware of the excellence of divine art, for it reveals itself in this innumerable and yet distinct and well-ordered variety of the heavenly host (p. 52).

And now what Calvin says suggests that one who accedes to this tendency and in these circumstances accepts the belief that God has created the world—perhaps upon beholding the starry heavens, or the splendid majesty of the mountains, or the intricate, articulate beauty of a tiny flower—is quite as rational and quite as justified as one who believes that he sees a tree upon having that characteristic being-appeared-to-treely kind of experience.

No doubt this suggestion won't convince the skeptic; taken as an attempt to convince the skeptic it is circular. My point is just this: the Christian has his own questions to answer, and his own projects; these projects may not mesh with those of the skeptical or unbelieving philosopher. He has his own questions and his own starting point in investigating these questions. Of course, I don't mean to suggest that the Christian philosopher must accept Calvin's answer to the question I mentioned above; but I do say it is entirely fitting for him to give to this question an answer that presupposes precisely that of which the skeptic is skeptical—even if this skepticism is nearly unanimous in most of the prestigious philosophy departments of our day. The Christian philosopher does indeed have a responsibility to the philosophical world at large; but his fundamental responsibility is to the Christian community, and finally to God.

Again, a Christian philosopher may be interested in the relation between faith and reason, and faith and knowledge: granted that we hold some things by faith and know other things; granted that we believe that there is such a person as God and that this belief is true; do we also *know* that God exists? Do we accept this belief by faith or by reason? A theist may be inclined towards a *reliabilist* theory of knowledge; he may be inclined to think that a true belief constitutes knowledge if it is produced by a reliable belief producing mechanism. (There are hard problems here, but suppose for now we ignore them.) If the theist thinks God has created us with the *sensus divinitatis* Calvin speaks of, he will hold that indeed there is a reliable belief producing mechanism that produces theistic belief; he will thus hold that we *know* that God exists. One who follows Calvin here will also hold that a capacity to apprehend God's existence is as much part of our natural noetic or intellectual equipment as is the capacity to apprehend truths of logic, perceptual truths, truths about the past, and truths about other minds. Belief in the existence of God is then in the same boat as belief in truths of logic, other minds, the past, and perceptual objects; in each case God has so constructed us that in the right circumstances we acquire the belief in question. But then the belief that there is such a person as God is as much among the deliverances of our natural noetic faculties as are those other beliefs. Hence we *know* that there is such a person as God, and don't merely believe it; and it isn't by *faith* that we apprehend the existence of God, but by reason; and this whether or not any of the classical theistic arguments is successful.

Now my point is not that Christian philosophers must follow Calvin here. My point is that the Christian philosopher has a right (I should say a duty) to work at his own projects—projects set by the beliefs of the Christian community of which he is a part. The Christian philosophical community must work out the answers to *its* questions; and both the questions and the appropriate ways of working out their answers may presuppose beliefs rejected at most of the leading centers of philosophy. But the Christian is proceeding quite properly in starting from these beliefs, even if they are so rejected. He is under no obligation to confine his research projects to those pursued at those centers, or to pursue his own projects on the basis of the assumptions that prevail there.

Perhaps I can clarify what I want to say by contrasting it with a wholly different view. According to the theologian David Tracy,

> In fact the modern Christian theologian cannot ethically do other than challenge the traditional self-understanding of the theologian. He no longer sees his task as a simple defense of or even as an orthodox reinterpretation of traditional belief. Rather, he finds that his ethical commitment to the morality of scientific knowledge forces him to assume a critical posture towards his own and his tradition's beliefs. In principle, the fundamental loyalty

of the theologian quo theologian is to that morality of scientific knowledge which he shares with his colleagues, the philosophers, historians and social sciences. No more than they can he allow his own—or his tradition's—beliefs to serve as warrants for his arguments. In fact, in all properly theological inquiry, the analysis should be characterized by those same ethical stances of autonomous judgment, critical judgment and properly skeptical hard-mindedness that characterizes analysis in other fields.[3]

Furthermore, this "morality of scientific knowledge insists that each inquirer start with the present methods and knowledge of the field in question, unless one has evidence of the same logical type for rejecting those methods and that knowledge," Still further, "for tire new scientific morality, one's fundamental loyalty as an analyst of any and all cognitive claims is solely to those methodological procedures which the particular scientific community in question has developed" (6).

I say *caveat lector.* I'm prepared to bet that this "new scientific morality" is like the Holy Roman Empire: it is neither new nor scientific nor morally obligatory. Furthermore the "new scientific morality" looks to me to be monumentally inauspicious as a stance for a Christian theologian, modem or otherwise. Even if there were a set of methodological procedures held in common by most philosophers, historians and social scientists, or most secular philosophers, historians, and social scientists, why should a Christian theologian give ultimate allegiance to them rather than, say, to God, or to the fundamental truths of Christianity? Tracy's suggestion as to how Christian theologians should proceed seems at best wholly unpromising. Of course I am only a philosopher, not a modern theologian; no doubt I am venturing beyond my depths. So I don't presume to speak for modem theologians; but however things stand for them, the modern Christian *philosopher* has a perfect right, as a philosopher, to start from his belief in God. He has a right to assume it, take it for granted, in his philosophical work—whether or not he can convince his unbelieving colleagues either that this belief is true or that it is sanctioned by those "methodological procedures" Tracy mentions.

And the Christian philosophical community ought to get on with the philosophical questions of importance to the Christian community. It ought to get on with the project of exploring and developing the implications of Christian theism for the whole range of questions philosophers ask and answer. It ought to do this whether or not it can convince the philosophical community at large either that there really is

---

3. David Tracy, *Blessed Rage for Order* (Seabury, 1978), 7

such a person as God, or that it is rational or reasonable to believe that there is. Perhaps the Christian philosopher *can* convince the skeptic or the unbelieving philosopher that indeed there is such a person as God. Perhaps this is possible in at least some instances. In other instances, of course, it may be impossible; even if the skeptic in fact accepts premises from which theistic belief follows by argument forms he also accepts, he may, when apprised of this situation, give up those premises rather than his unbelief. (In this way it is possible to reduce someone from knowledge to ignorance by giving him an argument he sees to be valid from premises he knows to be true.)

But whether or not this is possible, the Christian philosopher has other fish to fry and other questions to think about. Of course he must listen to, understand, and learn from the broader philosophical community and he must take his place in it; but his work as a philosopher is not circumscribed by what either the skeptic or the rest of the philosophical world thinks of theism. Justifying or trying to justify theistic belief in the eyes of the broader philosophical community is not the only task of the Christian philosophical community; perhaps it isn't even among its most important tasks. Philosophy is a communal enterprise. The Christian philosopher who looks exclusively to the philosophical world at large, who thinks of himself as belonging primarily to *that* world, runs a two-fold risk. He may neglect an essential part of his task as a Christian philosopher; and he may find himself adopting principles and procedures that don't comport well with his beliefs as a Christian. What is needed, once more, is autonomy and integrality.

4. Theism and Persons

My third example has to do with philosophical anthropology: how should we think about human persons? What sorts of things, fundamentally, *are* they? What is it to be a person, what is it to be a *human* person, and how shall we think about personhood? How, in particular, should Christians, Christian philosophers, think about these things? The first point to note is that on the Christian scheme of things, *God* is the premier person, the first and chief exemplar of personhood. God, furthermore, has created man in his own image; we men and women are image bearers of God, and the properties most important for an understanding of our personhood are properties we share with him. How we think about God, then, will have an immediate and direct bearing on how we think about humankind. Of course we learn much about ourselves from other sources—from everyday observation, from introspection and self-observation, from scientific investigation and the like. But it is also perfectly proper to start from what we know as Christians. It is not the case that rationality, or proper philosophical method, or intellectual responsibility, or the new scientific morality, or whatever, require that we start from beliefs we share with everyone else—what common sense and current science teach, e.g.—and attempt to reason to or justify those beliefs we hold as Christians. In trying to give a satisfying philosophical account of some area or phenomenon, we may properly appeal, in our account or explanation, to anything else we already rationally believe—whether it be current science or Christian doctrine.

Let me proceed again to specific examples. There is a fundamental watershed, in philosophical anthropology, between those who think of human beings as *free*—free in the libertarian sense—and those who espouse determinism. According to determinists, every human action is a consequence of initial conditions outside our control by way of causal laws that are also outside our control. Sometimes underlying this claim is a picture of the universe as a vast machine where, at any rate at the macroscopic level, all events, including human actions, are determined by previous events and causal laws. On this view every action I have in fact performed was such that it wasn't within my power to refrain from performing it; and if, on a given occasion I did *not* perform a given action, then it wasn't then within my power to perform it. If I now raise my arm, then, on the view in question, it wasn't within my power just then not to raise it. Now the Christian thinker has a stake in this controversy just by virtue of being a Christian. For she will no doubt believe that God holds us human beings responsible for much of what we do—responsible, and thus properly subject to praise or blame, approval or disapproval. But how can I be responsible for my actions, if it was never within my power to perform any action I didn't in fact perform, and never within my power to refrain from performing any I did perform? If my actions are thus determined, then I am not rightly or justly held accountable for them; but God does nothing improper or unjust, and he holds me accountable for some of my actions; hence it is not the case that all of my actions are thus determined. The Christian has an initially strong reason to reject the claim that all of our actions are causally determined—a reason much stronger than the meager and anemic arguments the determinist can muster on the other side. Of course if there *were* powerful arguments on the other side, then there might be a problem here. But there aren't; so there isn't.

Now the determinist may reply that freedom and causal determinism are, contrary to initial appearances, in fact compatible. He may argue that my being free with respect to an action I performed at a time t, for example, doesn't entail that it was then within my power to refrain *from performing it*, but only something weaker—perhaps something like *if I had chosen not to perform it, I would not have performed it*. Indeed, the clearheaded compatibilist will go further. He will maintain, not merely that freedom is *compatible* with determinism, but that freedom *requires* determinism. He will hold with Hume that the proposition *S is free with respect to action A* or *S does A freely* entails that *S* is causally determined with respect to *A*—that there are causal laws and antecedent conditions that together entail either that *S* performs *A* or that *S* does not perform *A*. And he will back up this claim by insisting that if *S* is not thus determined with respect to *A*, then it's merely a matter of *chance*—due, perhaps, to quantum effects in *S*'s brain—that *S* does *A*. But if it is just a matter of chance that *S* does *A*, then either S doesn't really do *A* at all, or at any rate S is not responsible for doing *A*. If *S*'s doing *A* is just a matter of chance, then S's doing *A* is something that just *happens* to him; but then it is not really the case that he *performs A*—at any rate it is not the case that he is *responsible* for performing *A*. And hence freedom, in the sense that is required for responsibility, itself requires determinism.

But the Christian thinker will find this claim monumentally implausible. Presumably the determinist means to hold that what he says characterizes actions generally, not just those of human beings. He will hold that it is a *necessary* truth that if an agent isn't caused to perform an action then it is a mere matter of chance that the agent in question performs the action in question. From a Christian perspective, however, this is wholly incredible. For God performs actions, and performs free actions; and surely it is not the case that there are causal laws and antecedent conditions outside his control that determine what he does. On the contrary: God is the author of the causal laws that do in fact obtain; indeed, perhaps the best way to think of these causal laws is as records of the ways in which God ordinarily treats the beings he has created. But of course it is not simply a matter of *chance* that God does what he does—creates and upholds the world, let's say, and offers redemption and renewal to his children. So a Christian philosopher has an extremely good reason for rejected this premise, along with the determinism and compatibilism it supports.

What is really at stake in this discussion is the notion of agent causation: the notion of a person as an ultimate source of action. According to the friends of agent causation, some events are caused, not by other events, but by substances, objects—typically personal agents. And at least since the time of David Hume, the idea of agent causation has been languishing. It is fair to say, I think, that most contemporary philosophers who work in this area either reject agent causation outright or are at the least extremely suspicious of it. They see causation as a relation among *events;* they can understand how one event can cause another event, or how events of one kind can cause events of another kind. But the idea of a *person,* say, causing an event, seems to them unintelligible, unless it can be analyzed, somehow, in terms of event causation. It is this devotion to event causation, of course, that explains the claim that if you perform an action but are not caused to do so, then your performing that action is a matter of chance. For if I hold that all causation in ultimately event causation, then I will suppose that if you perform an action but are not caused to do so by previous events, then your performing that action isn't caused at all and is therefore a mere matter of chance. The devotee of event causation, furthermore, will perhaps argue for his position as follows. If such agents as persons cause effects that take place in the physical world—my body's moving in a certain way, for example—then these effects must ultimately be caused by volitions or un*dertakings—which,* apparently, are immaterial, unphysical events. He will then claim that the idea of an immaterial event's having causal efficacy in the physical world is puzzling or dubious or worse.

But a Christian philosopher will find this argument unimpressive and this devotion to event causation uncongenial. As for the argument, the Christian already and independently believes that acts of volition have causal efficacy; he believes indeed, that the physical universe owes its very existence to just such volitional acts—God's undertaking to create it. And as for the devotion to event causation, the Christian will be, initially, at any rate, strongly inclined to reject the idea that event causation is primary and agent causation to be explained in terms of it. For he believes that God does and has done many things: he has created the world; he sustains it in being; he communicates with his children. But it is extraordinarily hard to see how these truths can be analyzed in terms of causal relations among events. What events could possibly cause God's creating the world or his undertaking to create the world? God himself institutes or establishes the causal laws that do in fact hold; how, then, can we see all the events constituted by his actions as related to causal laws to earlier events? How could it be that propositions ascribing actions to him are to be explained in terms of event causation?

Some theistic thinkers have noted this problem and reacted by soft pedaling God's causal activity, or by impetuously following Kant in declaring that it is of a wholly different order from that in which we engage, an order beyond our comprehension. I believe this is the wrong response. Why should a Christian philosopher join in the general obeisance to event causation? It is not as if there are cogent *arguments* here. The real force behind this claim is a certain philosophical way of looking at persons and the world; but this view has no initial plausibility from a Christian perspective and no compelling argument in its favor.

So on all these disputed points in philosophical anthropology the theist will have a strong initial predilection for resolving the dispute in one way rather than another. He will be inclined to reject compatibilism, to hold that event causation (if indeed there is such a thing) is to be explained in terms of agent causation, to reject the idea that if an event isn't caused by other events then its occurrence is a matter of chance, and to reject the idea that events in the physical world can't be caused by an agent's undertaking to do something. And my point here is this. The Christian philosopher is within his right in holding these positions, whether or not he can convince the rest of a philosophical world and whatever the current philosophical consensus is, if there is a consensus. But isn't such an appeal to God and his properties, in this philosophical context, a shameless appeal to a *deus ex machina*? Surely not. "Philosophy," as Hegel once exclaimed in a rare fit of lucidity, "is thinking things over." Philosophy is in large part a clarification, systematization, articulation, relating and deepening of pre-philosophical opinion. We come to philosophy with a range of opinions about the world and humankind and the place of the latter in the former; and in philosophy we think about these matters, systematically articulate our views, put together and relate our views on diverse topics, and deepen our views by finding unexpected interconnections and by discovering and answering unanticipated questions. Of course we may come to change our minds by virtue of philosophical endeavor; we may discover incompatibilities or other infelicities. But we come to philosophy with pre-philosophical opinions; we can do no other. And the point is: the Christian has as much right to his pre- philosophical opinions as others have to theirs. He needn't try first to 'prove' them from propositions accepted by, say, the bulk of the non-Christian philosophical community; and if they are widely rejected as naive, or pre-scientific, or primitive, or unworthy of "man come of age," that is nothing whatever against them. Of course if there were genuine and substantial arguments against them from premises that have some legitimate claim on the Christian philosopher, then he would have a problem; he would have to make some kind of change somewhere. But in the absence of such arguments—and the absence of such arguments is evident—the Christian philosophical community, quite properly starts, in philosophy, from what it believes.

But this means that the Christian philosophical community need not devote all of its efforts to attempting to refute opposing claims and or to arguing for its own claims, in each case from premises accepted by the bulk of the philosophical community at large. It ought to do this, indeed, but it ought to do more. For if it does only this, it will neglect a pressing philosophical task: systematizing, deepening, clarifying Christian thought on these topics. So here again: my plea is for the Christian philosopher, the Christian philosophical community, to display, first, more independence and autonomy: we needn't take as our research projects just those projects that currently enjoy widespread popularity; we have our own questions to think about. Secondly, we must display more integrity. We must not automatically assimilate what is current or fashionable or popular by way of philosophical opinion and procedures; for much of it comports ill with Christian ways of thinking. And finally, we must display more Christian self-confidence or courage or boldness. We have a perfect right to our pre-philosophical views: why, therefore, should we be intimidated by what the rest of the philosophical world thinks plausible or implausible?

These, then, are my examples; I could have chosen others. In ethics, for example: perhaps the chief theoretical concern, from the theistic perspective, is the question how are right and wrong, good and bad, duty, permission and obligation related to God and to his will and to his creative activity? This question doesn't arise, naturally enough, from a nontheistic perspective; and so, naturally enough, nontheist ethicists do not address it. But it is perhaps the most important question for a Christian ethicist to tackle. I have already spoken about epistemology; let me mention another example from this area. Epistemologists sometimes worry about the confluence or lack thereof of epistemic *justification,* on the one hand, and *truth,* or *reliability,* on the other. Suppose we do the best that can be expected of us, noetically speaking; suppose we do our intellectual duties and satisfy our intellectual obligations: what guarantee is there that in so doing we shall arrive at the truth? Is there even any reason for supposing that if we thus satisfy our obligations, we shall have a better chance of arriving at the truth than if we brazenly flout them? And where do these intellectual obligations come from? How does it happen that we have them? Here the theist has, if not a clear set of answers, at any rate clear suggestions towards a set of answers. Another example: creative antirealism is presently popular among philosophers; this is the view that it is human behavior— in particular, human thought and language—that is somehow responsible for the fundamental structure of the world and for the fundamental kinds of entities there are. From a theistic point of view, however, universal creative anti-realism is at best a mere impertinence, a piece of laughable bravado. For *God,* of course, owes neither his existence nor his properties to us and our ways of thinking; the truth is just the reverse. And so far as the created universe is concerned, while it indeed owes its existence and character to activity on the part of a person, that person is certainly not a *human* person.

One final example, this time from philosophy of mathematics. Many who think about *sets* and their nature are inclined to accept the following ideas. First, no set is a member of itself. Second, whereas a property has its extension contingently, a set has *its* membership essentially. This means that no set could have existed if one of its members had not, and that no set could have had fewer or different members from the ones it in fact has. It means, furthermore, that sets are contingent beings; if Ronald Reagan had not existed, then his unit set would not have existed. And thirdly, sets form a sort of iterated structure: at the first level there are sets whose members are non-sets, at the second level sets whose members are non-sets or first level sets; at the third level, sets whose members are non-sets or sets of the first two levels, and so on. Many are also inclined, with Georg Cantor, to regard sets as *collections*—*as* objects whose existence is dependent upon a certain sort of intellectual activity—a collecting or "thinking together" as Cantor put it. If sets were collections of this sort, that would explain their displaying the first three features I mentioned. But if the collecting or thinking together had to be done by *human* thinkers, or any finite thinkers, there wouldn't be nearly enough sets—not nearly as many as we think in fact there are. From a theistic point of view, the natural conclusion is that sets owe their existence to *God's* thinking things together. The natural explanation of those three features is just that sets are indeed collections—collections collected by God; they are or result from God's thinking things together. This idea may not be popular at contemporary centers of set theoretical activity; but that is neither here nor there. Christians, theists, ought to understand sets from a *Christian* and *theistic* point of view. What they believe as theists affords a resource for understanding sets not available to the non-theist; and why shouldn't they employ it? Perhaps here we *could* proceed without appealing to what we believe as theists; but why *should* we, if these beliefs are useful and explanatory? I could probably get home this evening by hopping on one leg; and conceivably I could climb Devil's Tower with my feet tied together. But why should I want to?

The Christian or theistic philosopher, therefore, has his own way of working at his craft. In some cases there are items on his agenda—pressing items—not to be found on the agenda of the non-theistic philosophical community. In others, items that are currently fashionable appear of relatively minor interest from a Christian perspective. In still others, the theist will reject common assumptions and views about how to start, how to proceed, and what constitutes a good or satisfying answer. In still others the Christian will take for granted and will start from assumptions and premises rejected by the philosophical community at large. Of course I don't mean for a moment to suggest that Christian philosophers have nothing to learn from their non-Christian and non-theist colleagues: that would be a piece of foolish arrogance, utterly belied by the facts of the matter. Nor do I mean to suggest that Christian philosophers should retreat into their own isolated enclave, having as little as possible to do with non-theistic philosophers. Of course not! Christians have much to learn and much of enormous importance to learn by way of dialogue and discussion with their non-theistic colleagues. Christian philosophers must be intimately involved in the professional life of the philosophical community at large, both because of what they can learn and because of what they can contribute. Furthermore, while Christian philosophers need not and ought not to see themselves as involved, for example, in a common effort to determine whether there is such a person as God, we are all, theist and non-theist alike, engaged in the common human project of understanding ourselves and the world in which we find ourselves. If the Christian philosophical community is doing its job properly, it will be engaged in a complicated, many-sided dialectical discussion, making its own contribution to that common human project. It must pay careful attention to other contributions; it must gain a deep understanding of them; it must learn what it can from them and it must take unbelief with profound seriousness.

All of this is true and all of this is important; but none of it runs counter to what I have been saying. Philosophy is many things. I said earlier that it is a matter of systematizing, developing and deepening one's pre-philosophical opinions. It is that; but it is also an arena for the articulation and interplay of commitments and allegiances fundamentally religious in nature; it is an expression of deep and fundamental perspectives, ways of viewing ourselves and the world and God. The Christian philosophical community, by virtue of being Christian, is committed to a broad but specific way of looking at humankind and the world and God. Among its most important and pressing projects are systematizing, deepening, exploring, articulating this perspective, and exploring its bearing on the rest of what we think and do. But then the Christian philosophical community has its own agenda; it need not and should not automatically take its projects from the list of those currently in favor at the leading contemporary centers of philosophy. Furthermore, Christian philosophers must be wary about assimilating or accepting presently popular philosophical ideas and procedures; for many of these have roots that are deeply anti-Christian. And finally the Christian philosophical community has a right to its perspectives; it is under no obligation first to show that this perspective is plausible with respect to what is taken for granted by all philosophers, or most philosophers, or the leading philosophers of our day.

In sum, we who are Christians and propose to be philosophers must not rest content with being philosophers who happen, incidentally, to be Christians; we must strive to be Christian philosophers. We must therefore pursue our projects with integrity, independence, and Christian boldness.[4]

---

[4]. Delivered November 4, 1983, as the author's inaugural address as the John A. O'Brien Professor of Philosophy at the University of Notre Dame.

2

A LESSON FROM DIVINE HIDDENNESS OR, PAVE YOUR OWN WAY

Charity Anderson

Baylor University

When I was in graduate school, it was common to receive two pieces of advice with respect to research in philosophy of religion. First, that one ought not to write one's dissertation on a topic in philosophy of religion. The idea being that the best way to proceed is to establish one's career in a mainstream area of philosophy, get tenure, and then turn one's attention to philosophy of religion. This was often, though not always, coupled with a general—if slightly reductionist—picture of philosophy of religion according to which the way to do philosophy of religion is to take an idea from 'mainstream' philosophy, whether it be metaphysics, epistemology, etc., and apply it to a religious topic. While some good philosophy of religion has been produced by following this strategy—and I myself followed this advice for the most part early in my career—I now think this strategy proves too limiting. Or so as I shall suggest. The advice to steer clear of publishing in philosophy of religion pre-tenure may still be excellent practical advice—I don't mean to underestimate the difficult state of the job market. Here I wish to simultaneously affirm and push back slightly against the second piece of advice—namely, that the way to proceed in philosophy of religion is to do mainstream work and then apply it to a religious topic.

A core problem with the idea that philosophy of religion simply 'falls out' of generalist philosophy is that this method can lead to insufficient attention paid to phenomena deserving of attention. On this way of thinking, progress in philosophy of religion is inevitably dependent on and directed by whatever topics are of interest in generalist philosophy. Sometimes this is a welcome dependence, but not always.[1] Sometimes it means that philosophy of religion inherits a deference to the fads of the day. But the topics of interest to epistemologists or ethicists in any given year may not be what is required for progress in philosophy of religion.

As I proceed, I offer a reflection on one subarea of philosophy of religion with the aim of pointing to a way in which I think philosophy of religion could improve. Like Plantinga's advice, the reflection is specific to a moment in time. And, as any advice of this kind, it naturally involves speaking in broad strokes and generalizations. In short, the concern is that Christian philosophers of religion should be more self-directive. When the focus is too much on "applying mainstream ideas" or—as shall be my focus here—on "taking down atheistic arguments," this can have the effect of holding philosophers of religion back from the kind of independent thinking that leads to the production of insightful work. To explain what I mean, I'll draw on an example from the recent development of the problem of divine hiddenness.

One example of stagnant thinking in philosophy of religion can be seen in how the dialectic of the argument from divine hiddenness has unfolded over the last 30 or so years. As a phenomenon, divine hiddenness is something many people wrestle with—theists as well as non-theists. But the philosophical discussion has been, with some exceptions, surprisingly narrow. The stage was set by John Schellenberg in the 1990s, after which article after article has been written in response to his core argument. There are a large number of attempts to take down a premise of the Schellenberg argument by poking a hole in it. Generally, the means by which these attempted holes are poked is via a story that purports to vindicate God in light of hiddenness by offering a reason a person who loves someone might have to be hidden from them. (I'll refer to these stories as theodicies, though I realize that the term "theodicy" is typically use more narrowly. My usage will refer to stories which vindicate God in light of evil or in light of hiddenness, and also to stories which are merely possible as well as purportedly known to be true.)

Theodicies for divine hiddenness are numerous and vary widely. To give a sense of the spectrum, I'll mentioned just two. The first involves refraining from rescuing a person whose ship has capsized because there

---

1. To emphasize, I do not mean that no progress can be made by following this strategy. On the contrary, I think it is essential that philosophers of religion be up to date on ideas in mainstream philosophy and that application of generalist research can lead to important advances in philosophy of religion. My suggestion is that philosophy of religion should not consist merely in research of this type.

are pirates nearby—thus sparing a sure death by pirates compared to the mere possibility of drowning. The second appeals to the possibility of having an online relationship with what might turn out to be a Chatbot (and hence, a relationship where you don't know whether a person is on the receiving end).[2] These stories are advanced as replies to Schellenberg and generally fall under the heading of providing and making plausible a reason God might have to be hidden.

It doesn't take much to see that these stories won't go very far with respect to providing comfort to someone who struggles with God's absence. Many of these stories are far-fetched. Of course, to be fair, the stories aren't meant to bring comfort—the aim is to take down the argument.

Something that has been overlooked, in the midst of the pirates and Chatbots, is that the argument Schellenberg put forward is extremely strong in two respects. First, it relies on a key premise about God which Schellenberg argues to be *conceptually* true. Second, the conclusion is that God does not exist—rather than that hiddenness is merely some evidence against God's existence. It's worth noting two points here. In a context such as this, theists will be motivated to provide any story—however bizarre or implausible—to resist the conclusion. And second, to show the first premise is false it suffices to produce a story which is *conceptually possible*. In this way, there is a ready explanation for why the dialectic has proceeded as it has: the argument that served to set the stage for discussion led responses in this direction.

The problem I wish to draw attention to is that very few philosophers stepped back to notice that, structurally, philosophers of religion have been rehashing a similar debate that was conducted over 50 years ago and that commonly falls under the heading "the logical problem of evil." Long associated with the work of J. L. Mackie, the logical problem of evil involves an argument (or, more specifically, an inconsistent set of premises) which leads to the conclusion that there is a kind of inconsistency between God and evil. And, as anyone who has taken an undergraduate philosophy course will have read, this version of the problem is no longer in play—it was ended by Plantinga's free will defense. The rhetoric that describes the success of Plantinga's defense is impressive: the logical problem is now "dead." While I don't disagree that a conceptually possible story (whether we call it a theodicy or a defense—again, I'm treating the terms here as equivalent) is sufficient to put an end to the so-called logical problem

---

[2]. Andrew Cullison, "Two Solutions to the Problem of Divine Hiddenness," *American Philosophical Quarterly* 47 (2010); Travis Dumsday, "Divine Hiddenness and Special Revelation," *Religious Studies* 51 (2015).

of evil, I want to draw attention to the fact that a structurally similar discussion has been going on in the literature on divine hiddenness, more or less without notice.

This is surprising, to say the least. While the received narrative about the problem of evil emphasizes that we now (where "now" began roughly with Plantinga's free will defense and the work of Rowe) are advancing and responding to an evidential version of the argument from evil, the core argument used to depict the problem of hiddenness—the Schellenberg argument—bears a strong structural resemblance to the logical problem of evil. I suggest this is one explanation for the many, many theodicies for hiddenness in print. Philosophers of religion offer a story and suggest, "this story is conceptually possible," Schellenberg says that he is not convinced, and we go around again. When the goal of inquiry on a topic is focused so narrowly on convincing one individual, it is unsurprising that discussion reaches an impasse or becomes stale.

At this point, the stage-setting leads to the reflection I wish to offer. If philosophers of religion thought about the problem of divine hiddenness on its own terms, rather than to reacting to the formulation of the problem already in play, perhaps the literature would have taken a different path. Naturally, when one approaches a new topic the responsible thing to do is to consider what has already been written on the topic. And in this case, the literature will overwhelmingly point in one direction: towards the Schellenberg argument. After all, there are basically no alternative presentations of divine hiddenness and theists need a target.

But this approach is limiting, and in this case, the deference has hindered progress in discussion. As a rule of thumb, I suggest that if we are drawn to a topic because we think it is of existential importance but when engaging with the literature it feels like we have changed the subject somewhere along the way, it is worth stepping back to ask whether we have adequately captured the idea we started with. At that point, we may need to reconsider the framing of the topic.

My suggestion is that Christian philosophers of religion engage in more constructive and less reactive thinking—even with respect to arguments *against* theism. And, even if this means we have to do the work of constructing arguments against theism. In doing so, we may find that there are more plausible presentations of topics available.

Among the benefits of this approach are an expansion of how philosophers think about divine hiddenness along a few dimensions. First, there is the potential to capture existential features of divine hiddenness that theists struggle with. The Schellenberg argument is focused on God's hiddenness from non-theists, but we might construct more formulations of the problem which focus on features of particular importance to theists.³

Second, for theists interested in defending God in the face of anti-theistic arguments, there are advantages to interacting with the most plausible formulation of the argument. Responses that offer a theodicy that we think is false, but which nevertheless defeats a "logical" version of a problem, isn't of much help if there is an evidential argument that is unaddressed.

Consider that if there is some allegedly strong evidence that your friend committed a crime and when asked about it you respond simply that it is conceptually possible that aliens replaced her for a few minutes while the crime was committed. Although you may succeed in deflecting *some* argument or other—after all, it's conceptually possible that aliens could have such powers—this misidentifies the argument you should be focused on deflecting. If that's all you say, people would reasonably think that it was tantamount to admitting that you think the evidence against your friend is strong. After all, in offering a conceptually possible story of this kind, you didn't say anything to push back against the evidential significance of the case against your friend.

There's something rather strange about offering an extremely implausible story in defense of your friend (or God) when they are accused of something. While I've suggested that the presentation of the argument from hiddenness (given its structural similarity to the logical problem of evil) can explain why theists have responded in this fashion, this doesn't explain why philosophers of religion by and large failed to step back and reconsider the setup, rather than allow others to set the terms of debate. Capturing a problem in its most plausible formulation is an important step towards forming plausible responses.

I'm not saying that theists should never respond to pre-existing arguments. But we should not allow our philosophizing to be limited by such arguments. Instead, we should feel free to rewrite the arguments when needed. Another sign that we haven't hit on the most plausible formulation is if we begin by being drawn to the topic because it strikes us as important—whether for us or those we know—and it is resolved with an easy answer. This may be a sign that we did not begin with the best formulation of the problem in mind.

---

3. I am aware that there have been several recent essays addressing the dark night of the soul, and while they in some sense offer the kind of expansion I have in mind, they haven't generally been advanced as alternative problems or presentations of divine hiddenness. See, for example, Sarah Coakley, "Divine Hiddenness or Dark Intimacy?" in *Hidden Divinity and Religious Belief*, eds. Adam Green and Eleonore Stump (Cambridge: Cambridge University Press 2016), 229-245.

While it's natural to be inclined to defend God, I think one lesson we can learn from the literature on divine hiddenness is that it is not easy to hit the right formulation of various problems. Finding the right words to capture an idea or argument can take time. It's much easier to take someone else's presentation and start poking holes than it is to start from scratch. We need to step back and ask, "does this argument get at the phenomenon I was interested in?" If not, pave the way. I expect that this will lead to new directions and insightful research.

3

CHRISTIAN PHILOSOPHY AS A HELPING MINISTRY

Michael W. Austin

Eastern Kentucky University

I never met Alvin Plantinga, but I was able to attend a talk he gave at a meeting of the American Philosophical Association many years ago. Apart from his intellectual excellence, I was impressed by his character. Another philosopher was both demeaning and a bit antagonistic toward Plantinga during the discussion portion of his talk. Plantinga had the right mix of humor, humility, and charity in his interactions. It is a mix I've tried to imitate over the ensuing years, with varying degrees of success. There was also, of course, a heavy dose of philosophical excellence. Another fond memory I have of Alvin Plantinga is from my time as a PhD student at the University of Colorado. I sent him an email with questions about his views on regeneration and the Holy Spirit as it related to his work on warranted Christian belief. He was kind and charitable enough to give me, a graduate student he'd never met, a fairly lengthy and helpful reply. From what I can gather, this was typical of him during his time as a professional philosopher. This too is something I've tried to imitate over the years, demonstrating the value of persons—especially students—by giving them my time.

    As I'm sure all readers of this volume know, Plantinga's philosophical work is careful, rigorous, and aimed at truth. He has clearly been a person who wants to learn, to understand, to *know*. And, importantly, his vast and impressive body of work has been aimed at helping others do the same, in the academy as well as more public venues. This notion of helping others via Christian philosophy is sorely needed today, and provides a clear and compelling vision of the role of Christian philosophers in the church and the world. We will return to this below.

It was in part this desire to know (and to help others know) that led me to pursue graduate studies in philosophy and my vocation as a philosopher and professor. I wasn't a philosophy major during my undergraduate years at Kansas State University, but I took several philosophy classes, mostly in social and political philosophy. I loved each one of them. After graduating, I spent a year in Hungary working for a campus ministry, then came back home and did the same for several years in the United States. It was during my time as a campus minister that I first read J. P. Moreland's book, *Scaling the Secular City*. I was fascinated by the chapter explaining and defending the Kalam Cosmological Argument. Thinking about the nature of time, eternity, causation, and how these things could be employed as an argument for the existence of God was riveting to me. Like Plantinga, I wanted to learn, to understand, to *know*. It wasn't enough for me that there were followers of Jesus who knew such things. I wanted to know them for myself, to explore them for myself, to seek out truth and wisdom for myself. This desire played a major role in my decision to pursue graduate studies in philosophy.

It was around the time I began those studies at Talbot School of Theology's MA Philosophy program that I first heard the name of Alvin Plantinga. We read his *God, Freedom, and Evil* in a seminar on the problem of evil. During my time at Colorado, we read his newly published *Warranted Christian Belief* in a philosophy of religion class. But more than these and his other works, his "Advice to Christian Philosophers" has had a deep influence on me and how I practice my vocation as a Christian philosopher. In this chapter, I first offer some reflections on the influence of Plantinga's advice on me. I then offer some advice of my own, which is in many ways an amplified form of advice from another great Christian philosopher, Dallas Willard, advice that is also based in my nearly 30 years of doing Christian philosophy.

1. The Impact of Plantinga's Advice on Me

When I decided to pursue graduate studies in philosophy, my primary professional goal was to become a philosophy professor at a secular university. I sensed a call to teach and write in that environment, with the hope that I could have a positive influence for the kingdom of God on students and faculty. In this environment, I have chosen to do some writing that is implicitly Christian, work that rests on unstated theological foundations. But a lot of my work has been explicitly Christian, motivated in part by Plantinga's conviction, stated several times throughout his paper, that Christian philosophers are the philosophers of the Christian community. We are to serve that community as philosophers. This means in part that the topics we focus on as Christian philosophers are those that are of special concern to the Christian community. This need not be our sole occupation, but it is a significant one and demands at least a significant portion of our best efforts. This is a particular kind of autonomy that Plantinga urges us to exercise in our philosophical endeavors. We are to exercise that autonomy to meet our responsibilities to the wider philosophical world, but more fundamentally to meet our responsibilities to the Christian community and ultimately to God.

I think this is right. In my experience, there are topics of special concern to Christians that are also of concern to the wider philosophical world. Some of my own work exemplifies this. At times this has been intentional. As a philosopher at a public university, I've sought out common ground in my work as well as with my colleagues and students who don't share my Christian faith. This is vital. All too often, when Christians (both philosophers and others) adopt the "culture war" paradigm of engagement, we undercut good work we could do in partnership with God for the kingdom. We become antagonistic, strident, abrasive, and at times verbally abusive, in my experience. This should not be. When there is common ground, it is wise and good to recognize it and to work that ground.

On some issues, there is no common ground to be had. Disagreement, sometimes strong disagreement, is normal and to be expected. But the vast majority of my own colleagues who don't share my Christian faith, or are part of a very different Christian tradition than mine, are very gracious. I have had discussions over the years with colleagues about many philosophical, moral, religious, and political issues, including quite controversial ones, and they've nearly always been respectful. I've learned a lot from them, and I hope they've learned something from me as well. They are willing and able to talk about such issues, and to do so without ostracizing or belittling me simply because we have deep disagreements. For that, I am grateful. I know of other Christian philosophers who have had very different experiences, and have faced challenges that have not been a part of my vocational life.

Strangely, it is the disagreements I have had with other professing Christians that have been more volatile and heated. Some of my views are at odds with the views of other Christians, such as my work on Christian ethics and guns, American Christian nationalism, and my skepticism about the culture war paradigm and the associated bogeymen many conservative Christian thinkers take aim at these days, such as critical race theory, progressive Christianity, and "wokeism."[1] But such disagreement is to be expected. There is diversity of thought within Christian philosophy, just as there is within Christianity more broadly. Yet the manner in which we discuss such disagreements needs improvement, sometimes drastically so. I've learned some lessons via my missteps and sins. And I'm still growing in this, I hope.

There are important boundaries for authentically Christian philosophy, at least for me, such as the resurrection and divinity of Christ, the Trinity, and the authority of Scripture as a source of knowledge, but on so many issues there are several plausible Christian perspectives. Christian philosophers, as a group, should be exploring and examining them *together*, using the skills of our discipline. This requires humility about our own abilities and views, and humility towards others who disagree with us in good faith. Sadly, such humility is all too often in short supply.

A central focus of my research for the past 15 years or so has been the nature and value of humility.[2] My time reading, reflecting, and writing on this virtue has been personally convicting. It has also birthed in me the conviction that humility is a neglected virtue in philosophy generally, and, more problematically, in Christian philosophy in particular. In the next section, I'll expand on this and other ideas.

2. More Advice to Christian Philosophers

Early in his "Advice to Christian Philosophers," Plantinga says the following:

> "Who are you," you say, "to give the rest of us advice?" That's a good question. I shall deal with it as one properly deals with good questions to which one doesn't know the answer: I shall ignore it.[3]

The same question could easily be asked of me, and I shall follow Plantinga's example in how to deal with that question.

My first piece of advice will be unsurprising, given the focus of my own work: we must seek to cultivate the virtue of humility. I take humility to have both self-regarding elements and other-regarding elements. With

---

1. *God and Guns in America* (Eerdmans, 2020) and *American Christian Nationalism: Neither American Nor Christian* (Eerdmans, 2024).
2. *Humility and Human Flourishing: A Study in Analytic Moral Theology* (Oxford University Press, 2018); *Humility: Rediscovering the Way of Love and Life in Christ* (Eerdmans, 2024).
3. Alvin Plantinga, "Advice to Christian Philosophers," *Faith and Philosophy* 1 (1984): 254.

respect to the former, consider Romans 12:3, which says "For by the grace given me I say to every one of you: Do not think of yourself more highly than you ought, but rather think of yourself with sober judgment, in accordance with the faith God has distributed to each of you" (NIV). This can be a challenge, as the temptation to intellectual pride is ever-present for those of us who spend so much time reading, teaching, reflecting, and writing on difficult philosophical issues. We often more easily see the intellectual mistakes and carelessness present all around us, and without realizing it perhaps, we begin to elevate ourselves due to our knowledge, which has the tendency to puff up, as we know. A realization of our indebtedness to millennia of thinkers as well as those people in our lives who have helped us along the way should foster humility. Moreover, the realization that any intellectual ability or aptitude we have is a gift from God should help here as well.

The other-regarding aspect of humility, in relationship to other human beings, is captured in Philippians 2:1-11, in particular verse 4: "Let each of you look not to your own interests, but to the interests of others" (NRSVUE). Just as Jesus exemplifies (Phil 2:5-11), the humble person is disposed to put the interests of other people above their own. This might call for a sacrifice of time, effort, money, status, even what we think of as rightfully ours. But if we are imitating Christ, it is all on the altar. Humility towards others in the context of a life centered on God and a deepening union with Christ is true, good, and beautiful. It fosters genuine unity. And it is sorely needed. Progress in these dimensions of humility sets the stage for the next piece of advice I have related to our vocation and how we can serve others through it.

In his excellent book, *The Allure of Gentleness*, Dallas Willard puts into words what both he and Alvin Plantinga exemplified in practice, namely, the importance of helping others come to know things that matter.[4] We should do our work as Jesus would do it if he were in our shoes, which "means, above all, that we do it to help people, and especially those who *want* to be helped."[5] This is how Jesus did his work; we should follow his example. Christian philosophy should be thought of as a helping ministry. It should be thought of and engaged in as yet another way to love God, and love our neighbor.

What does it mean to do Christian philosophy as a helping ministry, as a form of neighbor love? It "means being humble" because "love will

---

4. Dallas Willard, *The Allure of Gentleness* (HarperCollins, 2015), 1-5. Willard is discussing apologetics, and while there are differences between Christian philosophy and Christian apologetics, everything Willard says here applies to both. I'll therefore take the liberty of applying his points to Christian philosophy.
5. Willard, *Allure of Gentleness*, 2.

purge us of any desire to win as well as of intellectual self-righteousness and contempt for the opinions and abilities of others,"[6] not to mention contempt for others themselves. We are not trying "to beat unwilling people into intellectual submission, but to be a servant of those in need."[7]

It also means that we do philosophy as "relentless servants of the *truth*."[8] We take false ideas to task wherever we find them, but not the people who hold them. As Willard says, "allegiance to truth—whatever the truth may be—permits us to stand alongside every person as honest fellow inquirers. Our attitude is therefore not one of 'us and them,' but of 'we.'"[9] Others are not our enemies in a culture war. While I reject this way of framing our relationship to culture, the best metaphor for the role of Christians in a culture war is not the soldier, rather, it is the medic. We don't inflict harm on others, but instead bring healing. We don't seek victory on the battlefield by attacking our supposed enemies, but rather bring healing in the field hospitals of the soul.

If we pursue philosophy (and the rest of our lives) not only for its own sake, but also as a means for bringing healing and redemption, then we will be able to look back on our years of service to God and his kingdom with gratitude. And perhaps, in the context of our vocations, we might hear those words all followers of the Way long to hear: "Well done, good and faithful servant."

---

6. Willard, *Allure of Gentleness*, 3.
7. Willard, *Allure of Gentleness*, 3.
8. Willard, *Allure of Gentleness*, 3.
9. Willard, *Allure of Gentleness*, 4.

4

ADVICE WELL-TAKEN

William Lane Craig

Talbot School of Theology

Other contributors to this volume can doubtless be depended on to offer analysis and philosophical reflection upon Plantinga's "Advice to Christian Philosophers." Instead, I should like to share something more of a personal memoir about the impact of Plantinga's advice upon my own philosophical career (or, as I prefer, ministry, since I view it as a calling from God).

I had completed my doctoral studies in theology at the University of Munich only one year before Plantinga delivered his epochal lecture. So I was just embarking upon a career as a Christian philosopher when I read Plantinga's advice. I had already absorbed during my undergraduate days at Wheaton College the vital importance of the integration of my faith and learning. I was, moreover, mindful of Scripture's condemnation of those who "loved the praise of men more than the praise of God" (John 12.43). And I admired the Apostle Paul for his heroic boldness in proclaiming the gospel in the face of seemingly overwhelming opposition. So Plantinga's advice met in me with a prepared heart, and his appeal for greater autonomy, integrality, and boldness on the part of Christian philosophers resonated deeply within me. I determined that I would heed Plantinga's advice and so direct my efforts as a Christian philosopher. His call for greater autonomy, integrality, and boldness among Christian philosophers thus helped to chart my path from the beginning.

Many years later, when I published my trilogy on God and time, I included the following dedication:

To
ALVIN PLANTINGA
who by his work and his life has pointed the way

That dedication signaled my indebtedness and heartfelt gratitude to Plantinga for showing us—showing *me*—how to be a Christian philosopher.

Notice that in my dedication I mentioned both his work and his life. Not only was Plantinga's philosophical work characterized by the autonomy, integrality, and boldness that he called for, but his personal life exemplified that Christian character that should be exhibited by Christian philosophers. In 1985 I participated, along with Plantinga, in a remarkable interdisciplinary conference organized by Roy Varghese in Dallas. During the course of the conference, I arranged to meet personally with Plantinga so that I could ask him several questions I had about his philosophical positions. We had just begun to talk when a staff member of the conference came to us and said, "Dr. Plantinga, the Press are here and are asking to interview you." My heart sank. But to my utter shock, Plantinga replied, "Well, tell them to go away! Tell them I'm doing something more important: we're talking philosophy." You can imagine how that made me, as a young philosopher, feel! Alvin Plantinga considered it more important to talk with me than to do a published interview!

Years later, Plantinga's gracious character was on full display at a Wheaton Philosophy conference I attended. A philosopher of no renown was assigned to deliver a comment on Plantinga's paper, and he was obviously intimidated at the prospect. Before reading his comment, he nervously expressed his apprehension. "I'm afraid Al's going to wipe the floor with me!" His ensuing critique was a tissue of obvious errors. When Plantinga rose to respond, I wondered what he was going to say. He began by turning to the commentator and addressing him by name, saying, "No one's going to wipe the floor with anybody." He paused and then added, "In fact, I feel pretty wiped out myself by your critique!" Of course, that wasn't true; but I thought to myself, "What incredible graciousness!" That's Alvin Plantinga.

But this essay is supposed to be about his advice, not his life. Since Plantinga's original address is peppered with examples, let me give a few of my own to illustrate how his advice has influenced my own work. Fresh out of my doctoral studies, I wondered what research project I ought to undertake. I chose the coherence of theism, beginning with divine omniscience, particularly divine foreknowledge of future contingents. Even though the Bible explicitly attributes foreknowledge (*prognōsis*) to God and provides numerous illustrations of God's foretelling future contingents like Judas' betrayal and Peter's threefold denial before the cock crows twice, an astonishing number of Christian philosophers have denied to God such knowledge of the future. Such unbiblical compromise betrays a lack of integrity on their part. Instead, they ought to explore, just as Plantinga has done, ways of defending the compatibility of divine foreknowledge with human freedom, as well as the metaphysical possibility of God's knowing future contingents, or at least admit that they do not know the solution. In my work I defended not only an Ockhamist solution to the problem, but even more fundamentally the Molinist doctrine of middle knowledge, which brings with it enormous theological benefits concerning divine providence, predestination, and other doctrines. Whatever one thinks of the success of my arguments, such an approach at least exhibits the integrity that Plantinga called for, whereas the denial of divine foreknowledge of future contingents does not.

After seven years, I turned my attention to the study of divine eternity, exploring God's relationship to time. I soon discovered that the philosophy of time and space is one of those areas of philosophy that requires a bold autonomy on the part of the Christian philosopher. Mainstream philosophy of time is shaped by Quine's so-called naturalized epistemology, which sees legitimate metaphysics as an extension of the natural sciences. As a result, the common, almost unquestioned, assumption among philosophers of time is that time is that quantity which is treated under that name in physics. Even many Christian philosophers writing on divine eternity acquiesce in this assumption. But the assumption is obviously wrong. If God, existing alone sans the universe, were to count down to creation, "... 3, 2, 1, *fiat lux*!" then clearly there would be a temporal sequence in his contents of consciousness wholly in the absence of any physical reality. (If it be thought that God is immutable, then just substitute angels experiencing a succession of thoughts.) I take this to be a knock-down argument against the widespread belief that time itself is a physical quantity.

In other words, Isaac Newton was right in distinguishing between time and our physical measures of time. Thus thrust into Newton's arms, I was stunned to discover that the metaphysical basis for Newton's doctrine of absolute time lay in his theism! In the *Scholium* to his *Principia Mathematica*, Newton clearly explains that because God is eternal and omnipresent, absolute time and space are concomitant effects of God's being. This stunning realization meant that the widely trumpeted destruction of absolute time by Albert Einstein's special theory of relativity is spurious. For Einstein had no way of knowing that God's absolute time does not exist. A careful reading of his early papers on relativity reveals that his rejection of absolute time, space, and motion was predicated on a verificationist epistemology that he inherited from Ernst Mach, the very sort of verificationism so roundly criticized in Plantinga's address. Verificationism has passed away, but in its place stands naturalized epistemology, which will not countenance time apart from physics. Never mind for now how the relation between time itself and physical time is to be resolved, the overriding point of the illustration is that the Christian philosopher exploring God's relationship to time must be prepared to challenge the very foundations of contemporary philosophy of time and the naturalized epistemology that underlies it.

Another illustration emerged from my subsequent study of divine aseity. Although the Bible teaches clearly that God is the sole ultimate reality, the Creator of all things other than himself, some Christian philosophers accept the reality of uncreated abstract objects, objects which, as Plantinga put it in *The Nature of Necessity*, exist just as serenely as your most robust concrete objects. The acceptance of untold infinities of infinities of uncreated abstract objects makes God's creation of the physical universe *ex nihilo* an utter triviality. Plantinga himself came to embrace a divine conceptualism concerning such putative abstract objects, as already evident in his advice to Christian philosophers. But a more fundamental challenge to Platonism is to call into question the neo-Quinean criterion of ontological commitment that allegedly requires such an ontology. There is no good reason to think, and good reasons to doubt, that we are ontologically committed to the values of variables bound by the existential quantifier or to the referents of singular terms in sentences we take to be true. Christian philosophers who countenance an ontology of uncreated objects of any sort exhibit a lack of integrality with their faith; but challenging the prevalent neo-Quineanism requires autonomy and boldness.

So much for my examples of the influence of Plantinga's advice in my own life and work! Plantinga's advice to Christian philosophers has shaped my work from the beginning and continues to do so until this day. I thank God to have been born a contemporary of this great man.

We have also been asked to share any further advice that we ourselves might have for Christian philosophers. In fact, I do have one such piece of advice. It is that we Christian philosophers give greater heed to biblical theology. Plantinga advised us to exhibit greater integrality in our work, to think about issues from a Christian point of view. But Plantinga did not discuss what determines a Christian point of view. It is the conviction of the Christian Church that our ultimate authority for Christian doctrine is the teaching of inspired Scripture. Even the authority of ecumenical councils is ultimately derivative from the final authority of Scripture. Therefore, we Christian philosophers need to put some effort into understanding and submitting to the teaching of Scripture.

I have been alarmed at the ignorance of or indifference to scriptural teaching by many Christian philosophers. As philosophical theologians at best, many of us do not seem to be greatly interested in biblical theology. Very typically, we reflect philosophically upon an issue independently of scriptural teaching, not bothering to determine what the Bible teaches about a subject.

Illustrations come all too readily to mind. Consider once more God's omniscience. In chatting with one Christian philosopher about my work on divine omniscience, I asked him, "How can Christian philosophers deny that God has foreknowledge, when the Bible explicitly states that he has foreknowledge?" He smiled and said, "Bill, you know that Christian philosophers don't care what the Bible teaches!" We both laughed, but inside I felt a certain sadness. Could it be true that Christian philosophers really do not care?

Or consider some Christian philosophers' espousal of Platonic realism about *abstracta* in contradiction to the biblical teaching that God alone is uncreated. Their attempts to reconcile their position with biblical teaching on the grounds that biblical authors did not have abstract objects in mind fails to appreciate that whatever lay in the domain of their quantifiers unknown to them, nonetheless they intended to assert that all things apart from God have been created by God, that God and God alone is an uncreated being. If we were to tell them that abstract objects are just as real as people or rocks, they would doubtless have said that they, too, must then have been created by God.

Or again, the doctrines of divine simplicity and impassibility espoused by some of us Christian philosophers are unbiblical, not merely in the sense that, say, the doctrines of divine necessity or timelessness are unbiblical, that is, not explicitly taught but nevertheless permitted by the biblical text, but in the sense that they are positively anti-biblical. The Bible teaches that God has a diversity of attributes and is multi-personal. Moreover, he is affected by his creatures in what he knows, loves, and wills. Strong doctrines of divine simplicity and impassibility are rooted historically, not in the Bible, but in neo-Platonism and represent a perversion of biblical teaching.

Or consider the doctrine of the atonement. I have found that fellow Christian philosophers who write on this subject are often woefully ignorant of biblical teaching. The typical procedure is to develop a doctrine of the atonement based upon how reconciliation is achieved between human parties to a dispute. Such a methodology is horribly distorted, not merely because of the disanalogies between the persons involved (human and divine), but even more fundamentally because the biblical doctrine of atonement is not primarily about reconciliation. Christian philosophers typically treat the atonement in the etymological sense of the term of "at one-ment" or reconciliation. But the biblical words in Hebrew and Greek for "atonement" or "to make atonement" have to do mainly with cleansing or expiation of impurity and sin. German theologians nicely mark this distinction by distinguishing between *die Sühne* and *die Versöhnung*, but in English we are not so blessed. Thus, incredibly, the work of many, if not most, Christian philosophers on the doctrine of the atonement has almost nothing to do with the biblical concept of atonement. They usually develop their atonement theories independently of biblical teaching and then turn to the Bible to find proof texts in support of their theory.

These examples illustrate an important weakness of contemporary Christian philosophy. The reason our work often lacks integrality is because we are too often ignorant of or indifferent to the teaching of Scripture. We might try to excuse our indifference on the grounds that we are not biblical scholars, after all, but philosophers. But this excuse is empty. One need not know the biblical languages in order to benefit from reading expert commentaries written by biblical scholars who do know such languages and can exegete the text for us. We just need to do our homework.

In fact, reading biblical theology can be extremely interesting for a Christian philosopher because of our training in conceptual analysis, which biblical scholars usually lack. One will sometimes find them overlooking important distinctions, e.g., between death as a consequence of sin and death as a punishment for sin or propositional faith in contrast to personal faith. Many biblical theologians do not understand the differences between anthropological dualism (which the Bible teaches) and Platonic dualism (which it does not). We can thus help one another in our common quest for an adequate worldview. But we cannot do so if we ignore our sister discipline.

In his advice to Christian philosophers Plantinga emphasized that as Christian philosophers we are to serve the Christian community. We shall be much more effective in our service to the Church if we make an effort to familiarize ourselves with biblical theology.

5

FROM JUSTIN MARTYR TO ALVIN PLANTINGA AND BACK AGAIN: ADVICE FROM THE FIRST CHRISTIAN PHILOSOPHER

Edward Feser

Pasadena City College

1. Introduction

Alvin Plantinga's 1984 essay "Advice to Christian Philosophers" has become something of a classic, given the boldness of the advice and the eminence of the one who gave it.[1] What advice would the *most* eminent Christian philosophers of the past have given us? Would it be the same as Plantinga's? It would, for example, be interesting to know what might have been said by arguably the greatest of all Christian philosophers, namely St. Thomas Aquinas.

However, despite my reputation as a staunch Thomist, Aquinas's views are not what I want to discuss here. Rather, I propose that we consider those of the very first Christian philosopher, St. Justin Martyr (albeit Aquinas would, I think, say more or less the same thing on this topic as Justin). The advice he would give is, we will see, if anything bolder still than Plantinga's, even if Plantinga's advice is in large part well-taken.

In what follows, I will first summarize the key points made by Plantinga in his famous essay. Then I will draw out from Justin's writings what I

---

1. Alvin Plantinga, "Advice to Christian Philosophers," *Faith and Philosophy* 1 (1984): 253–71. The essay was reprinted in Michael D. Beaty, ed., *Christian Theism and the Problems of Philosophy* (University of Notre Dame Press, 1990). I will be quoting from the latter.

take to be the most relevant parallel themes, so as to set the stage for a compare and contrast. We will see that Justin's position implies a partial endorsement of Plantinga's advice, though also, in part, a correction of it. I am certain that Plantinga will welcome such constructive criticism, offered as it is in the spirit of honest philosophical inquiry and Christian brotherhood—iron sharpening iron, and all that.

2. Independence, Integrity, and Courage

Plantinga was writing at a time when both metaphysically robust philosophy in general, and philosophy sympathetic to Christianity in particular, were seeing a revival in the circles of academic analytic philosophy after decades of having been relegated to the sidelines by logical positivism and related movements. Plantinga himself had, of course, contributed mightily to these revivals. In "Advice," he expresses gratification that "Christianity is on the move, and on the move in philosophy, as well as in other areas of intellectual life."[2] Still, he identifies three areas where he thinks Christian philosophers can and ought to do better. They need, he says, to show more independence, more integrity, and more courage.[3]

What he means by showing more integrity and courage is straightforward enough. Christian philosophers ought to do their philosophical work in a way that is compatible with their Christian convictions and unafraid in the face of secular hostility to those convictions. What requires more explanation is exactly what Plantinga has in mind by his first piece of advice, when he says that "Christian philosophers and Christian intellectuals generally must display more autonomy—more independence of the rest of the philosophical world."[4]

He elaborates as follows. First, the specific way Christian philosophers ought to show more independence is that they need to be less deferential to the views prevailing in mainstream secular philosophy about what counts as a respectable topic of philosophical investigation, a respectable range of opinions on philosophical topics, and a respectable way of arguing for an opinion. One way many Christian philosophers fail to show such independence, says Plantinga, is that they devote the bulk of their attention to whatever topics and controversies currently happen to dominate discussion in contemporary secular philosophy, rather than to the topics a Christian would naturally find most important. For example, they may focus on an issue like the indeterminacy of translation, scientific

---

2. Plantinga, "Advice," 15.
3. Plantinga, "Advice," 16.
4. Plantinga, "Advice," 16.

realism, or Rawls's theory of justice (some of the topics Plantinga mentions as especially fashionable at the time he was writing) rather than the philosophical questions raised by Christian doctrine.

Another way Christian philosophers fail to show sufficient independence is by being too ready to reinterpret Christian claims in terms that a secular philosopher might find acceptable. Plantinga gives the example of a Christian philosopher influenced by Quine who proposes conceiving of God as a *set* of some kind, on the grounds that Quineans are willing to admit sets into their ontology. Such a proposal really amounts to a distortion of Christian teaching rather than an articulation or defense of it. What is needed, says Plantinga, is "less accommodation to current fashion and more Christian self-confidence."[5]

But Plantinga is critical even of the suggestion that Christian claims ought or need to be defended *at all* in the face of the secular world's skepticism. He writes:

> Many Christian philosophers appear to think of themselves *qua* philosophers as engaged with the atheist and agnostic philosopher in a common search for the correct philosophical position vis à vis the question whether there is such a person as God... the Christian philosopher... will think, or be inclined to think, or half inclined to think that as a philosopher she has no right to this position unless she is able to show that it follows from, or is probable, or is justified with respect to premises accepted by all parties to the discussion—theist, agnostic and atheist alike. Furthermore, she will be half inclined to think she has no right, as a philosopher, to positions that presuppose the existence of God, if she can't show that belief to be justified in this way.[6]

In opposition to this, Plantinga says, he "want[s] to urge... that the Christian philosophical community ought *not* to think of itself as engaged in this common effort."[7] Indeed, the Christian "has a right to take the existence of God for granted and go on from there in his philosophical work."[8] For all philosophers "come to philosophy with pre-philosophical opinions; we can do no other" and "the Christian has as much right to her pre-philosophical opinions as others have to theirs."[9] Indeed, "we have a perfect right to our pre-philosophical views."[10] Hence the Christian can and ought to take belief in God as *basic*, a conviction in light of which

---

5. Plantinga, "Advice," 21.
6. Plantinga, "Advice," 23-24.
7. Plantinga, "Advice," 24.
8. Plantinga, "Advice," 23.
9. Plantinga, "Advice," 33.
10. Plantinga, "Advice," 34.

other claims are to be evaluated rather than something that itself requires justification.

Here Plantinga is deploying a certain conception of what philosophy is, and a certain conception of what knowledge of God involves. Philosophy, says Plantinga, "is a matter of systematizing, developing and deepening one's pre-philosophical opinions."[11] Expanding on this claim, he writes:

> Philosophy is in large part a clarification, systematization, articulation, relating and deepening of pre-philosophical opinion. We come to philosophy with a range of opinions about the world and humankind and the place of the latter in the former; and in philosophy we think about these matters, systematically articulate our views, put together and relate our views on diverse topics, and deepen our views by finding unexpected interconnections and by discovering and answering unanticipated questions.[12]

To be sure, he immediately goes on to allow that philosophy may lead us to change our minds, and even that it could in principle turn out that some philosophical argument could pose a problem for Christian belief. But the emphasis throughout the essay is on the notion that philosophy is the enterprise of more systematically articulating one's pre-philosophical body of beliefs rather than either criticizing or justifying them.

Where it comes to articulating one's pre-philosophical belief in God, specifically, Plantinga suggests that one way this might be done is to adopt Calvin's thesis that we know of God by way of a divinely implanted instinct.[13] He acknowledges that the skeptic will not find this plausible, and also says that he is not claiming that a Christian must agree with Calvin on this point. His emphasis, though, is on the theme that however one spells out the epistemology of theism, the Christian can—and, it seems, in Plantinga's view should—do so in a way that allows belief in God to count as a conviction for which no argument need be given. This is, of course, a well-known theme of the "Reformed epistemology" Plantinga spelled out in another work at around the same time the "Advice" essay appeared.[14]

What, then, does specifically Christian philosophy amount to for Plantinga? He characterizes it as "the project of exploring and developing the implications of Christian theism for the whole range of questions philosophers ask and answer."[15] Among the examples he offers is one drawn

---

11. Plantinga, "Advice," 36-37.
12. Plantinga, "Advice," 33.
13. Plantinga, "Advice," 24-25.
14. For example, see Alvin Plantinga, "Reason and Belief in God," in *Faith and Rationality*, eds. Alvin Plantinga and Nicholas Wolterstorff (University of Notre Dame Press, 1983).
15. Plantinga, "Advice," 28.

from set theory. He suggests that "what [Christians] believe as theists affords a resource for understanding sets not available to the nontheist," namely taking them as "collections collected by God... result[ing] from God's thinking things together."[16] It is "neither here nor there," he adds, whether most set theorists would find this plausible. In general, Plantinga says, while a Christian philosopher *might* be able to convince a secular philosopher of the truth of his theistic commitments, he need not try to do so:

> But whether or not this is possible, the Christian philosopher has other fish to fry and other questions to think about... Justifying or trying to justify theistic belief in the eyes of the broader philosophical community is not the only task of the Christian philosophical community; perhaps it isn't even among its most important tasks.[17]

To be sure, Plantinga also says that Christian philosophers "must listen to, understand, and learn from the broader philosophical community" and that they "must be intimately involved in the professional life of the philosophical community at large, both because of what they can learn and because of what they can contribute."[18] But he emphasizes once again that they "need not and ought not to see themselves as involved, for example, in a common effort to determine whether there is such a person as God."[19]

Plantinga's conception of philosophy appears to make of it a set of techniques for analyzing and systematizing a set of beliefs, whatever those beliefs happen to be. There is nothing distinctively anti-Christian or anti-theistic about it, but also nothing distinctively Christian or even theistic about it either. Hence, it seems that what he thinks Christian philosophers can learn from, and contribute to, the larger philosophical community essentially boils down to further refinements of these neutral techniques. It apparently does *not* involve anything relevant to theism or Christianity per se.

As we will see, this is deeply at odds with St. Justin's conception of Christian philosophy, and in my view it is also deeply mistaken. Plantinga insists that he "[doesn't] mean to suggest that Christian philosophers should retreat into their own isolated enclave, having as little as possible to do with nontheistic philosophers."[20] But the trouble is that he seems to think that at those times when they do leave the enclave and interact

---

16. Plantinga, "Advice," 35.
17. Plantinga, "Advice," 28.
18. Plantinga, "Advice," 28, 36.
19. Plantinga, "Advice," 36.
20. Plantinga, "Advice," 36.

with other philosophers, they should leave their distinctively theistic and Christian positions behind. He would not consign Christian *philosophers* to a ghetto, but it seems he would consign Christian *philosophy* to one. To me, and certainly to Justin Martyr, this does a disservice to both Christianity and philosophy alike. Let's turn, then, to Justin's own position.

3. Justin Martyr and Christian Philosophy

Justin was a philosopher before he was a Christian, and remained one afterward. Naturally, he saw no conflict, but that is not merely because he thought being a Christian was *consistent* with being a philosopher. Rather, he regarded Christianity as the *culmination* of sound philosophy. Even apart from the influence of Christian revelation, philosophy had, in Justin's view, naturally led the greatest thinkers to knowledge of God's existence, and of at least something of his nature. And while not all philosophers had such knowledge, that was precisely because their grasp of the nature of their enterprise was defective. In his *Dialogue with Trypho*, Justin writes:

> Philosophy is indeed one's greatest possession, and is most precious in the sight of God, to whom it alone leads us and to whom it unites us, and they in truth are holy men who have applied themselves to philosophy. But, many have failed to discover the nature of philosophy, and the reason why it was sent down to men; otherwise, there would not be Platonists, or Stoics, or Peripatetics, or Theoretics, or Pythagoreans, since this science of philosophy is always one and the same...
>
> Man cannot have prudence without philosophy and straight thinking. Thus, every man should be devoted to philosophy and should consider it the greatest and most noble pursuit; all other pursuits are only of second or third-rate value, unless they are connected with philosophy...
>
> Philosophy... is the knowledge of that which exists, and a clear understanding of the truth; and happiness is the reward of such knowledge and understanding.[21]

Clearly, Justin takes philosophy, correctly pursued, to amount to a body of knowledge, not merely a method for systematizing whatever pre-philosophical beliefs we happen to have. Indeed, it may require us to abandon such beliefs. In his *First Apology*, Justin says that "reason directs

---

21. Justin Martyr, *Dialogue with Trypho*, 2–3, in *The Fathers of the Church, Volume 6: Writings of Saint Justin Martyr*, trans. by Thomas B. Falls (Catholic University of America Press, 1948), 149, 152. Hereafter, all citations will be given as "Justin, *Dial.* 2–3 (Falls, 149, 152)."

those who are truly pious and philosophical to honour and love only what is true, declining to follow traditional opinions, if these be worthless."[22] No less clearly, he takes the content of the body of knowledge that philosophy yields, when rightly pursued, to include theism. The philosophical tradition that had the greatest influence on Justin was Middle Platonism, which contained not only ideas from Plato himself that Justin regarded as converging with Christian teaching about the divine nature, but had also appropriated the Aristotelian argument for God as the unmoved mover of the world.[23] Through philosophy, he thought, we can know that there is an uncaused, transcendent, unchangeable, eternal, non-spatial, impassible, incorruptible, ineffable creator and ruler of the natural order.[24]

By no means did Justin deny that Christian teaching afforded insight into the divine nature that the philosophers had not known. But he regarded what they *had* been able to discover as a gateway to the reception of the divine revelation given through Christ. In effect, he judged philosophy to provide what later Christian theologians would call the *praeambula fidei* or "preambles of faith." Through philosophy, we can determine that there really is a God who might reveal himself through a prophet backed by miracles. Since it is what God reveals that we then go on to accept on the basis of faith (in the sense of trust in the authority of the infallible divinity who has given the revelation), that there is a God in the first place is something that precedes faith. Divine revelation then adds to, and corrects the defects in, the philosophical knowledge about the divine nature that had set the stage for it. Philosophy and theology are thus not separate enterprises, but continuous with one another. As L. W. Barnard summarizes Justin's position:

> Justin Martyr made no clear distinction between theology and philosophy in the strict sense. There was, for him, but one wisdom, one philosophy, which had been revealed fully in and through Jesus Christ. This involved however no clear break with Greek philosophy, the best elements in which were a preparation for the Gospel.[25]

Yet even the *praeambula fidei* are in fact only half of the story of the argumentational stage-setting that must precede knowledge of divine

---

22. Justin Martyr, *First Apology*, 2, in *Ante-Nicene Fathers*, Vol. 1, eds. Alexander Roberts, James Donaldson and A. Cleveland Coxe, trans. Marcus Dods and George Reith (Christian Literature Publishing Co., 1885). Hereafter, all citations will be given as "Justin, 1 *Apol*. 2 (Dods and Reith)."
23. For detailed discussion of the Greek philosophical influences on Justin, see L. W. Barnard, *Justin Martyr: His Life and Thought* (Cambridge University Press, 1967), chapter III.
24. See Barnard, *Justin Martyr*, chapter VI, especially pp. 79-83, for discussion of what Justin thought could be known about the divine nature through philosophical arguments.
25. Barnard, *Justin*, 27.

revelation. We also need what later theologians would call the "motives of credibility." While the preambles of faith tell us that there really is in fact a God who might reveal certain truths to us, the motives of credibility gives us reasonable grounds for judging that he has in fact done so. These would include evidence that miracles really have occurred, so that the prophet through whom the miracles were worked can be judged truly to be speaking with divine authority. Justin had much to say about this, putting heavy emphasis especially on the thesis that Old Testament prophecies had been fulfilled by the details of the life and death of Christ, thus confirming that he really had taught with divine authority.

Thus, central to Justin's work as a Christian philosopher was the task of what is today called *apologetics*, which is concerned with establishing the rational credentials of the Christian religion. This fusion of the philosophical and theological enterprises is evident even in the titles of his most famous works, the *First Apology* and *Second Apology*, and in his having come to be known to history as Justin *Martyr*. Plato's famous *Apology* is about Socrates's defense of true philosophy even to the point of death. Justin's *Apologies* are about the defense of the culmination of philosophy in Christianity, also to the point of death, which he would eventually suffer because of his work. The Christian philosopher, for Justin, simultaneously emulates both Christ and Socrates in being willing to sacrifice his life for the sake of the truth.[26] Barnard writes of the earliest Christian Apologists:

> *Apologia*, or the case for the defence... was based on the magnificent defence which Socrates had made at his trial before the people of Athens in which he showed the essential rationality of his position. The Christian Apologists therefore set themselves the wider task of showing how Christianity was the embodiment of the noblest conceptions of Greek philosophy and was the truth *par excellence*...
>
> In addition to the refutation of calumnies and the presentation of Christianity as a rational faith the Apologists were also concerned with the questionings of thoughtful men.[27]

Eusebius, the Father of Church history, noted that "Justin... *in the guise of a philosopher*, preached the truth of God, and contended for the faith."[28] At the beginning of the *First Apology*, Justin addresses the emperor Antoninus Pius and the future emperors Marcus Aurelius and Lucius Verus, and appeals to the latter two precisely *as fellow philosophers* to hear out the case he makes. He aims to convince them through rational arguments appealing

---

26. Cf. *1 Apol.* 5, 46; *2 Apol.* 3, 10.
27. Barnard, *Justin*, 3.
28. *Ecclesiastical History*, IV.11, quoted in Barnard, *Justin*, 12. Emphasis added.

to "the strongest and truest evidence."[29] These arguments he hopes to be compelling to his interlocutors even though they do not initially share his convictions. He says that even though "it is not easy suddenly to change a mind possessed by ignorance," nevertheless rational considerations can be put forward "for the sake of persuading those who love the truth, knowing that it is not impossible to put ignorance to flight by presenting the truth."[30] Nor in Justin's view is this merely something the Christian philosopher *may* attempt to do, it is something he *ought* to do. "We will now offer proof," he writes, "not trusting mere assertions"; and again, "we do not make mere assertions without being able to produce proof."[31]

As Thomas Falls points out, whereas earlier Fathers of the Church addressed their writings to fellow Christians, "St. Justin is considered to be the first prominent defender of the Christian faith against non-Christians and the enemies of the Church."[32] Nor is it any accident that the first Christian philosopher would also be the first of the Fathers to address the non-Christian world, given that he saw philosophy as affording the Christian common theological and moral ground by which to be understood by that world, and methods of rational argumentation by which to convince it. Falls notes:

> [Justin] was not only the first Christian writer to apply the categories and to utilize a philosophical terminology in Christian thought, but he was also one of the first to attempt to reconcile faith with reason... In combining Plato's world of ideas with the Word-concept of the Holy Scripture, he became the originator of the philosophical exposition of the Logos.[33]

As Falls observes, Justin thus inaugurated a project that continued through Augustine and Aquinas. Writes Barnard, "speculative thought and Christian philosophy begin with Justin."[34]

4. Conclusion

Certainly Justin would warmly endorse Plantinga's call for more independence, integrity, and courage among Christian philosophers. As we have seen, he was critical of the errors some philosophers of his day had made, and he was famously devoted to refuting heretics within the Church

---

29. Justin, *1 Apol.* 30.
30. Justin, *1 Apol.* 12.
31. Justin, *1 Apol.* 30, 53.
32. Falls, Foreword to *The Fathers of the Church, Volume 6: Writings of Saint Justin Martyr*, 9.
33. Falls, *The Fathers of the Church*, 17–18.
34. Barnard, *Justin*, 26.

no less than to rebutting attacks on the Church from without. Thus, like Plantinga, he would surely urge contemporary Christian philosophers to show greater independence from the conventional wisdom among secular philosophers, and greater integrity as Christians. As to courage, Justin was attracted to Christianity in part precisely because the Christians of his day were "fearless in the face of death and of every other thing that was considered dreadful."[35] Defying the Church's persecutors, he wrote "you can kill, but not hurt us," and by his own martyrdom showed himself an exemplar of Christian courage.[36]

Yet in other respects, Justin's position was very different from Plantinga's. Plantinga's conception of philosophy emphasizes its role in systematizing whatever set of pre-philosophical beliefs one happens to have. Justin's conception of philosophy emphasizes that it is concerned first and foremost with what is actually true, and thus may require jettisoning one's pre-philosophical beliefs. Plantinga denies that Christian and non-Christian philosophers are engaged in a common project of establishing God's existence. Justin takes this project to be central to philosophy by its very nature. Plantinga rejects the idea that Christian philosophers have any obligation to provide arguments that their secular colleagues might find convincing. Justin insists that the Christian philosopher should back up his assertions with rational arguments. Plantinga regards apologetics as "not the only task of the Christian philosophical community; perhaps it isn't even among its most important tasks." Justin put apologetics at the center of his work as a Christian philosopher, and indeed invented Christian philosophy precisely as an essentially apologetic enterprise.

Needless to say, on these matters I think Plantinga is wrong and Justin is right. Indeed, I think this part of Plantinga's advice is bad and even harmful to the cause of Christianity. For, intentionally or not, it encourages a fideism which in my view threatens to make Christian teaching appear unmoored from objective reality and grounded in contingent cultural prejudices, subjective preferences, or the like. No doubt this difference of opinion reflects in part larger disagreements about the relationship between faith and reason that exist between Catholics like myself and Calvinists like Plantinga. But Justin was writing centuries before the Reformation, indeed very near the beginning of the Church. *His* views can hardly be dismissed as nothing more than the prejudices of a Thomist! And it seems to me that, in any event, the advice of the first Christian philosopher remains something contemporary Christian philosophers ought to consider very seriously.

---

35. Justin, *2 Apol.* 12, (Falls, *The Fathers of the Church*, 132).
36. Justin, *1 Apol.* 2.

6

A GLANCE BACK AND A LONG LOOK FORWARD

Gregory E. Ganssle

Talbot School of Theology

Like many others, I stumbled into philosophy through trying to answer people's questions and objections to Christianity. I never took a philosophy class as an undergraduate. I did encounter some of the models of defending the gospel with intellectual honesty. My reading was filled with people like C. S. Lewis and Francis Schaeffer. I served with Campus Crusade for Christ (now Cru) for many years on various campuses. As I attempted to share the gospel with students, I became enthralled with their objections. I was struck particularly with two kinds of thoughts. First, I wanted to develop answers to the specific questions I encountered. Second, I began to wonder how the students, mostly between eighteen and twenty-one years old, got the ideas they had. One day, I walked out of a dorm room of a convinced moral relativist, and I thought to myself, "Where did he get those ideas? He did not make them up!" After something like four years of thinking and reading, it occurred to me that I was doing philosophy. Maybe, it was time that I took a class. I enrolled in Intro to Philosophy as a twenty-five year old campus minister in a room filled mostly with first year students.

I tell my students that philosophy can be like heroin. You think you can dabble safely, but you just might get hooked. I got hooked. A few years after this first class, I was a part-time MA student at the University of Rhode Island. My main professor, Don Zeyl, introduced me to the Society of Christian Philosophers and the work of Alvin Plantinga, as well as that of Bill Alston, Nick Wolterstorff, Peter van Inwagen, Bob and Marilyn Adams, and others. I first encountered Plantinga's essay, "Advice to Christian Philosophers," around 1986. The Society of Christian Philosophers and Plantinga's essay were life-changing encounters for me. It is an honor for me to reflect after four decades on his important words to us.

Plantinga urged the community of Christian philosophers in three ways. First, he exhorted us to show more autonomy in our work. Rather than allowing contemporary philosophical interest to dictate our agendas, we should also take up the projects that are important to the Christian community. He emphasizes that there are a range of questions that are important to the church, even if they are not important to anyone else. It is the Christian philosophers that must take up these questions. Second, he encouraged us to show more integrity in our work. That is, we should pursue all of our philosophical work in light of our Christian convictions. We do not have to defend these convictions *before* we can turn to applying them to various philosophical projects. Third, Plantinga urges us to show more courage. We must entrust our work and our careers to the Lord.

Beneath Plantinga's specific advice is a fundamental commitment. A Christian philosopher has a stewardship. We have been given training and skills that make us especially fit to tackle specific tasks. And as Paul reminds us, "it is required of stewards that they be found faithful" (1 Cor 4:2). Plantinga's advice is an admonishment to faithfulness. We could say that the governing question for Christian philosophers ought to be "What does it mean to be a philosopher who follows Jesus faithfully?" Plantinga suggested it involves, at least, those qualities: autonomy, integrity, and courage.

In the forty years since his essay was published, Christian philosophy has taken Plantinga's advice. The results have been astounding. This movement of Christian philosophers has contributed to the flourishing of academic philosophy as a whole. This flourishing goes well beyond the philosophy of religion. Almost every area of philosophy has benefited from the rigorous engagement of Christians. The new field of Analytic Theology emerged largely because philosophers began to address issues that are important to the church. It has truly been an amazing story. Scholars in other disciplines have adapted Plantinga's charge to their own projects. Two generations of philosophers are benefitting from the movement that was launched by Plantinga and the other early leaders of the Society of Christian Philosophers. This amazing development gives us many things to ponder. Two items in particular come to mind.

The first item is a posture. Reflecting on all that has happened in Christian philosophy prompts a posture of deep and abiding gratitude. First, of course, gratitude to God. The movement of Christian philosophy is something that God, in his providence, accomplished. It is a privilege for all of us to participate. Second, we are prompted to gratitude to the early leaders of the Society of Christian Philosophers. Their courage and determination opened the way in academic philosophy so that our generation could follow. We must ponder how grateful we are.

The second item is a crucial question: What should we put our hands to for the *next* forty years? In 2064, two more generations of Christian philosophers will have emerged. When they look back at our time, for what will *they* be grateful? What will they wish we had pursued more faithfully? We can think about this question in relation to academic philosophy, the church in particular, and in relation to the general culture.

In order to think about this question, let's consider the parable of the soils.[1] As we know from Jesus' own explanation, the farmer sows the Word. The soils have different degrees of receptiveness to the seed. Some soil is hard. Some is rocky. Some is overgrown with thorny plants. Some is pretty good soil. The seed that falls on the good soil takes root and grows into a harvest. There is a question that Jesus did *not* ask as part of this parable, but that every person who listened to him understood. The question is: *what does the farmer do next year?* Everyone who heard Jesus knew the answer. What is the answer?

Next year, the farmer goes out *before* he sows the seed, and he chops the hard ground, he pulls out the rocks and uproots the vines. That is what the farmer does next year. The reason that everyone who heard Jesus knew this answer is that they knew about farming firsthand. Many of them spent long days in the fields chopping ground, pulling thorns and digging up rocks. I think Jesus did not ask this question because it was obvious to everyone who heard. Part of the farmer's task is to prepare the soil.

The preparation of the soil involves more than pulling out those things that prevent the seed from taking root. It involves putting things into the ground that help the seed germinate. A farmer today prepares the seed by coating it in nutrients in order to give it the best chance for growth and a good harvest. The role a faithful follower of Jesus has is more than pulling out the bad things. It includes putting in good things. We do what we can to make the soil healthy.

The question posed for the next forty years of Christian philosophy can be framed in terms of the soil metaphor. What needs to be uprooted

---

1. This parable is found in Matt 13: 3–9; Mark 4: 1–9; Luke 8:4–8.

in philosophy, or in the culture, so that the seed of the gospel will find fertile soil? What nutrients must we develop and mix throughout the soil? In hindsight, we can identify what we needed forty years ago. Plantinga and the other early members of the Society of Christian Philosophers explored many topics, but there was a focus on three crucial items. These items represent obstacles to the growth of religious belief. They were the Problem of Evil, the reasonability of belief in God, and the respectability of Christian philosophy. The first two involved philosophical issues that both had a long tradition of investigation and which affected the confidence of believers throughout the church. The third issue was an obstacle only for professional philosophers.

Plantinga himself, as well as a host of others, strategically addressed the challenge of evil and the reasonability of belief in God. The contours of these discussions have been dramatically and permanently changed. To be sure, there is still lots of work to be done in these areas, but it is no longer simply assumed that these issues decisively undermine theistic belief. The respectability of Christian philosophy was tackled mostly by example. While believing philosophers occasionally argued for Christian philosophy directly, for the most part, they simply did excellent work. The rigor and clarity of the work required thoughtful responses in the broader philosophical community. I bring up these examples as reminders. We are deeply grateful that these leaders took up these topics and pursued them with excellence. Their work paved the way for our presence in the academy.

Turning to the future, in forty years, what will Christian philosophers wish we had faithfully pursued? There are rocks in the soil that we must faithfully continue to dig out.

First, there will always be the task of articulating and defending the basic Christian story in the broader philosophical world. In each generation of philosophers, there will be many who for various reasons consider the Christian story unreasonable or false. This fact involves both perennial topics such as the problem of evil and how to articulate the reasonableness of Christian belief. Furthermore, new challenges to Christian belief will emerge in the academy, and new opportunities to commend belief in Jesus will present themselves. Good philosophy of religion will always be needed.

In addition to the continued defense of the reasonability and truth of Christianity, we also need to defend its *goodness*. Nietzsche is famous for his quip "What is now decisive against Christianity is our taste, no longer our reasons."² Nietzsche, of course, was delighted with the growing revulsion of educated people to the Christian story. Today, the notion that Christianity is bad or distasteful is a powerful deterrent from considering it on its merits. Development in this area is already emerging through discussions of the Axiology of Theism. Much more is needed. As Paul encouraged the Thessalonian church, we must "excel still more" (1 Thess 4:10).

If we drill more deeply below the soil on which the word is sown today or tomorrow or seven years from, now, we eventually get to some foundational issues that contribute to shaping the resistance or receptivity to the gospel for generations. Following David C. Mahan, we can call these issues the Fault Lines of Culture.³

The metaphor of the fault line is apropos. A fault line involves three features. First, fault lines lie deep below the topsoil. They are invisible to the casual observer. Second, a fault line is a location of dramatic movement. Tectonic plates press against each other and the foundation of the ground shifts. People notice shifts at this level only when they shake up the surface. A third feature of a fault line is that it is a location of division. The motion is in some part due to the divide. This metaphor helps us turn our attention away from the latest cultural manifestation of rejection of Christianity to the locations where the shift in terrain originates.

There are several issues that rightly count as the Fault Lines of Culture. Mahan identifies five. For Christian philosophers thinking about executing our calling faithfully for the next generations, I want to think about the Fault Line of the Self or Human Identity. Identity issues have taken center stage in our cultural conversation. Although we must provide thoughtful and charitable engagement in this conversation, we must also dig more deeply. Philosophy takes up human identity largely through ethical theory and philosophy of mind. Two trends in these areas have been helpful. First, in ethics there has been a rebirth of virtue ethics and the role of human flourishing. In contemporary times, this is often dated from Elizabeth Anscombe's paper "Modern Moral Philosophy."⁴ Since that paper came out, Aristotelian approaches have been widely developed and discussed. Christian philosophers have played a major role in this trend.

The second area is philosophy of mind. Versions of substance dualism are receiving renewed attention. These discussions have helped identify

---
2. Friedrich Nietzsche, *The Gay Science* ed., Bernard Williams, trans., Josefine Nauckhoff. *Cambridge Texts in the History of Philosophy* (Cambridge University Press, 2001): section 132.
3. David C. Mahan, *Fault Lines Workbook*, 2014.
4. G. E. M. Anscombe, "Modern Moral Philosophy," *Philosophy*, vol. 33 (1958): 1-19.

criteria for an adequate concept of the human person. Human beings are agents who act for reasons. We have an irreducible first-person perspective. These facts must be accounted for in any metaphysics of the mind. Part of preparing the soil involves challenging accounts of human nature that are inadequate. Christian philosophers are leading the way here.

How can this Fault Line be engaged faithfully? What nutrients need to go into the soil regarding the self? In the space that remains, I want to commend one long-term project. This project will have to overflow the boundaries of academic philosophy and involve a host of related disciplines. It will be a public-facing project. In summary, we need to revitalize a Christian Existential Humanism.

Each of these terms must be explained. First, we need to revitalize Humanism. Humanism places the nature, concerns, and flourishing of human beings at the center. Many people of my generation remember the popularity of *secular* humanism. The secular version of humanism argues that humanistic commitments are best established, grounded, defended, and explored within a secular framework. It was all the rage in the early eighties for evangelicals to be alarmed about secular humanism. To be honest, I was alarmed with the best of them. What the secular humanists were right about was the need for a well-grounded humanism. What they were wrong about was that a secular framework was adequate to this task.

We need a robust *Humanism*. That is, we need to explore and defend the notion of being human. There are two directions, at least, from which pressure against a robust humanism comes. First there is pressure from reductionistic accounts of being human. These accounts may be defended philosophically or scientifically. A recent example is the book *Determined* by Robert M. Sapolsky.[5] In Sapolsky's view, human beings are determined biologically, and there is not sufficient freedom to ground real moral responsibility. Morality, too, winds up being an illusion.

The other direction from which attacks come is from transhumanism. Transhumanism is a continuation of the enlightenment project of harnessing technological advances to transform human living. The editors of the *Transhumanist Reader* offer the following characterization: "Transhumanism is a class of philosophies that seeks the continued evolution of human life beyond its current human form as a result of science and technology guided by life-promoting principles and values."[6] The cultural plausibility of transhumanism arises from the fact that most naturalistic pictures of the world cannot ground a fixed human nature. In

---

5. Robert M. Sapolsky, *Determined: A Science of Life Without Free Will* (Penguin Press, 2023).
6. Max More and Natasha Vita-More, ed., *The Transhumanist Reader: Classical and Contemporary Essays on the Science, Technology, and Philosophy of the Human Future* (Wiley Blackwell, 2013): 1.

naturalistic Darwinism, for example, human beings are purely biological, and constantly developing. In the words of the apostle John, "it has not appeared as yet what we shall be" (1 John 3:2). Human nature is a moving target. Another impetus for transhumanism is the continued exponential growth in both medical and computer related technologies. These tools, epitomized by things like generative AI, seem to allow for the boundaries between current and future humanity to be transgressed at will.

The Christian vision of what it means to be human begins with our doctrine of creation. In the beginning God created the heavens and the earth. He made us in his image. Image-bearing grounds a fixed nature and an objective purpose. It is on these theological pillars that we begin to build our distinctly Christian picture of what it means to be human.

The humanism we revitalize must be *existential*. By calling for an existential humanism, I am not channeling Jean Paul Sartre. Plantinga himself argued against his foundational quip that existence precedes essence.[7] I am arguing for more of a Kierkegaardian existentialism. Kierkegaard, under the pseudonym Johannes de Silentio, bemoans the fact that he cannot understand Abraham. To understand someone is to put him under a category. For Kierkegaard, such categories are shattered by the individual self's immediate relation to the primary meaning maker of the cosmos. Thus, he asks: "Is there a teleological suspension of the ethical?" and "Is there an absolute duty to God?" The individual stands before God as an individual, and not merely as a member of a class or species.

In addition, our humanism must be existential in that it must be adequate to a particular human life. This life—the one that humanism recommends—is a good life for a particular human being. It is livable, achievable, and experientially self-justifying. What I am calling existential humanism is humanism that fits particular human beings. As we are able to articulate it and demonstrate it, we see that it is, in the words of Paul, "good, acceptable and perfect" (Rom 12:2). It is good for us. Acceptable in that it is a fitting life for a particular human being and it is perfect—not in the sense that there are no flaws in life, but in the sense that it is complete, whole, it is the flourishing life.

Lastly, our existential humanism must be *Christian*. In the context of this essay, it must demonstrate that the Christian vision of life is good for us. It is good to us. It is the best life that can be lived and it is available to us all.

---

7. Alvin Plantinga, "On Existentialism," in Alvin Plantinga, *Essays in the Metaphysics of Modality* ed. Matthew Davidson (Oxford University Press, 2003): 158–175.

All of this is a call to invest some of our time, or for some of us to invest all of our time, in exploring, rediscovering, articulating and defending a rich Christian existential humanism. We need to diagnose the subterranean movements that will inevitably cause severe shaking on the surface. We must identify the rocks and thorns related and we must dig them out, we must cultivate the soil and pour the health of a rich Christian existential humanism throughout.

We are reading this book because forty years ago a small group of philosophers took a careful look at their context and opportunities and the faithfully pursued their calling. In forty years, I pray others will say the same about our generation of Christian philosophers.[8]

---

8. I would like to thank Rick Langer and David Horner for comments on this essay.

7

ADVICE FOR CHRISTIAN PHILOSOPHERS: REFLECTIONS ON THE CHANGES IN LANDSCAPE

Marina F. Garner

Loma Linda University

The philosophical landscape of 2024 markedly differs from that of 1984. Christian philosophy has experienced significant growth since the 1980s, marked by frequent annual and bi-annual conferences and the establishment of at least four North American academic journals. Christian philosophers gained mainstream attention, appearing on television and becoming influential figures on platforms like YouTube. Christian philosophy transitioned from being championed by fringe thinkers to evolving into a robust community with its own norms and humor. How does this substantial shift impact our reading of Alvin Plantinga's seminal work, "Advice to Christian Philosophers"? I will delineate three reflections on this essay and its contemporary relevance, informed by my personal observations.

In his essay, Plantinga outlines a potential academic journey for young Christians interested in philosophy. He envisions these aspiring philosophers pursuing graduate degrees at prestigious, non-Christian universities, where they would grapple with the "burning questions of the day." Post-graduation, Plantinga suggests, these individuals may continue to explore the same topics, feeling that deviating from them is only "marginally respectable." This trajectory, he thinks, could lead to the development of Christian philosophers who either fail to adequately address the needs of the Christian community or do so in a manner overly influenced by prevailing non-Christian presuppositions or defensive postures toward Christian beliefs. While this narrative resonates with many, I want to share my own journey as a contrast to this perspective.

My passion for philosophy, particularly its relevance to Christian inquiries, began during my college years. Following a conversion experience in my teens, I pursued a major in theology at a Seventh-Day Adventist university in Brazil. As one of the few Christians, and the only practicing one, in my immediate family, I faced relentless questioning from my atheist brothers and agnostic father about the rationality of my faith. It was amidst this tumultuous period that I discovered Christian apologetics, serving as a lifeline amid the waves of doubt. Delving into this branch of Christian philosophy for two years, I eventually decided to pursue a master's degree in Philosophy of Religion, offered at Trinity Evangelical Divinity School (TEDS) at that time.

Arriving at TEDS with the anticipation of a curriculum heavily focused on arguments for God's existence or against moral relativism, I was surprised to find my perspective on Philosophy of Religion, or Christian philosophy, broaden significantly. Over those two years, I delved into debates concerning Christian ontology, theories of religious epistemology, and the dilemma of biblical and philosophical dualism versus materialism. It became apparent to me that philosophy, in its entirety, served to enrich the Christian faith, aligning with Plantinga's assertion that it clarifies, systematizes, articulates, relates, and deepens our "pre-philosophical opinion" about God's existence, Jesus's divinity, and the accuracy of biblical truths.

Most significantly, philosophy equipped me with a sophisticated language and arsenal of arguments to articulate what I believed. I observed a shift in my approach to religious debates with my family and noticed a corresponding change in their reactions.

From that point, I realized that academia was my true calling and applied to several doctoral programs, primarily seeking advisors committed to questions beneficial to the Christian community. Regrettably, I wasn't accepted into any of those programs, or if I was, the financial burden was beyond my means. Instead, I was accepted into the Religious Studies program at Boston University, specializing in philosophy of religion. Although my advisor shared my Christian faith, he encouraged me to explore beyond the confines of Christian-centric questions.

My department, too, was wary of the Christian philosophy trajectory and its accompanying presuppositions. They aimed to expose me to a diverse range of philosophical dialogues, even those I did not find to be very "philosophical" at all. I delved into Indian philosophy and Foucault,

I wrote about the philosophy of love, engaged with Neo-Aristotelian Ethics and Metaphysics (not exclusively Christian metaphysics), and even learned Arabic to be competent to read the works of Muslim philosophers in their original language. This exposure shattered my bubble, revealing the vastness of philosophy and, more specifically, philosophy of religion. This shift is evident in the topic of my dissertation: the exploration of shame as virtue and pride as vice in the works of Aristotle, Thomas Aquinas, and Abu Hamid al-Ghazali. I realized that not all philosophy directly serves Christianity, nor does it need to in order to hold intrinsic value. My journey, unlike the fictional student in Plantinga's essay, was progressive, moving from a narrow definition and scope of philosophy to a broader understanding, rather than regressive. This experience afforded me insights into the practice of Christian philosophy.

First, I learned that Christian philosophy did not need to be bound to a narrow set of questions formulated in the 1970s and 1980s. Upon perusing various Christian philosophy journals, it becomes apparent that discussions often revolve around perennial topics like the Problem of Evil, rational evidence for God's existence, God's relationship to time, and similar themes. While these debates, popularized by figures like Richard Swinburne, Alvin Plantinga, and William Lane Craig, are undeniably captivating and warrant attention, they seem to dominate our discourse to the exclusion of other inquiries. Although there are occasional deviations from these themes, they remain exceptions rather than the norm.

This tendency may have been influenced, in part, by Plantinga's exhortation in his essay to prioritize serving the Christian community with its unique questions and concerns, rather than being seduced by the fashionable topics of mainstream philosophical circles. However, I would argue that Plantinga's plea could have been more nuanced. Philosophy and Christianity share a fundamental trait: their scope extends to all facets of life. Together, they offer a lens through which virtually anything can be analyzed and understood—the sky is *not* the limit. So why do we limit ourselves to just a handful of questions?

Before college, and especially after marrying a pastor and serving several churches in southern Brazil, I observed a recurring practice within the church community. On Saturday afternoons, we held meetings exclusively for the youth. While the primary aim was to steer them away from ungodly activities performed during the weekend, there was also a strong emphasis on fostering community and enhancing biblical literacy. During these gatherings, it was customary for the pastor to solicit suggestions from the young Christians regarding topics to be discussed. Without fail, certain themes always surfaced and these were the usual suspects: 1) media, 2) dating, and 3) end-time events. Regardless of the church's location or the demographic makeup of the youth, the responses remained remarkably consistent. Faced with this predictability, my husband and I confronted a dilemma: should we simply cater to the perceived needs of our community by addressing these topics, or should we adopt a different approach? We opted for the latter. Drawing upon our seminary education, we recognized that we had insights into profound theological questions that, although unfamiliar to these young Christians, were crucial for nurturing a robust relationship with God and the church. We started addressing different, new, and fresh (to them) topics, and the youth were enthusiastic.

I see an analogous reality within Christian philosophy today. We often find ourselves grappling with the same timeless questions, and we face a choice: do we persist in seeking innovative answers to these questions, or do we venture into uncharted territory by posing different, yet equally pertinent, questions for our community? By doing so, we can initiate a whole new array of conversations and perspectives. Those pursuing training in non-Christian philosophy departments should be encouraged to introduce fresh questions and methodologies to the discourse. I am not suggesting that we abandon the foundational questions that underpin our beliefs, but only that we do not linger solely on them.

Second, I learned that Christian philosophy needn't adopt a defensive posture. Plantinga's counsel to Christian philosophers to assert more autonomy from the broader philosophical community stemmed from the reactive atmosphere of the 1980s, characterized by a surge in atheistic philosophy. With limited spaces for Christian philosophers to convene and amidst pressure to defend Christian premises using philosophical tools, Christian philosophers often dispensed much academic energy to defending the faith. However, the landscape of North American philosophy has shifted. The prevailing trends in philosophy pose little threat to core Christian beliefs, necessitating less emphasis on defense and allowing for greater integration. In fact, certain fashionable topics in non-Christian philosophy can offer valuable insights or shed light on aspects of the Christian faith, given its all-encompassing nature. Moreover, as Christian philosophers we often find ourselves in academic environments where we share similar religious convictions, creating opportunities to engage with challenging ideas that may broaden perspectives lest we remain comfortable in the high quality of our overly complicated arguments. Though the Christian projects "may not mesh with those of the skeptical or unbelieving philosopher," properly applied to the Christian context, these projects may be enlightening and provide greater depth to our faith.

Third, I learned that there is a distinction between using philosophy as a tool for deconstruction versus using it for reconstruction. One of the practices that I see Plantinga criticizing in the essay "Advice to Christian Philosophers," is that of reconceptualizing Christian theological beliefs using categories and theories that are antithetical to Christianity. This criticism remains relevant alongside the suggestion to introduce new topics, questions, and philosophical tools to Christian philosophy. The key to reconciling these perspectives lies in properly discerning the various uses of philosophical tools. The "deconstructionist" aim of philosophy, not to be confused with the deconstructivist movement spearheaded by Jacques Derrida, involves clarifying, classifying, and deepening the meaning of beliefs through philosophical questions. Conversely, the "constructivist" aim pertains to the philosophical terms, categories, systems, or theories employed to answer these questions. Engaging in Christian philosophy often entails utilizing "secular" philosophy in its deconstructivist function, but not necessarily in its constructivist role. In fact, Christian philosophers are tasked with introducing their "pre-philosophical assumptions" during the constructivist phase, as Plantinga astutely observes. He hints at this process when he suggests that a Christian philosopher "thinks about the topics of current concern in the broader philosophical world, he will think about them in his own way, which may be a different way." Rather than discarding fashionable philosophical deconstructivist questions, we should carefully consider how to undertake constructivist work that aligns with our core beliefs and values. This approach enables us to navigate the interplay between deconstruction and reconstruction within Christian philosophy effectively.

Plantinga's enduring plea to Christian philosophers to boldly and courageously engage in "systematizing, deepening, [and] clarifying Christian thought on these topics" remains profoundly relevant even four decades later. However, the context and emphasis of this advice have evolved over time. In the 1980s, the message may have been primarily about embracing one's religious presuppositions without shame and serving the cause and community with boldness and courage. While this advice still holds true, the current state of Christian philosophy suggests a need for a shift in emphasis. Given the recent history of Christian philosophy and its perceived isolation from the broader philosophical community, perhaps the emphasis should now be placed on taking ideas that are currently in vogue and using them to raise new and fresh questions. However, these questions should be courageously answered on the basis of strong Christian presuppositions. In other words, Christian philosophers should not shy away from engaging with contemporary philosophical trends but should do so while firmly grounding their responses in Christian principles. This approach allows for both innovation and fidelity to core beliefs—qualities that Plantinga has beautifully exemplified in his own work.

8

THE CHRISTIAN (PUBLIC) PHILOSOPHER AS A BORDER-WALKER

Paul M. Gould

Palm Beach Atlantic University

When Alvin Plantinga delivered the John A. O'Brien Professor of Philosophy inaugural address at the University of Notre Dame on November 4, 1983, he began with the observation that Christianity is on the move within philosophy.[1] And it was. Largely due to the influence of Plantinga, Nicholas Wolterstorff, and William Alston, theism, along with Christian theism, was being taken seriously in academic philosophy. The question of God's existence was no longer viewed as meaningless, thanks to the waning grip of logical positivism. Christianity was at least considered *possibly* true. Still, the intellectual landscape was largely and profoundly nontheistic and often anti-theistic. Within this cultural and intellectual milieu, Plantinga famously argued that Christian philosophers need to courageously exercise more autonomy from the rest of the philosophical world and more integrity or wholeness as Christians. Regarding autonomy, the idea was that Christian philosophers should feel more freedom to do philosophy from a distinctively *Christian* perspective. Regarding integrity, the ideas was that Christian philosophers should seek to integrate the deliverances of faith with the deliverances of philosophy.

In 1983 this was all excellent and needed advice. It is still good advice for those of us who are philosophers today. It's good advice for any of us, really, who find ourselves in multiple communities. We ought to seek to serve the Christian community and the broader community with integrity,

---

1. Alvin Plantinga, "Advice to Christian Philosophers," *Faith and Philosophy* 1.3 (1984): 253.

conviction, and courage. What about now, in 2024? If I were Plantinga—and of course I am not—I'd expand the advice to Christian philosophers in at least two ways.

The first expansion involves the *scope of communities* the Christian philosopher is called to serve. In 1983, Plantinga spoke of two communities in which Christian philosophers belong and serve: the philosophical community and the Christian community [Figure 1].

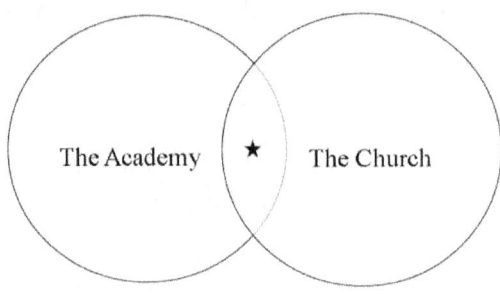

Figure 1: Plantinga's Two Communities

I'd expand that list to three: the philosophical community, the Christian community, and the wider culture [Figure 2].

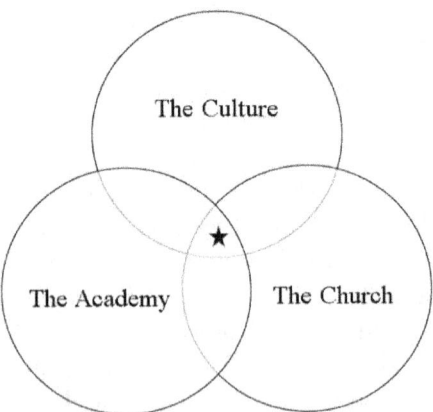

Figure 2: Gould's Three Communities

Christian philosophers inhabit and travel between three intersecting communities. We are, to borrow a metaphor from the artist Makoto

Fujimura, *border-walkers*.² In earlier times, border-walkers were "individuals who lived on the edges of their groups, going in and out of them, sometimes bringing back news to the tribe."³ This is an apt-description of the Christian philosopher. We are viewed with suspicion by most, outsiders by some, in each of these communities: the predominantly secular academy tolerates us as long as we play by the rules, much of the evangelical church views us as annoying gadflies, and the culture at large wants nothing to do with our ethics. We're misunderstood, marginalized, and maligned. But we remain, and for many of us, cheerfully and eagerly with a deep sense of calling and gratitude to God. We bring back—through our teaching and writing, podcasting and video interviews—"news" of a world full of deep beauty, mystery, and enchanted goodness.

The second expansion involves the *scope of concern* the Christian philosopher is called to address. Plantinga spoke of our calling to defending the *truth* of theism or the *rationality* of belief in God. Of course, this is part of our calling as Christian philosophers. We've picked up this call, and done quite well over the past 40 years or so, demonstrating the rationality of belief in God and the coherence of Christian doctrine. In 2004, the atheist philosopher Quentin Smith noted this groundswell of theistic philosophy in the academy, lamenting the facts that many of the leading philosophers in the various sub-disciplines in philosophy were Christians and that theism was not only taken seriously, but that theistic philosophers were now on the offensive, arguing for the rational superiority of theism over naturalism.⁴ This is all well and good. Christian philosophers have earned a place at the academic table within the university. The challenge will be saving that place without losing a sense of our identity as Christians (more on this below). But we should care about more than truth and rationality. There are also objections, prominent of late, to the goodness and beauty of Christianity. These objections come from all three communities. Thus, Christian philosophers need to address those related areas too by living a good and beautiful life and helping others see the truth, goodness, and beauty of Jesus and the gospel. This suggests a second way in which Christian philosophers are border walkers. Just as the artist walks the terrain of the beautiful and in their art helps us see reality as it is, the Christian philosophers walks the terrain of what I'll call the "sacred order" and in our philosophy help others see the connections between the sacred and the so-called mundane or everyday orders of

---

2. Makoto Fujimura, *Culture Care: Reconnecting with Beauty for Our Common Life* (InterVarsity Press, 2017), 58.
3. Fujimura, *Culture Care*, 58
4. Quentin Smith, "The Metaphilosophy of Naturalism," *Philo* 4.2 (2001): 195-215.

reality.⁵ Thus, the Christian philosopher, as a border-walker between the sacred and mundane orders, reveals the unity and connectedness of reality, helping others *understand* the sacredness of all things in Christ and *unite* with God, self, and the world for the flourishing of all [Figure 3].

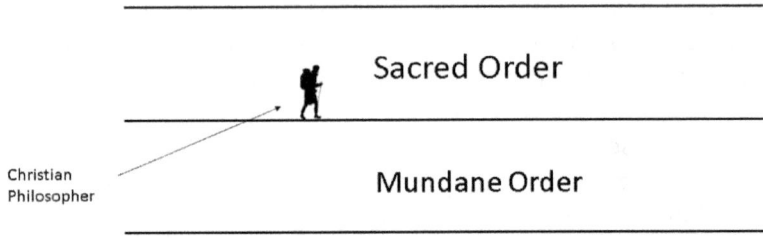

Figure 3: The Christian Philosopher as Border-Walker

In the remainder of this short essay, I shall expand the metaphor of the Christian philosopher as a border-walker by clarifying and defending two theses and issuing a warning.

1. Public-Facing Philosophy

Barry Lam distinguishes between "peer-facing" philosophy and "public-facing" philosophy.⁶ This distinction picks out our philosophical posture, which in turn, shapes the content of our philosophy. There are three possibilities: a philosopher can be wholly peer-facing, wholly public-facing, or partly peer- and partly public-facing. Consider first the wholly peer-facing philosopher. She will only write for academic presses and journals. Teaching will be viewed as secondary, perhaps even a necessary evil, since publications are most valued in the academy. She'll prize rigor, possibly at the expense of clarity, undoubtedly at the expense of accessibility. The goal in her writing and teaching is epistemic justification; she seeks to survive the reader and listener.⁷ Her research agenda will be largely driven by whatever is currently "in play" at the cutting edge of her sub-

---

5. The idea of the artists as people who walk the terrain of the beautiful is from Barbara Nicolosi, "The Artist: What Exactly is an Artist, and How Do We Shepherd Them?" in *For the Beauty of the Church*, ed. W. David O. Taylor (Baker, 2010), 113. Elsewhere I've given a more fine-grained description of the sacred order as "as *the realm of God and the enacted plan of God to create, sustain, and redeem the universe in Christ*" ["Christian Metaphysics and Platonism" in *Four Views on Christian Metaphysics*, ed. Timothy Mosteller (Cascade, 2022), 3].

6. Barry Lam "Nonfiction and Narrative Popular Philosophy," *Daily Nous* (September 7, 2020), accessed at https://dailynous.com/2020/09/07/nonfiction-narrative-popular-philosophy-guest-post-barry-lam/.

7. The idea of trying to survive the reader is from Michael Lewis, as quoted in Lam, "Nonfiction and Narrative Popular Philosophy."

specialty where new knowledge, or at least new ways of thinking about old problems, are explored. By contrast, the wholly public-facing philosopher will write for non-academic audiences, value clarity and accessibility (and perhaps but not necessarily rigor), will write or teach with other goals in mind beyond epistemic justification (such as to produce joy or inspire or educate the reader or listener), and will select research agendas and topics in light of the issues and concerns of the community she seeks to serve.[8] And of course, the philosopher that is partly peer- and partly public-facing will be a combination of the two at distinct times.

I now defend the claim that all Christian philosophers have responsibilities to all three communities and thus ought to be partly peer- and partly public-facing. I offer three reasons. First, as Plato's freed prisoner reminds us, there are obligations to all three communities placed upon us *qua* philosopher. We do not seek knowledge and wisdom for our flourishing only. Our obligation—to truth, goodness, beauty, and ultimately to God—extends beyond ourselves to those around us in the academy, church, and culture. Wisdom and knowledge ought to be pursued *for the flourishing of all*. As Plato describes, the job of the philosopher is to "spread happiness through the city by bringing the citizens into harmony with each other" and thus, we "must go down to live in the common dwelling place of the others" (*Republic* VII, 519$_e$2-3).[9] The freed prisoner's "upward journey" (*Republic* VII, 517$_b$3) to the source of all reality is not his final resting place, at least in this life.[10] Those of us who have been nourished on the good, true, and beautiful and who walk the terrain of the sacred order must cross back into the mundane realms to liberate those still in captivity to ignorance and folly, and not just among our academic peers.

Second, there are obligations to all three communities placed upon us *qua* Christian. Just as Jesus was sent by the Father into the world, Christians are sent by Jesus into the world (John 17:18, NIV). We are missionaries, one and all, compelled by love to represent Christ to the unbeliever, wherever they are found (2 Cor 5:14-15, 20, NIV). Our missionary call, then, extends "into all the world" (Mark 16:5; see also Matt 28:19-20, NIV). As Christ followers, we follow in the footsteps of Jesus who "came down from heaven" and gave himself "for the life of the world" (John 6:51, NIV). Given this missionary call, again, we ought to care about the heart and minds of those in the academy, church, and culture.

---

8. The discussion about the different aims (i.e., epistemic justification vs. joy) of the peer-facing vs. public-facing philosophy is from Lam, "Nonfiction and Narrative Popular Philosophy."
9. Plato, *Republic*, in *Plato: Complete Works*, ed. John Cooper (Hackett, 1997), 1137.
10. Plato, *Republic*, 1135.

Finally, there are obligations to all three communities placed upon us qua *Christian philosopher*. Paul reminds us that the spiritual battle partly involves the call to "demolish arguments and every pretension that sets itself up against the knowledge of God" (2 Cor 10:5, NIV). Christian philosophers have a unique calling, as trained experts in metaphysics, epistemology, logic, and ethics, to lead in the Christian community in defending and commending the faith to others in the academy and the public sphere. The Christian philosopher is a border-walker who dwells—sometimes at the center, sometimes at the margins—in three overlapping domains of discourse. And of course, there are many false ideas and bad arguments coming from all three communities. The Christian philosopher can and should take the lead in addressing, and sometimes demolishing bad ideas and arguments for the sake of truth and the gospel.

This re-casting of the Christian (public) philosopher as a *border-walker* between three inter-related communities and two realms of reality imposes a heavy burden upon us. It means that we'll need to be conversant with theology, academic philosophy, and how ideas and thought patterns express themselves within the public sphere. In addition to the "peer-facing" philosophy many of us do so well as we teach and write in and for the academy, we'll need to learn how to do "public-facing" philosophy too, teaching and writing for the church and for the public sphere. Importantly, we'll need to work to be translators, communicating the technical concepts and truths discovered within academic philosophy to help those in the church and public see and understand truth, goodness, and beauty for the flourishing of all. All Christian philosophers ought to be partly public-facing philosophers.[11] This entails that the Christian philosopher ought not adopt a wholly peer- or public-facing posture. We are philosophers "in the middle" who walk the borders of *all three* communities.

2. Public Philosophy

The notions of "peer-facing" and "public-facing" have to do with our posture, our learned stance toward the communities we find ourselves called to serve. The notion of "public philosophy" has to do with our gesturing and pointing, i.e., the kinds of philosophical activities we engage in and the kinds of philosophical works we produce. While all of

---

11. Of course, this was Plantinga's point too in 1983. He argued that our primarily responsibility was to the Christian community. As I've framed it, this means that we ought to be partly peer-facing and partly public-facing. I've just expanded the scope of communities that we ought to publicly face to the church and culture.

us are called to be partly public-facing (our posture), *not all of us are called to work primarily in the area of public philosophy* (our gesturing and pointing).[12] Following Myisha Cherry, let's define "public philosophy" as "[the sharing of] philosophical ideas in an accessible way with the world."[13] On this understanding of public philosophy, a public philosopher is a philosopher whose *primary* audience for disseminating philosophical ideas is the non-philosophical world.

To clarify, I distinguish between "academic philosophy" and "public philosophy" such that the former is the kind of philosophy that is published in academic presses and journals and read by professional philosophers and the latter is published in more popular presses and journals and read by the mythical "educated lay reader." With this distinction in hand, we can distinguish between two kinds of philosophers in the middle (i.e., two kinds of partly peer- and public-facing philosophers). There are those who are primarily called to be academic philosophers and secondarily public philosophers and those who are primarily called to be public philosophers and secondarily academic philosophers [Figure 4].

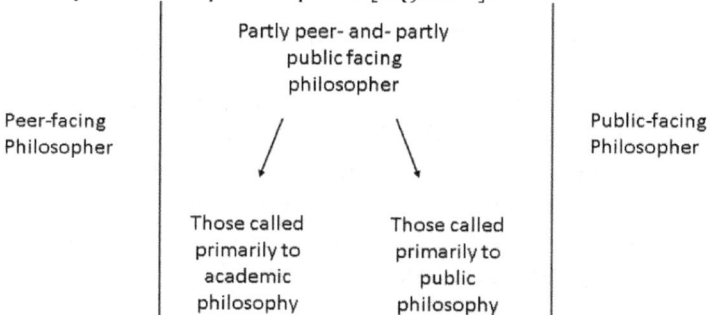

Figure 4: Kinds of Philosophers

Not all of us are called to be public philosophers. Some of us are called to be academic philosophers. But, as I've set things up, all of us are philosophers in the middle, doing some academic and some public philosophy, all motivated out of love for God and in service to others. For some, the bulk of our philosophy work will be peer-focused, full of technical jargon, and published in academic presses and journals. For others the split between peer-focused and public-focused will be more evenly split. And of course, for those called to do public philosophy, some

---

12. The distinction between posture and gesture is from Andy Crouch, *Culture Making* (InterVarsity Press, 2008), chap. 5.
13. Myisha Cherry, "Coming Out of the Shade," in *Philosophy's Future: The Problem of Philosophical Progress*, eds. Russell Blackford and Damien Broderick (John Wiley & Sons, Inc., 2017), 25.

are called to serve more directly in their writing and teaching the Christian community and others the culture beyond the church's doors.

This is good news. There is freedom in Christ and freedom in Christian philosophy! All of us ought to do *some* academic and *some* public philosophy. And since *ought* implies *can*, this means all of us can do academic and public philosophy. I suspect that Plantinga and those who helped orchestrate the so-called renaissance in Christian philosophy that led to Quentin Smith's lament where those primarily called to do academic philosophy (and of course, Plantinga, Alston, and Wolterstorff are exemplars of this kind of philosophy). I also suspect that it is time for those called to be public philosophers to pick up that call and do the work that philosophy demands of them. Many Christian philosophers are leading the way in this: producing and appearing on podcasts, radio interviews, YouTube channels, and even television, bringing their philosophical meat to feed the (knowledge and wisdom) starving masses. But much more can and needs to be done.

3. Power and the Temptation to Idolatry

As academics, Christian philosophers possess what the sociologist James Davison Hunter calls "symbolic capital."[14] We're credentialed, knowledgeable, accomplished, and members (for those in the academy) of one of the most powerful culture-shaping institutions in the world. We possess a kind of power or influence in virtue of our (earned) symbolic capital. Hunter describes the kind of power symbolic capital provides as follows:

> It starts as credibility, an authority one possesses which puts one in a position to be listened to and taken seriously. It ends as the power to define reality itself . . . . it is the power of "legitimate naming."[15]

Identifying a kind of capital that is not economic or political helps articulate what was so wrong with Marco Rubio's 2015 comment at the Republican presidential debate that "we need more welders, and less philosophers."[16] Welders can help put cars and computers together, but philosophers, get to *name* welders, philosophers, cars, and computers (following Peter van Inwagen, welders and philosophers are complex objects since they are living things, cars and computers are merely "atoms

---

14. James Davison Hunter, *To Change the World* (Oxford University Press, 2010), 35–37.
15. Hunter, *To Change the World*, 36.
16. Quoted in Cherry, "Coming out of the Shade," 22.

arranged car-wise" and "atoms arranged computer-wise"). Welders don't have that kind of power, a kind of magician's power to name reality itself.

My first point in this last section then, is that Christian philosophers possess a kind of power. My second point is that this is a good thing, a gift from God, meant to be stewarded and nourished for the flourishing of all. "Power is for flourishing," according to Andy Crouch. "This means power is a gift worth asking for, seeking and—should we receive it—stewarding."[17] The idea that power is a gift to be sought and stewarded might sound, at best, naïve and odd and, at worst, delusional and dangerous. After all, one of the central dividing lines many (secular) philosophers have drawn in their priestly duty of naming reality is that between the oppressed and the oppressor. If these are the only two options, it is hard to make sense of the idea of power as a gift. A more theologically grounded perspective on power, however, helps us understand better the nature and value of power. In power, God creates a world full of beauty, order, and abundance for the flourishing of all (Gen 1 and 2). Moreover, God has created humans, as divine image-bearers to possess "the same kind of delighted dominion over the teeming creatures as their Maker" (Gen 1:26-28).[18] Christians are "icons," image-bearers that "serve as living, breathing representations of the living God who breathed creation into existence."[19] Thus, according to Crouch, image bearing, and power, is for flourishing.[20]

The problem, and this is my final point in this section, is that there is a strong temptation to misuse this power (resulting in injustice) and a strong temptation to seek our own glory instead of God's (resulting in idolatry).[21] While everyone struggles with idolatry, the temptation is especially strong for Christian philosophers, i.e., those of us called to be partially peer-facing and partially public-facing. On the one hand, we succeed in the academy to the degree that we publish and bring attention and prestige to ourselves and our institution. On the other hand, we also get attention and accolades from those in the church (or the public sphere more broadly) that value the knowledge about perennial issues that we are so well equipped to address. It is difficult in this cultural milieu, a culture that values celebrity, to keep our identity squarely on Christ. Thus, we can only successfully be partially peer-facing and partially public-facing philosophers if we are first and foremost God-facing philosophers.

---

17. Andy Crouch, *Playing God: Redeeming the Gift of Power* (InterVarsity Press, 2013), 37.
18. Crouch, *Playing God*, 35.
19. Crouch, *Playing God*, 88.
20. Crouch, *Playing God*, 35.
21. Crouch argues injustice and idolatry are the same thing. See Crouch, *Playing God*, 71-73.

Plato's language describing education as a kind of turning of the soul toward the good (*Republic* VII, 518$_d$3-5) is not far from the truth then.[22] The Christian philosopher is a Christ follower. Our ultimate allegiance is to God. It is through God that we faithfully—and iconically—face the communities we are called to serve. And those communities in turn, will not primarily look *at* us, but *through* us to Christ.[23]

---

22. Plato, *Republic*, 1136.
23. "Icons are not meant primarily to be looked *at*; they are meant to be looked *through* [Crouch, *Playing God*, 96].

9

CONTEXT COLLAPSE, IDEOLOGICAL CAPTURE, AND WINSOME NON-VIOLENCE

Adam Green

University of Oklahoma

Alvin Plantinga's "Advice to Christian Philosophers" is first and foremost an exercise in applied virtue theory. He looks at the state of philosophy circa 1984 and then singles out three virtues that Christians who are philosophers need to exemplify more of or enact better. These are autonomy, "integrality," and courageous self-confidence.[1]

These virtues are not chosen at random but rather as responses to the recent history and overall trajectory of philosophy at that time as interpreted by Plantinga. The then recent death of verificationism, for instance, should teach us that all the handwringing done during the heyday of logical positivism over the seeming unverifiability of religion was for naught.[2] Attempts by Christians to accommodate verificationism have now been revealed to be a waste of intellectual energy if not to have been of dubious faithfulness. What is popular in philosophy at a time will not remain so. To be a Christian, by contrast, is to be committed to truths which have weathered many intellectual fashions over the last several millenia.

At the same time, grad school and the profession at large has a strong socialization effect such that, whether one intends to or not, one will find oneself with projects, methods, and assumptions that are in significant tension with Christian faith unless one dedicates oneself to a different way

---

1. Alvin Plantinga, "Advice to Christian Philosophers," *Faith and Philosophy* 1, no.3 (1984): 253-271.
2. Plantinga, "Advice to Christian Philosophers," 258.

of inhabiting the profession.³ Being caught up in the biases of the day is the norm, not the exception. One needs, instead, to cultivate an ability and a willingness to part ways with the mainstream (autonomy). This more ambivalent relationship with the mainstream is in the service of pursuing a set of philosophical positions *qua* Christian philosopher that cohere well one with another and with one's faith tradition (integrality). This willingness to depart from the philosophically fashionable or disregard the platitudes of secular thought is not done as a kind of side hobby or private interest. Still less does the Christian consent to describe their work as something other than real philosophy (aka "that's just… theology"). Rather, one should boldly present an alternative way of being a thinking person to the world, letting the world make of it what they will (courageous self-confidence).

For Plantinga, it does not matter if one cannot convince a nonbeliever of what a Christian believes. Though a Christian philosopher may have a responsibility to the profession of philosophy, it is not fundamental in the way one's responsibility to the faith is.⁴ Moreover, whatever common ground one may find with the agnostic or the atheist, there will be a certain thinness or fragility to that common ground, or at least there should be so long as one has really integrated one's faith into how one sees the world. Thus, for Plantinga, the Christian philosopher should pursue projects that make sense from within a Christian framework and employ assumptions and methods in the pursuit of those projects that are fitting as judged from an insider's point of view. They ought to do this with confidence in the value of what they are doing, in part, because what philosophy does is deepen what one thinks one knows pre-philosophically, and the pre-philosophical positions that the Christian philosopher seeks to deepen are, or should be, Christian.⁵

In my own contribution, I will follow Plantinga's format, even if my recommendations are a little different. In particular, I will suggest that the relevant social context that the Christian philosopher has to navigate as we knock on the door of the mid 21st century is, in important respects, different from the one Plantinga took himself to be in, and my diagnosis will lead me to highlight different virtues as guiding lights. To cut to the chase, the two factors to navigate which I will highlight are context collapse and ideological capture.

---

3. Plantinga, "Advice to Christian Philosophers," 254-255.
4. Plantinga, "Advice to Christian Philosophers," 262; 270-271.
5. Plantinga, "Advice to Christian Philosophers," 268.

"Context collapse" is a function of the technology of communication, especially social media.[6] In the digital age, in principle, any speech act can outlive its utterance. Any conversation, talk, or thought expressed at random can be recorded, removed from its context, recast in another context, and widely broadcast. The increasing ghettoization of long-form writing, with the development of thought, point and counterpoint that such forms foster and the promotion instead of sound-bite sized assertions of perspective, weakens the social scaffolding necessary for creating a unique communicative context in which to situate a thought. One needs to be prepared for any thought one might communicate in any moment to be extracted from its native context and broadcast in a way that is either neutered of context or that is situated against the pre-existing low-fi contexts available in popular culture. One needs to be prepared for a collapsing of context that is unintentional ("context collision") or that may be engineered with ill intent ("context collusion").

Human language is deeply and subtly context dependent. What is appropriate in a private conversation may not be appropriate outside of it. One might not hold a statement made in a fraught, emotional moment to the same standards one would at another time. Different standards are relevant at different stages of the lifespan or when one is speaking in or outside of a specific role. We state our thoughts poorly in ways that may function well enough within the context of a conversation or within the history of a relationship. The very same words can be powerful or trite depending on the exact way they are said. For different audiences, one might shape a message to make contact with their unique interests and background knowledge. As we all know, language taken out of context is a potent source of misunderstanding and harm. The same locutions can have different illocutionary force, different implicatures, and different perlocutionary force in different contexts.

One of the effects of context collapse is that it incentivizes either pre-filtering one's speech so as to express only what is likely to survive perverse uptake or building in so much qualification into each local unit of communication that one's speech becomes in effect un-poachable by those who might seek to take it out of context. The problem with the former is that pre-filtered speech is likely to be simple, dumbed down, take no conversational risks, be restricted to universal idioms, and move quickly to a conclusion. The problem with the latter is that it restricts one's audience, raises the processing costs of engagement on that audience, risks breeding a different kind of miscommunication because it is overly

---

6. Cf. Jenny Davis and Nathan Jurgenson, "Context Collapse: Theorizing Context Collusions and Collisions," *Information, Communication, & Society* 17 (2014): 476–485.

complicated, vitiates language of its affective power, and makes for a kind of speech that is resistant to not only perverse but also productive forms of uptake and distribution.

The problem of context collapse is only made worse by our second problem, ideological capture.

Sally Haslanger says that "in the most basic sense ideologies are representations of social life that serve in some way to undergird social practices."[7] In effect, there are things we do only because of how we think about them and their role in our collective life. Let us use that as a starting but not an ending point. This is not quite narrow enough. It does not capture the respects in which it is epistemically if not morally risky to be caught in the grips of an ideology and thus why "ideology" lends itself to pejorative use.[8] Yet, it is possible to be too heavy handed in one's account. Tommie Shelby, for instance, defines ideology as, "a widely held set of loosely associated beliefs and implicit judgments that misrepresent significant social realities and that function, through this distortion, to bring about or perpetuate unjust social relations."[9] Surely, contra Shelby, it is possible for an ideology to be held by a few people, be more or less integrated, be more or less explicit, concern matters that are more or less significant, and to fail to produce significant social harm. Yet, at the same time, whatever ideologies are, they frequently produce what Shelby takes to be definitive of them, which itself bears explaining. In what follows, I will take inspiration from Charles Taylor's analysis of accounts of secularization and the displacement of religion in the modern world, which he critiques as not so much wrong as too simple and convenient to be true.[10] An ideology is a kind of simplification story. In particular, it is a simplification story that of its nature streamlines the processing of stimuli that correlate with in-groups and out-groups, primes in-group based responses to such stimuli, and allows for coarse-grained coordination across members of an in-group.

Collective action requires communication amongst members, and when a group takes itself to be competing with other groups, then communication must be efficient, both in terms of the salience of what gets communicated to the group and in the informational load of

---

7. Sally Haslanger, "Ideology, Generics, and Common Ground," in *Feminist Metaphysics*, ed. Charlotte Witt (Springer Verlag, 2010): 179–207. 180.

8. This is related to Tommie Shelby's distinction between the evaluative and nonevaluative uses of the terms "ideology" and "ideological" (156-157) but even in a nonevaluative account of ideology, I think we need something that explains why the same term lends itself to evaluative uses. See Tommie Shelby, "Ideology, Racism, and Critical Social Theory," *The Philosophical Forum* 34 (2003): 153–188.

9. Tommie Shelby, "Racism, Moralism, and Social Criticism," *DuBois Review* 11 (2014): 57–74. 66.

10. Cf. Charles Taylor, *A Secular Age* (Harvard University Press, 2007).

communication. If too much information is communicated without useful markers that help one prioritize what is of relevance to the group, then the processing costs are too high and the chance of missing vital information in the informational noise inevitable. If what is communicated is too complex, then, once again, processing costs go up and the chance of errors in transmission likewise multiply. Thus, there is a strong incentive in competitive and pressurized group contexts to simplify messaging and to suppress information that might delay an adaptive response.

But, of course, whether the salience of group competition is more important than competing concerns is a contingent matter and in no small part a matter of perspective. If we felt unthreatened by out-groups or attached a higher value to ends other than those concerned with protecting the in-group, then we might judge the costs of more nuanced and complete evidence gathering and communication worth the price. Absent such circumstances, however, understandably but regrettably, the incentive to prioritize the in-group/out-group lens, defer to it whenever it may be salient, and thereby oversimplify reality in a way biased towards one's own group takes over. It is against this backdrop that we can characterize the second problem, that of ideological capture.

Ideological capture occurs when some domain of inquiry or practical action, one which could be and often should be decided in a way that is blind to in-group/out-group dynamics, gets subsumed into a broader ideological conflict. The phenomenon is familiar enough. The potential ethical abuses of some emerging technology spark discussion that is quickly subsumed into monolithic ideological stances on government regulation sparking a struggle that fails to make contact with the particulars of the technology and its probable societal impact. A curricular decision about how to teach history in schools quickly get subsumed into conflicts over whether history will be taught in a way that accords with the simplification stories one or more groups tell about themselves to either locate their group as the culmination of what is good about the past or to create a buffer between one's group and the proverbial sins of the fathers.

It is easy enough to see how ideological capture and context collapse interact perversely. If one operates in a context where there is a strong temptation to subsume domains of inquiry and practical action to ideological conflict, thereby giving reign to in-group biases, and one also operates in a communicative environment in which speech contexts are unstable and permeable, then the context that all speech acts get collapsed into is an ideologically loaded one. Moreover, the pressure that is already present due to context collapse to simplify one's speech makes contact with the way ideology presents a simplified view of the world. Given that one's potential interlocuters are ready to filter what one says through an ideology and spread it only if it seems in-group relevant, one's choices are, or at least can seem to be, either being complicit in ideological speech, thereby participating in ideological capture by extending the effective range of an ideology or to simply fail to communicate by uttering something that is unlikely to get uptake with any sort of fidelity of transmission.

One of the potential problems with Plantinga's advice from his famous paper is that following it can easily lead to talking only to oneself or to some small cabal of like-minded Christian philosophers. Confidently investigating matters of interest to Christians out loud and in public does not by itself make one a good communicator. In fact, having an insider conversation out loud, however boldly, invites the outsider to misrepresent what one is saying—its nature, its scope, its nuance—in no small part because of the way that language is context dependent. As Christian philosophy has grown from something of a renegade intellectual project to a major force in the discipline, having insider conversations out loud can under certain circumstances become obnoxious and offensive as those with less power in the discipline experience Christian philosophers as conducting themselves as if, say, other religions or spiritual orientations generally are not there or do not matter.

Calls to globalize the philosophy of religion have, not infrequently, come with a rebuke of what is perceived as Christian triumphalism, aka an expectation that Christians get to dictate what happens in a whole domain of philosophy that one would have thought should be open to anyone with an interest in both philosophy and religion.[11] There is a certain irony here. Plantinga's advice was given in no small part to offer succor and direction to Christians who were used to secular academe ignoring them or forcing them to engage in the discipline only if and to the extent that they could make their interests and concerns intelligible on secular grounds. But it has contributed to a state of play in the philosophy of religion where both proponents of the globalization of philosophy of religion as well as those in favor of the marginalization of philosophy of religion as a whole accuse Christian philosophers of having done the same thing Plantinga was standing up against, of creating a situation in which some are silenced and excluded or else only included if they are willing to play on an ideologically tilted field.

---

11. By way of illustration, Plantinga is the most quoted philosopher in the 2017 book *Renewing Philosophy of Religion*, and the reason philosophy needs to be renewed according to the contributors to that volume is that it is dominated by Christians operating in a Plantingian mode. In fact, one of the essays, that by J. Aaron Simmons, takes Plantinga's "Advice to Christian Philosophers" as the foil against which to articulate its critique (154ff). Paul Draper and J. L Schellenberg (eds.), *Renewing Philosophy of Religion: Exploratory Essays* (Oxford University Press, 2017).

Given this analysis of the situation that Christian philosophers have to navigate, I will be nominating two virtues that I wager would help one navigate context collapse without succumbing to an ideological simplification story. To be clear, although one can imagine cases in which an increase in a virtue might be on balance bad (e.g., the courageous Nazi), I am committed to an increase in any virtue being desirable absent strong countervailing reasons to think otherwise. Nonetheless, virtue talk and virtue-based action interpretation is easily twisted or politicized. For instance, Plantinga's recommendation of courageous self-confidence and autonomy to many contemporary readers looks like license to be closed-minded and arrogant. There is no reason to think that someone possessed of virtuous self-confidence and autonomy would be closed-minded and arrogant, and, of course, it would be both unfair and inaccurate to accuse Plantinga of valorizing these vices. If, however, a certain kind of Plantinga-inspired conservative Christian philosopher is in the outgroup of a more progressive philosopher, Christian or no, then ideological pressure will take the virtue talk of the conservative and interpret it as the corresponding vices. Self-confidence becomes arrogance. Autonomy becomes closed-mindedness.

Moreover, if we grant that in-group biases and related simplification stories are an important danger, it becomes important that pursuing an independence of influence from people who are not in one's group (aka pursuing Plantingian autonomy) lends itself to participating in these vices as does trying to be courageously self-confident in speaking one's truth in the presence of those who are not in a position to receive it. Again, the point is not that autonomy or courageous self-confidence as understood by Plantinga are bad or even that we should not cultivate them. To the contrary, to my mind, Plantinga's essay depicts a form that virtue can and often does need to take. Rather, the point is that holding up these virtues as the ones to steer by is not especially helpful if our salient problems are context collapse and ideological capture, and all other things being equal, pursuing them preferentially can actually make the problem worse because in-group bias is fully consistent with feeding off the animus or misunderstanding of out-groups and taking a certain kind of pride in performing one's in-group identity in front of them.

Let us briefly touch on the other side of the coin. One might think that the natural approach to navigating a highly polarized and pluralistic context would be to cultivate humility and open-mindedness, both of which have generated very fruitful analytic literatures. I wholeheartedly agree that more humility and open-mindedness would be a good thing and that one should try to cultivate these traits. Yet, humility and open-mindedness are vulnerable to ideological capture along certain obvious lines, in particular as a critique or intervention proffered by more progressive or secular philosophers to "fix" Christian philosophy's recalcitrant conservatives and traditionalists.

When person A tells another person B that they should be more humble and open-minded, this naturally conveys the message that A doesn't think person B knows what they think they know and certainly that what person B thinks they know is not as important as person B thinks. Suppose a Christian philosopher who takes an important part of their identity to be that Christianity is true, important, and worth defending is told by someone, say someone more secular or more progressive than themselves, that philosophy as done by Christians is insufficiently open-minded and lacking in humility. How is this likely to be received? The Christian philosopher in question already knows that believing Christianity to be true, important, and worth defending is not something she should be expecting people who are in her outgroup to agree to, certainly not as she herself understands these claims. At best, an out-group member finding one to be insufficiently humble and open-minded sounds like mere disagreement about the truth claims definitive of the in-group/out-group difference cloaked in the guise of a critique of their character. It would be understandable if she found the marshalling of virtue talk in this case to be coercive or question-begging, a way of trying to press a pluralistic, de-committed perspective on her. In short, because of the relevance of ideological capture, even the promotion of virtues like humility and open-mindedness can function as, or be reasonably perceived to be, an illicit attempt by one side to seize the rhetorical high ground.

Self-confidence, autonomy, humility, and open-mindedness are all vitally important. Here, however, I will be suggesting that winsomeness and non-violence are uniquely well-placed to address a context characterized by context collapse and ideological capture.

There is no philosophical literature on winsomeness and certainly there is some significant plasticity to its use. I primarily have in mind how one might describe a certain kind of circumspect speech or writing as winsome. Someone doesn't just put things well. They do so in a way that connects with their audience by inviting them into a recognizably shared human experience. Winsome speech shares with humility an attentiveness to human limits. It may even "own" them as the most prominent current account of intellectual humility emphasizes we should,[12] but the valence is

---

12. See Dennis Whitcomb, Heather Battaly, Jason Baehr, and Daniel Howard-Snyder, "Intellectual Humility: Owning Our Limitations," *Philosophy and Phenomenological Research* 94 (2017): 509–539.

different. A winsome person is at peace with their limits, is appreciative of the good that is found within them, and models how to have perspective on one's socially embedded existential concerns in a way that is uptake friendly for others whose circumstances may be different. Winsomeness is particular enough and nuanced enough to make contact with lived reality, but it's aim is still to draw out something of universal human relevance.

A winsome communicator may not have the power to undo context collapse as a social phenomenon, but they are less susceptible to its negative effects for two reasons. First, because they are aware of and foreground those aspects of their context that are relevant to grappling with their subject matter, it should be harder to poach parts of their speech without either conveying the intended context or else making perspicuous that violence has been done to the original text. Second, because the winsome communicator gravitates toward universal truths grounded in shared human experiences, they are less likely to spur misunderstanding when those who quote them switch contexts and audiences.

Furthermore, attempting to be more winsome in one's speech cuts athwart ideological capture and its perverse incentives. If one owns one's context, including one's group memberships, while seeking to prioritize shared human experiences and existential concerns, then even if one's perspective is intrinsically a group-mediated one, one does not wear it in a way that presumes hostility to the out-group. One does not communicate to rally the base to keep the demonized other at bay and does not obsess over new ground the enemy might be on the verge of taking. If one successfully makes contact with shared experiences and shared concerns, one has reason to think the other can engage in uptake that is not perverse. Thus, the incentive to self-protect in one's speech either by dumbing it down and rendering it generic or else by making it over-qualified is reduced.

Let us turn to the second trait. Non-violence is, of course, opposed to violence, but the violence I am concerned with here is epistemic and related to communication. Consider, for instance, Kristie Dotson's description of "epistemic violence" below:

> Epistemic violence is a failure of an audience to communicatively reciprocate, either intentionally or unintentionally, in linguistic exchanges owing to pernicious ignorance. Pernicious ignorance is a reliable ignorance or a counterfactual incompetence that, in a given context, is harmful.[13]

---

13. Kristie Dotson, "Tracking Epistemic Violence, Tracking Practices of Silencing," *Hypatia* 26 (2011): 236–257. 242.

This failure to reciprocate of which Dotson speaks could take different forms, some but not all of which are intuitively described as "violent." Here are two kinds of cases where the application seems apt to me. First, the attempt to deny or make overly difficult the uptake of the perspective of another person into a social space of reasons is a kind of violence in much the way that physically removing someone from a space and/or barring them from entry can be described as violent. Second, because we make up our minds in part through social processes and because we are not impervious to the influence of others, epistemic and otherwise, the influence of another can be coercive, that is, can do violence to the mind's processes of coming to its own conclusions through as honest and skilled an assessment of the evidence as one can manage. Epistemic violence, then, can take the form of a violation of the integrity of another person's mind.[14]

A commitment to epistemic non-violence is not merely an absence of epistemic violence anymore than the methods of Gandhi or Martin Luther King are adequately picked out by pointing out that they did not go around thwacking people upside the head. Rather, epistemic non-violence is a commitment to do well in that domain where doing poorly looks like silencing or epistemic coercion. This involves a disposition to recognize and disvalue when others are being silenced or excluded and to oppose intellectual manipulation or coercion even on behalf of the truth. It requires a desire to interact with others in a way that is marked by gentleness, respect, and reciprocity. This does not preclude thinking one is right or wanting to convince others of what one believes. Rather, it is an orientation away from silencing or intellectually coercion and towards non-violent ways of engaging others. This orientation ought to influence one's attention, affections, methods, and ideals. The epistemically non-violent person does not easily feel threatened by others arguing positions they think are false and prioritizes small gains achieved by means organic to the psyche of the other person rather than simply dominating a dialectical space.

Non-violence discourages ideological capture by either deflating the sense of threat that amplifies the salience of one's in-group/out-group psychology or else calling into question any ideological simplification story that would represent someone as a threat despite their interacting with one non-violently. When it comes to physical violence, the key to

---

14. There are cases of a failure to reciprocate that do seem to stretch the idea of violence too far but for which neglect would still be an apt analog. I set this topic to the side for present purposes as I do not have space to broach the tricky topic of what epistemic duties we may have to members of out-groups relative to us and what virtues may be most germane to fulfilling such duties.

whether or not non-violent protest is effective appears to be whether it succeeds in sapping the motivation of enforcers, those who enact violence directly on others on behalf of a violent regime.[15] One of the reasons that the track record of non-violent protest in the 20th century is as good as it has been is that the violent repression of non-violent persons is aversive to the average person and feeling like one's commitments demand violently repressing the non-violent is fertile ground for reconsidering those commitments.[16] One should not assume that the deep-seated biological aversion to violently attacking another human who is not a physical threat will be as strong in the case of epistemic violence, but the underlying logic is the same.

By contrast, non-violence by itself does not help directly with context collapse. One's words can still be taken out of context and misunderstanding engendered. Yet, at the same time, non-violence makes it less likely that, when one's words are taken out of context, that they will cause harm. There is less potential for harm in non-violent speech. Moreover, if one's words are both winsome and non-violent, then there is every reason to think they will typically be uptake friendly even in the sort of impoverished communicative context defined by context collapse.

---

15. Cf. Sharon Nepstead, *Nonviolent Revolutions* (Oxford University Press, 2011).
16. Peter Ackerman and Jack Duvall, *A Force More Powerful* (St. Martin's Press, 2000).

10

ON THE MORAL AND INTELLECTUAL HABITUS OF THE CHRISTIAN PHILOSOPHER

Ross D. Inman

Southeastern Baptist Theological Seminary

In his 1983 address "Advice to Christian Philosophers," Al Plantinga encouraged the Christian philosophical community to exhibit more autonomy, integrity, and Christian courage.[1] In doing so, Plantinga encouraged his fellow Christian philosophers—both individually and collectively—to cultivate a certain *habitus*, a way of being in the world that is distinctively Christian in its moral and intellectual posture. By "habitus", I mean the deeply ingrained moral and intellectual tendencies that shape how the Christian philosopher thinks, perceives, feels, and interacts with his or her social environment. In this sense, every Christian philosopher has a habitus. The guiding question here is the precise shape of one's habitus, whether it is properly ordered and oriented toward what is God-serving and others-serving, or whether it is disordered and oriented toward what is self-serving and vicious.

In this brief chapter I offer some personal reflection on how the Christian philosophical community might best carry out Plantinga's admonishment in "Advice to Christian Philosophers" to cultivate a well-formed—indeed Christ-shaped—habitus. Given Plantinga's emphasis on the need for Christian philosophers to cultivate courage, I'll focus on the intellectual virtue of courage with a specific eye on the intellectual character traits that both *hinder* as well as *help* its cultivation. While the Christian philosophical community remains in dire need of the Christian courage called for by

---

[1]. Alvin Plantinga, "Advice to Christian Philosophers" in *Faith and Philosophy* 1 (1984): 254.

Plantinga some forty years ago, I'm convinced that such unwavering courage is only the fruit of a Christ-shaped moral and intellectual habitus that finds its roots deeply planted in the seedbed of intellectual humility. To carry forth Plantinga's enduring vision of a courageous Christian philosophical community, then, Christian philosophers must work to lay aside intellectual vainglory and cowardice and to put on the virtue of intellectual humility; we must strive, above all, to become *certain kinds of people in heart and mind*.

1. Christian Philosophy in the Presence of a Window and a Skylight

Philosophers who carry the name of Christ should be guided by the two commandments upon which all of the Law and the Prophets depend (Matt 22:36-40); they are first and foremost to be lovingly oriented toward God with every fiber of their being, and secondly, to be lovingly oriented toward others. Borrowing a metaphor from the Swiss theologian Karl Barth, we can depict this two-fold aim of the Christian philosophical life as follows: Christian philosophers should operate in the presence of both a *window* and a *skylight*.[2] In general, skylights keep us open and responsive to the natural light that streams in from above. Christians who pursue the philosophical task in the absence of a skylight, an openness and responsiveness to the supernatural light that streams in from above—the "wisdom from above," as James might put it (Jas 3:13-18)—cut themselves off from the larger moral context that gives *Christian* philosophy its distinctively Christ-oriented aim and texture.

Windows, on the other hand, keep us attentive and accountable to what is going on outside of our own residences; they orient us to the needs, cares, and concerns of others, to those both inside and outside the Christian philosophical community. Since Christian philosophers are *Christians* first and *philosophers* second, they are summoned by their Lord to be responsive and accountable to the needs and concerns of their fellow image-bearers, including those outside the academic community who will never don academic regalia. While pursuing their philosophical task in front of an open window can help Christian philosophers remain attuned to the needs and concerns of others, such a posture can also can present unique challenges to the habitus of Christian philosophers.

I want to explore several ways in which the Christian philosopher's natural and virtuous desire to be attentive and responsive to others can

---

2. Karl Barth, *Evangelical Theology: An Introduction* (Eerdmans, 1963), 161.

be easily twisted into two signature vices of an ill-formed habitude—the vices of intellectual vainglory and cowardice. I'll then consider two corresponding signature virtues of a well-formed, Christ shaped habitus—intellectual humility and courage. I'll end by suggesting that only in the presence of light flooding in from both a window in front *as well as* a skylight above can Christian philosophers maintain a virtuous, Christ-shaped habitus and thereby carry forward Plantinga's charge to embody distinctively Christian courage in our academic communities and beyond.

2. Some Signature Vices of a Disordered Habitus: Intellectual Vainglory and Cowardice

As those who work in the professional philosophical guild know all too well, the life lived within the halls of the academy is marked not only by great joy and rich accomplishment, but also by many potential moral dangers, toils, and snares. Yet I'm convinced that the professional philosophical life can be—and indeed should be—an ongoing occasion for moral and spiritual transformation. If we let it, the vocational philosophical life lived in humble submission to Christ and in loving service to one another can aid in the uprooting of vice and the cultivation of virtue.

Let me try to unpack some of these moral dangers, toils, and snares as well as their correctives by way of a personal confession. I myself have felt the very powerful pull in academic life toward the vice of *intellectual vainglory*, the *excessive* desire to be well-regarded by one's intellectual peers. While a desire to be well-regarded by one's academic peers is both natural and healthy, intellectual vainglory is the *inordinate* and *unhealthy* preoccupation with intellectual image; the intellectually vain person remains deeply unfulfilled unless they're well thought of by their wider social and intellectual community.

The temptation to vainglory in an intellectual context is, of course, both ancient and modern. St. Augustine, reflecting on the spiritual condition of his younger and more vulnerable self, tells us in his *Confessions*: "I wanted to distinguish myself as an orator for a damnable and conceited purpose, namely, delight in human vanity."[3] In his spiritual autobiographical essay "A Christian Life Partly Lived," Plantinga candidly illustrates the pervasiveness of intellectual vainglory within the culture of professional, academic philosophy:

---

3. Augustine, *Confessions*, trans. Henry Chadwick (Oxford University Press, 1998), 38.

> We philosophers are brought up to practice our craft in a sort of individualistic, competitive, even egotistical style; there is enormous interest among philosophers in ranking each other with respect to dialectical and philosophical ability, deciding who is really terrific, who is pretty good, who is OK, who is really lousy and so on. Your worth, at any rate *qua* philosopher, tends to depend on your ranking, as if your main job is to try to achieve as high a ranking as possible.[4]

Philosophers in the grip of intellectual vainglory are enslaved to peer recognition; their perceived value tends to rise and fall with the ever-shifting valuation of their academic peers. As such, the intellectually vain are often willing to turn a blind eye to truth, simply for the sake being seen to be in line with the intellectual status-quo.

As C. S. Lewis describes so well in his profound essay "The Inner Ring" (delivered to fellow academics at the University of London in 1944), we naturally crave the fellowship of the inner ring—the tight and selective circle of "movers and shakers" in our valued social communities—and we greatly fear to be found outside of it.[5] There are, of course, a host of these inner rings to be found throughout the professional, philosophical guild, whether in graduate school or among professional societies like the American Philosophical Association, the Society of Christian Philosophers, the American Catholic Philosophical Association, or the Evangelical Philosophical Society.

One particularly well-defined inner ring within the halls of academia, one that was often alluring to me in graduate school and the few years beyond, concerns the quality and the length of one's CV; the sheer number and quality of publications attached to one's name keeps one safely within the scholarly inner ring. There is a very strong temptation to carry out one's intellectual work *solely* for the sake of the peer applause that comes with professional success. One can easily become inordinately consumed with publishing on the "right" topics in the "right" journals or landing the "right" book contracts with the "right" academic publishers—and, of course, it is equally important that we have been seen to be doing these things. Sadly, many often act as if the sole measure of the quality, depth, and enduring value of their philosophical work—even their very selves—resides in the often-temperamental hands of a pair of anonymous peer reviewers. The shift from a perfectly healthy desire to contribute to the scholarly, philosophical conversation to an *inordinate* need to be

---

4. Alvin Plantinga, "A Christian Life Partly Lived" in *Philosophers Who Believe* (InterVarsity Press, 1993), 79.
5. C.S. Lewis, "The Inner Ring" in *The Weight of Glory and Other Addresses* (HarperCollins Publishers, 2001), 141-157.

recognized and regarded by one's intellectual peers is ever so subtle yet pernicious.

Other academic inner rings circle around currently fashionable views in our respective philosophical subdisciplines, be it social ontology or social-political philosophy. And given our current cultural moment, more theologically conservative Christian philosophers should expect to increasingly find themselves on the outside of a very many of these inner rings, whether they be found in non-Christian or even explicitly Christian circles. We must watch and pray lest our proper love to be well-regarded by our academic peers be twisted into a perverse form of intellectual vainglory.

One of the perils of intellectual vainglory is that it can become the seedbed for further vices that are detrimental to a truly Christ-shaped moral and intellectual habitus. If one is in the grip of the ever-present notion that Christian philosophical work is primarily *performative*—that is, as a way of signaling to one's academic peers that one is gifted or savvy enough to be a part of the inner ring—then one will miss the deeply formative power of the Christian philosophical life as love of and service to God and neighbor.

Along these lines, consider the vice of *intellectual cowardice*.[6] The person who exhibits intellectual cowardice shrinks back from pursuing valuable intellectual goods (like truth, knowledge, wisdom, or understanding) out of fear of detriment to one's social standing. It is, of course, the intellectually vain person that is most susceptible to the vice of intellectual cowardice, given their inordinate concern for social-standing and peer approval; indeed, intellectual cowardice is crouching at the door of the intellectually vain. What makes intellectual cowardice so deadly for the habitus of the Christian philosopher is that it tends to manifest itself in the form of resistance to intellectual reproof and examination. And, of course, the failure to open oneself up to intellectual correction (perhaps out of deep pride or arrogance) inevitably stunts proper intellectual, moral, and spiritual growth.

3. A Few Signature Virtues of a Properly Ordered Habitus: Intellectual Humility and Courage

Intellectual humility and courage serve as virtuous correctives to the signature vices of intellectual vainglory and cowardice. Very roughly,

---

6. For more on the vice of intellectual cowardice and its corresponding virtue of intellectual courage, see Robert C. Roberts and Jay Wood, *Intellectual Virtues: An Essay in Regulative Epistemology* (Oxford University Press, 2007), ch. 8.

intellectual humility is the stable disposition to acknowledge and own one's cognitive limitations; an enduring readiness to live out one's intellectual dependence on others for the flourishing intellectual life.

Christian philosophers who, by the grace of God, clothe themselves with intellectual humility operate out of a deep awareness and confidence in who they *are*, and who they are *not*; where their source of identity and significance *is* found, and where it is *not*. Christian philosophers with a habitus marked by such humility are gripped by the fact that in Christ they have "died to the elemental spirits of the world," which includes much of the prideful intellectual posturing and grandstanding that's often rendered a virtue in the wider philosophical guild. They remain open and responsive to others, but their value, worth, and significance are not *tethered* to the recognition and applause of their intellectual peers. This is precisely what the Christian philosophical life lived in the presence of *both* a window and a skylight looks like.

It is precisely because of the divine light cascading down from above that the follower of Christ can rest assured that their life is first and foremost "hidden with Christ in God" (Col 3: 3), and thus that their posture toward their academic peers need not be one of grandstanding or unhealthy competition or comparison. Rather it's a posture of other-centeredness, marked by love, humility, meekness, and gratitude; gratitude that we have the great privilege to labor alongside one another, ultimately for the glory of the triune God and the display of the beauty, truth, and goodness of "the gospel of the glory of the blessed God" (1 Tim 1:11).

Thus, the intellectually humble person lives out of a posture of receptivity and openness to both God and others. Since the intellectually humble recognize and own their creaturely limitations and finitude in light of their openness to and dependence on God above, they are likewise open to both the success and the reproof of their intellectual peers. Such humble dependence creates a posture that naturally brings with it a freedom from arrogance and an unhealthy devotion to be well-regarded by others. For the humble, Philippians 2:3 is a guiding maxim in the philosophical life: "Do *nothing* from selfish ambition or conceit, but in humility count others better than yourselves. Let each of you look not only to his own interests, but also to the interests of others." For the intellectually humble, the collaborative pursuit of a deeper understanding of and alignment to reality is far more valuable than keeping up with intellectual appearances.

By my lights, intellectual humility is the indispensable seedbed for the kind of bold and unwavering courage called for by Plantinga in his "Advice to Christian Philosophers." Without a habitus shaped by intellectual humility, Christian courage will be cut off at the root, unable to thrive in any enduring or sustainable form. The intellectually courageous person is ready and willing to suffer potential loss for the sake of some greater intellectual good such as truth, knowledge, understanding, or wisdom. But if one remains firmly in the grip of intellectual vainglory, such willingness will be quickly overtaken by the weightier desire to maintain social standing and be well-regarded by one's academic peers at all costs.

With respect to our own contemporary academic context, this kind of intellectual courage in the face of potential social harm—potential harm to our professional reputation or wider academic respectability—can only be displayed when we love intellectual goods more than the favorable applause of our academic peers. If we fail to value truth over the length of our CV, our professional advancement, or how we're perceived by the wider academic guild, we'll no doubt risk very little in the face of social opposition.

Indeed, it is only the Christian philosopher who is receptive to the clarifying light that streams in from the skylight above—with regard to *who* (and *whose*!) they are and where their ultimate value and worth lies—that can cultivate and maintain a Christ-shaped moral and intellectual habitus and steer clear of the vices of intellectual vainglory and cowardice. In the absence of a wider and more compelling moral vision that conveys who we truly are (and are not) in relation to God and others, we cannot reasonably expect to embody the bold and unwavering courage called for by Plantinga. When the Christian philosophical life is uprooted from the seedbed of intellectual humility, intellectual vainglory and cowardice will inevitably reign supreme in our contemporary context.

Let me close with a brief application of what intellectual courage might look like in one's current academic context. While I was still in graduate school, an older and much wiser philosopher on the Way of Christ once wisely pointed me to Proverbs 14:4: "Where there are no oxen, the manger is clean, but abundant crops come by the strength of the ox."[7] Applying this verse to the all-too painful and vulnerable process of cutting one's scholarly teeth in graduate school, he said, "In order to see some academic growth and increase, you might have to put up with a bit of crap in your academic manger." I have carried this sound bit of wisdom with me throughout my young philosophical career; indeed, it still rings true this very day (as my own students can attest!). A clean "philosophical manger" might mean that you've never put yourself out there, you've never risked your perceived social status among your intellectual peers for the sake of

---

7. I refer here to my friend and fellow Christian philosopher, Robert Garcia.

a greater intellectual good; perhaps, out of fear of peer disapproval and ridicule, you never actively contribute in your philosophy seminars, you've never submitted a paper to present at an academic conference, or you've never subjected your own beliefs to the critical examination of your peers.

In the absence of a deep and abiding intellectual humility and courage—a Christ-shaped habitus—there will inevitably be the presence of what is commonly called "imposter syndrome"—the deep-seated fear of being exposed as the "unqualified, clumsy, inadequate scholarly outsider we secretly fear that we are," as author Joli Jensen puts it.[8] While in graduate school, many of us are confronted with our own deep feelings of inadequacy and quickly learn how to hide these feelings from others, lest our cover be blown and others find out that we are nowhere near as competent as others think that we are. But it is important to see that imposter syndrome is the natural fruit of an inordinate desire to maintain intellectual appearances at all costs; as such, imposter syndrome is ultimately rooted in a form of intellectual vainglory. Jensen, describing imposter syndrome from the inside as it pertains to academic writing, notes:

> Writing is a form of self-exposure; it makes us available for scrutiny, criticism, and evaluation. Since our writing feels like a measure of our 'selves,' we become paralyzed by the perceived gap between who we fear we really are and who we think we need to appear to be. Writing might reveal our fraudulence.[9]

And for those that are enslaved to maintaining intellectual appearances, exposure is to be avoided at all costs.

As with life in general, there are certain laws of return in the intellectual life that you can count on: if you never courageously risk putting yourself out there, you'll likely never grow and yield fruit as a Christian philosopher. Of course, this posture of intellectual courage requires deep-seated intellectual humility and an ongoing confidence in one's identity in and union with Christ. So, in the spirit of Plantinga's original "Advice to Christian Philosophers," let me encourage my fellow Christian philosophers to pursue their work from a distinctively Christ-shaped moral and intellectual habitus, a posture of humble reliance and openness to God and others, an openness that frees us to joyfully work and risk alongside one another and before a watching world, to give and receive correction with gratitude and humility. When our grace-renewed spiritual reflex leads us to draw our deepest value from our union with Christ, *then*,

---

8. Joli Jensen, *Write No Matter What: Advice for Academics* (University of Chicago Press, 2017), 52.
9. Jensen, *Write No Matter What*, 53.

and only then I believe, can we reasonably hope to embody Plantinga's vision of a courageous Christian philosophical community in our own day.

We must remember that the kind of resilient courage flagged by Plantinga cannot be cultivated by increased technical savvy or by amassing publications in top-tier, peer-reviewed journals or university presses. Rather, it is only when Christ is increasingly formed in each of us (Gal 4:19; Col 2:19) that we can expect to be a Christian philosophical community that remains bold and courageous in the face of potential social harm and increased marginalization. When we devote ourselves to the steady cultivation of a sure and stable Christ-shaped habitus in humble reliance on the riches of divine grace (1 Cor 3:6–7; Col 2:19), the vices of intellectual vainglory and cowardice gradually lose their luster. Intellectual courage is the natural fruit of a life securely rooted in Christ and in a Christ-shaped habitus marked by intellectual humility. *This* is how we embody the courageous, Christian philosophical life called for by Plantinga, both in front of a window and underneath a skylight.

11

PLANTINGA'S MANIFESTO: SPARKING A REVOLUTION

J. P. Moreland

Talbot School of Theology

I have been entrusted with the job of reflecting on Alvin Plantinga's revolutionary essay "Advice to Christian Philosophers" from three perspectives: (1) How did Plantinga's essay impact me personally? (2) How did his essay impact Christian philosophy? (3) What advice do I have to Christian philosophers 40 years after the essay's publication? I consider this to be a treasured honor and sacred duty. However, I shall begin with some background for understanding the impact of Plantinga's article followed by a description of four truths/values contained in the article and exemplified by Plantinga's life and work in general.

1. Background Context for Plantinga's Article

In 1984 when Plantinga's article was published, the intersection of two chains of historical events were well underway towards secularizing the public square in North America and marginalizing the Christian community. First, two worldviews were rapidly advancing towards cultural prominence—versions of philosophical naturalism and postmodern constructivism. Each in its own way fomented a progressive societal understanding—implicit and explicit—of the nature and limits of knowledge. The result was the claim that there is no knowledge of reality outside the hard sciences. Second, the church was adopting an anti-intellectual approach to Christianity's truth claims, an approach that protected the church from the dominant narratives of naturalism and PoMo. The church retreated from culture, adopted an understanding of faith as a private choice based on emotions to believe Christian teaching, and in the words of Oz Guinness, became its own gravedigger.

Something needed to be done and that something needed to start at the top among Christian intellectuals. Founded in 1978 by Plantinga, William Alston, and others, the Society of Christian Philosophers was a good start. Its purpose was to promote fellowship between Christian philosophers and to provide occasions for intellectual interchange among them on issues that arise from their joint commitment. The Society has always had a big-tent approach to membership, being open to anyone who considers himself or herself to be a Christian and a philosopher. In my opinion, this was the right approach for the time. On the downside, the theological looseness of this perspective did not have the sort of punch needed to generate a movement that stood out boldly against the prevailing ideologies of the time and to serve as a role model for others in the church to follow. What was needed was something that could foment a revolution that was constituted by a proper commitment to the authority of the Bible and theological conservatism.

This is where Plantinga's essay enters the scene. While it did not spark the beginning of renewal of Christianity in philosophy, it clearly laid out a mission, a perspective of what Christian philosophers ought to be about, and a call to embody a set of truths/values to be mentioned shortly. His essay took biblical truth claims at the core of historic Christianity to be a part of a knowledge tradition. As a result, and in this sense, it had significant implications for integrating one's work with one's Christianity.

In Mark Noll's important book *The Scandal of the Evangelical Mind*, he notes that Christian philosophers have "made their presence felt in the world of scholarship more substantially than intellectuals in any other discipline."[1] Among other things, Noll recommended that if Christian scholars wanted to engage in better, bolder, and appropriate integration of Christianity with their academic disciplines, they would do well to take a page from Christian philosophers who were leading the charge.

2. Four Important Truths/Values from Plantinga's Article and Broader Life

In my view, Plantinga's essay was seminal to this integrative task with far-reaching implications ranging throughout the academic disciplines.

---

1. Mark Noll, *The Scandal of the Evangelical Mind* (Eerdmans, 1994), 236. Cf. 233–253.

While much can be said about his essay, from my personal perspective, there were four important truths/values explicitly or implicitly resounded in it and, more generally, by Plantinga's life and work.

2.1 Be Excellent in Your Philosophical Work

The aspects of this are particularly striking and important. First, because Plantinga is an exceptional, first-rate philosopher, he had the respect, the gravitas, the stature to sound a clarion call to Christian philosophers that needed to be taken seriously. One may not agree with this or that point in Plantinga's body of work—including this essay—but no Christian philosopher can ignore it when Plantinga writes something. This is especially true of an essay like this in which he is giving "advice" for others to follow.

Second, Plantinga embodies the kind of philosophical excellence that makes him an ideal role model for other Christian philosophers—especially graduate students and younger brothers and sisters who are beginning their career. From the way he conducted himself, the way he wrote with precision, the manner with which he tackled an issue, and the way he exemplified a distinctively Christian approach to his work, Plantinga is the Platonic Form (with apologies to my nominalist friends) of a role-model of how to do Christian philosophy and be a *Christian* philosopher. Through his teachings and writings, he has mentored an untold number of philosophers both Christian and non-Christian. Who can measure the ripple effect of the excellence he exhibited?

Third, Plantinga's excellence and, more particularly, the precise nature of this particular article are expressions of his self-understanding according to which he saw his work as a vocation. It was a central facet as to why he believes he was put on this earth. As a result, he approached philosophy as part of his discipleship under the authority of the Lord Jesus and His Word. In an important and relevant article, Paul Moser distinguishes two approaches to doing philosophy: the discussion mode and the obedience mode.[2]

Roughly, the discussion mode is involved in a perennial focus on talking about questions, options, claims, and arguments, seemingly done for its own sake. In my opinion, Christians who adopt the discussion mode road are easily caught up in focusing on their career, their academic reputation

---

2. Paul Moser, "Jesus and Philosophy: On the Questions We Ask," *Faith and Philosophy* 22.3 (July 2005): 261–283.

in the guild, and so forth. The obedience mode is done under the authority of Jesus, especially under His love commands. According to Moser:

> So, under Jesus's teachings, we no longer have business as usual in philosophy. The discipline of philosophy then takes on a purpose foreign to philosophy as we know it, even as practiced by Christian philosophers. Under the authority of Jesus, philosophy becomes agape-oriented ministry in the church of Jesus and thus reflective of Jesus himself. In this respect, Jesus is Lord of philosophy.[3]

I am not suggesting that Plantinga would agree with everything in Moser's article or in the way he tweaks doing philosophy under the love commands of Jesus. Nevertheless, it is clear that Plantinga did philosophy under the obedience mode. He was on a mission in doing philosophy and he saw entering the battle between the kingdom of darkness and the Kingdom of God as what resided in the background of the topics he addressed and the views he adopted.

2.2 Identify With and Do Your Philosophy Primarily for the Theologically Conservative Christian Community That Embraces the Truth of Historic Christianity

In his paper and more generally, Plantinga has consistently identified himself as member of the more orthodox, Christian community. He says this in his paper: "Christian philosophers, however, are the philosophers of the Christian community; and it is part of their task as Christian philosophers to serve the Christian community."[4]

Plantinga eschewed revisionist versions of Christianity that made it politically correct and acceptable to secular academic colleagues. Whether he intended it or not, I do not know. But, in fact, he served as a spokesperson for that community. He sought to be faithful to Scripture and to the Lord Jesus. As an illustration, Plantinga notes that many Christian philosophers caved in regarding Verificationism and revised Christian assertions accordingly. He asserts that "This hand wringing and those attempts to accommodate the positivist were inappropriate."[5]

As a result, he was sometimes insulted as being nothing but a Fundamentalist. There are several legitimate meanings of this term, but these insults indicate that many viewed him as far too conservative and non-progressive in his Christian beliefs. Interestingly, in one place he

---

3. Moser, "Jesus and Philosophy," 261.
4. Alvin Plantinga, *Warranted Christian Belief* (Oxford University Press, 2000), 255.
5. Plantinga, *Warranted Christian Belief*, 258.

actually defended the notion of being a Fundamentalist by claiming that at the end of the day, the term is used by critics as a pejorative, stigmatizing term of abuse equivalent to "son of a bitch."[6]

There were two basic ways Plantinga's paper and his general stance exemplifies his commitment to identifying with and being faithful to the theologically conservative Christian community: (1) He identified with, was a spokesperson for, and sought to defend this community. (2) He adopted, delineated, and defended orthodox Christian doctrine understood in a conservative way and in keeping with the main affirmation of the historic Christian church.

Regarding (1), while I cannot find it, and it may be apocryphal, rumor has it that Plantinga wrote or lectured somewhere that the Christian philosopher has at least two important responsibilities: (a) to protect our more uneducated brethren from using bad arguments for what may be true conclusions; (b) to defend our more uneducated brethren and their orthodox biblical beliefs among our academic colleagues, e.g., at APA meetings. Apparently, he pointed out that it takes no courage to do (a), but it takes a lot of courage and commitment to the Lord to do (b). This advice is an excellent model for all of us regarding how to prioritize and conduct our role as *Christian* philosophers who belong to a community.

Regarding (2), Plantinga notes that attempts to reshape Christian claims, to graft Christian thought onto a fundamentally and decidedly alien worldview contrary to a Christian worldview "...will seriously compromise, or distort, or trivialize the claims of Christian theism."[7] Later, he connects this counsel with personal integrity: "[W]e must display more integrity. We must not automatically assimilate what is current or fashionable or popular by way of philosophical opinions and procedures; for much of it comports ill with Christian ways of thinking."[8]

To cite one example of this, while there are different notions of biblical inerrancy, Plantinga seems to hold to a robust view of biblical authority that is at least a very close cousin to a widely accepted understanding of inerrancy.[9] He seems to think that Scripture is inspired in such a way that God can be said to be its principle author, and that what the divine author says in Scripture can be counted on to be true, since God wouldn't assert falsehood.

Consider these statements from his *Warranted Christian Belief*:

---

6. Plantinga, *Warranted Christian Belief*, 244-245.
7. Plantinga, *Warranted Christian Belief*, 256.
8. Plantinga, *Warranted Christian Belief*, 268-269.
9. For a statement and clarification of this widely accepted definition, see J. P. Moreland, "The Epistemic Advantage of Lost Autographic Tokens of the Bible," *Philosophia Christi* 23:1 (2021):187-93.

First, there is Scripture, the Bible, a collection of writings by human authors, but specially inspired by God in such a way that he can be said to be its principal author.[10]

...he arranged for the production of Scripture, the Bible, a library of books or writings each of which has a human author, but each of which is also specially inspired by God in such a way that he himself is its principal author. Thus, the whole library has a single principal author: God himself.[11]

But a traditional Christian also believes, for example, that the Gospel of John and Paul's epistle to the Romans and the book of Acts are divinely inspired and hence authoritative for Christian belief and practice. Indeed, he will believe this of the entire Bible. The whole Bible is a message from the Lord to humankind; this entire book is authoritative for Christian belief and practice.[12]

2.3 Do Philosophy with Appropriate Christian Boldness and Courage

Adolfo Lopez-Otero, a Stanford Engineering professor and a self-described secular humanist offers advice to thinking Christians who want to impact the world:

> When a Christian professor approaches a non-believing faculty member...they can expect to face a polite but condescending person [with a belief that they possess] superior metaphysics who can't understand how such an intelligent person [as yourself] still believes in things which have been discredited eons ago.[13]

He goes on to say that "[Christian professors] cannot afford to give excuses...if they are honest about wanting to open spiritual and truthful dialogue with their non-believing colleagues—that is the price they must pay for having declared themselves Christians."[14]

While Lopez-Otero's remarks are directed to Christian professors, his point applies to all thinking Christians: If we claim that our Christian views are true, we need to back that up by interacting with the various ideas that come from different academic disciplines.

---

10. Plantinga, *Warranted Christian Belief*, 205.
11. Plantinga, *Warranted Christian Belief*, 243.
12. Plantinga, *Warranted Christian Belief*, 376.
13. Adolfo Lopez-Otero, "Be Humble, but Daring," *The Real Issue* 16 (September/October 1997): 10.
14. Lopez-Otero, "Be Humble, but Daring," 11.

This takes boldness and courage, and Plantinga's article and general perspective exhibit both and call us to do the same. Indeed, his paper is peppered with admonitions to be bold and courageous. For example, he says Christian philosophers must exhibit "Christian courage, or boldness, or strength, or perhaps Christian self-confidence. We Christian philosophers must display more faith, more trust in the Lord."[15] Elsewhere, he advises that "The Christian philosopher does indeed have a responsibility to the philosophical world at large; but his fundamental responsibility is to the Christian community, and finally to God."[16]

The opposite of this is the revisionist tendency among many Christian philosophers and scholars in other disciplines. There is politically correct pressure suddenly to "find" that the Bible all along taught what our secular friends and peers tell us it should teach if we are going to be culturally and academically respectable. There is a sober-mindedness that should accompany any self-identifying Christian philosopher/scholar regarding these matters, since our laity often look to us or consider us as representative spokespersons of the Christian tradition. To many laypeople, it seems hardly a coincidence that just when the progressive secularly informed culture puts pressure on us to believe that P, even though the history of biblical interpretation supports ~P, we conveniently discover that we have misunderstood the scriptures all along!

I think the Christian community expects more courage out of its leaders than this, and we run the risk of making our own desired views of biblical interpretation more authoritative than the text itself. It is as though some exegetes have a desired view they want to sustain, and they fiddle with the Bible until they get it to turn out the "right" way.

I am not arguing that the current revisionist views are false, though I believe that to be the case. What I am urging us to consider is the unintended consequences of embracing the revisionist positions—the marginalization of Christian doctrine and ethics (after all, if we "find" the church was wrong for two thousand years at just the time when it is convenient to make such a discovery, what does this say about the epistemic and alethic status of the views we just happened not to have revised at present) and the placement of Christianity outside the cultural plausibility structure.

I do not mean to be harsh, but I have a sense that the revisionist approach to Christianity does not so much reflect the fact that certain historical doctrines are no longer plausible. Rather, I think the problem with this approach is a spiritual one—the revisionist is cowardly, does not

---

15. Plantinga, *Warranted Christian Belief*, 254.
16. Plantinga, *Warranted Christian Belief*, 262.

want to be perceived negatively by academic colleagues, and has placed respect for and success in his/her career over being a distinctively *Christian* philosopher who embodies the list I present above. Plantinga's paper, life, and work are the polar opposites of this revisionist perspective, and that is why his boldness and courage—and his call to us to be the same way—are so crucial today as the university becomes increasingly hostile to Christianity.

2.4 When Integrating Christian Truth Claims with Those from Other Sources, Give Appropriate, Strong Weight to the Former, Especially the Ontological and Epistemological Aspects of a Christian Worldview

In what I call conceptual integration, one's theological beliefs, especially those derived from careful study of the Bible, are blended and unified with important, reasonable ideas from one's profession or college major into a coherent, intellectually satisfying Christian worldview. As St. Augustine wisely advised, "We must show our Scriptures not to be in conflict with whatever [our critics] can demonstrate about the nature of things from reliable sources."[17]

When problematic truth claims arise from sources outside Christian ones, there is a need for the Christian to think hard about them in light of the need for knowing the truth, strengthening the rational authority of Christian theism, and placing it squarely within the plausibility structure of contemporary culture. Let us use the term "theology" to stand for any Christian idea that seems to be a part of a Christian worldview. When one addresses problems like these, there will emerge a number of different ways that theology can interact with an issue in a discipline outside theology. I have addressed these ways elsewhere.[18] Two are especially relevant to this chapter.

2.4.1 The Complementarity View

Propositions, theories, or methodologies in theology and another discipline may involve two different, complementary, non-interacting approaches to the same reality. Sociological aspects of church growth, certain psychological aspects of conversion may be sociological or

---

17. Augustine *De genesi ad litteram* 1.21. Cited in Ernan McMullin, "How Should Cosmology Relate to Theology?" in *The Science and Theology in the Twentieth Century*, ed. Arthur R. Peacocke (University of Notre Dame Press, 1981), 20.

18. J. P. Moreland, "Series Preface," in Garrett J. DeWeese, *Doing Philosophy as Christian* (InterVarsity Press, 2011), 9–28.

psychological descriptions of certain phenomena that are complementary to a theological description of church growth or conversion.

2.4.2 The Direct Interaction View

Propositions, theories, or methodologies in theology and another discipline may directly interact in such a way that either one area of study offers rational support for the other or one area of study raises rational difficulties for the other. For example, certain theological teachings about the existence of the soul raise rational problems for philosophical or scientific claims that deny the existence of the soul. The general theory of evolution raises various difficulties for certain ways of understanding the book of Genesis. Some have argued that the Big Bang theory tends to support the theological proposition that the universe had a beginning.

The complementary view has a place in the overall task of integration, but today it is being used almost exclusively by many Christian scholars and employed at times when it should not be. As a result, whether intended or not, the effect is to place Christian claims in what Francis Shaeffer used to call the "Upper Story," a realm where claims are taken by blind faith *sans* any support from reason and evidence. Consequently, Christian truth claims are taken out of the realm of reason and placed in the realm of faith as it is currently understood, viz., blind faith and emotion.

Another result is that the metaphysical and epistemological components of a Christian worldview are set aside, and integration focuses on ethics. Given the currently ubiquitous depiction of the fact/value separation, this shift of focus is one way Christian thinkers become Christianity's gravedigger. Moreover, this shift comes perilously close to the NOMA view (non-overlapping magisterial). NOMA and the overuse of the complementary view result in insulating Christian claims from problematic so-called deliverances of reason. The price that is paid for this way of protecting Christianity is that its claims are no longer regarded as intellectually serious.

When you read Plantinga's paper it becomes clear that he did not accept this overuse of the complementary view. Instead, implicit in his integrative approach was the direct interaction view and Plantinga regularly used the metaphysics and epistemology of Christianity as he understood them to provide grounds for rejecting revising the historical, traditional claims of a biblical and theologically conservative Christian worldview.

3. The Impact Plantinga's Essay Had on Me Personally

I became a Jesus follower in November 1968 during my junior year as a physical chemistry major at the University of Missouri through the ministry of Cru (Campus Crusade for Christ). Upon graduation, I turned down a full ride to do a PhD in nuclear chemistry at the University of Colorado and joined the staff of Cru from 1970–1975 and 1979–1984. As I witnessed and discipled young believers, I turned to self-identified Evangelical philosophers and apologists for help. However, most of them published books or articles in Evangelical presses and they did not participate in the APA or other standard professional societies. But when I saw (especially) Plantinga start the Society of Christian Philosophers and, later, publish his essay, it gave me confidence, boldness, and a sense of pride about my conservative Christian worldview. Plantinga actually changed my life in the ways I mentioned above. While I did not and do not agree with some of his views, nevertheless, he became a role-model for me that eventually led me to get my MA and PhD in philosophy.

Here's a story that illustrates his impact on me. In 1981 I was in the middle of doing an MA in philosophy at the University of California Riverside. I was taking a seminar on Hume from Bernd Magnus (1937–2014). When discussing Hume's Fork as Magnus understood it, I raised my hand and said that the Fork was self-refuting. Magnus' patronizing response went this way: He said that when he was a graduate student, if he and other graduate students heard someone employ self-refutation against a view, they knew the person must be an undergraduate since sophisticated, well-trained philosophers recognize this as a cheap way to deal with a position. Yikes!

Well, as it happened, three weeks later Plantinga was a colloquium lecturer for the department. The room was packed with graduate students and virtually all the philosophy faculty in attendance. Given Plantinga's physical and academic stature, there was an air of intimidation in the room, and I noticed that Magnus never made eye-contact with Plantinga. Plantinga was analyzing classical foundationalism, and he pointed out (as he often did) that its fundamental epistemic principle was self-refuting. No one called him sophomoric or unsophisticated. Instead, not a single person had a response to his employment of self-refutation. Plantinga held court that day and, as I walked away, reflecting on Magnus's comment to me and lack of comment to Plantinga, I thought to myself, "Maybe I'm not as stupid as I think!" Brother Al gave me a boost of courage that day, and I stand in his debt for that!

4. The Impact of Plantinga's Essay on Christian Philosophy

Space considerations require me to be brief here. But at least three results were fostered and magnified by his essay: (1) The essay made it respectable and a Christian duty to be a traditional Christian with a conservative biblically based worldview, especially for those going into philosophy. (2) The essay fomented a movement in which a large and growing number of people pursued a doctorate in philosophy in order to be faithful to Jesus and His Word, to serve the Christian community and, secondarily, the profession, and to use scriptural teaching and historical Christianity in doing their work. (3) Plantinga's example helped to revive the quality of the Evangelical Philosophical Society and its journal *Philosophia Christi*, as well as contributing to the outbreak and academic quality of apologetics ministries all over the country and beyond.

5. My Advice to Christian Philosophers

Let me begin by affirming the four truths/values I listed above. I urge Christian philosophers to internalize and habituate them, to make them a part of their character, and to see their philosophical work as a calling from the Lord Himself by employing them.

In addition, I encourage my co-laborers to strike a balance according to their own sense of gifting, passion, and calling between engaging in technical, scholarly work and popular writings and lectures meant for thinking Christians in our churches and parachurch ministries as well as for thinking unbelievers. In this latter activity, we become to some degree public intellectuals who address important societal issues from a biblical worldview perspective and weigh in on these as philosophical ambassadors for Christ.

Next, don't be too quick to wave the white flag of surrender and give up too much theological territory in light of academic pressure or difficulties raised against the faith. There is too little courage among Christian philosophers today and too much revisionism to make Christianity user-friendly for our progressive secular colleagues and culture. We have had far too much of that. As you write and speak, start with an audience of One, while secondarily incorporating an audience constituted by the theologically conservative Christian community and, lastly, serve the secular audience and the guild in general.

Finally, attend to your relationship with God and your spiritual life. Fall in love with Jesus, attach to Him, learn to be intimate with Him, and develop a heart to see Him loved, respected, and made famous. Pay close attention to your spiritual formation and make it a regular habit to read classic and contemporary books on how to cultivate a deep spiritual life and make progress in your journey. Let these books wash over your soul and bring life-giving flourishing to you.[19] I have long believed that we Christian philosophers often go wrong by turning our work into a matter of career and prestige. We too often forget that we are whole persons who need passionate intimacy with God as well as regular exposure to the teachings and practices that will form our lives and deeply Christianize our pilgrimage. Cultivate emotional intelligence and learn good relational skills.

---

19. I highly recommend the writings of Dallas Willard in this regard.

12

PHILOSOPHY AS CHRISTIAN SERVICE

Dolores G. Morris

University of South Florida

The contributors to this volume are an impressive lot. When I was invited to participate, I spent some time wondering what, if anything, I could add to the project. I suspect there are a few reasons for my inclusion. I recently wrote a book encouraging Christians to develop the skills of philosophical reasoning—to become, in some sense, Christian philosophers. The more obvious explanation is my personal connection to Plantinga. I was privileged to write my dissertation under his direction. In my years at Notre Dame, I spent a good deal of time in conversation with him—about work, but also in a small group Bible study, in a discussion group about his work on science and religion, and even over rounds of disc golf with friends. When Plantinga first delivered his advice to Christian philosophers, I was working my way through kindergarten. Unsurprisingly, it made no impact on my life at the time. Plantinga's life and work, in contrast, shaped my entry into Christian philosophy.

This likely explains my invitation to contribute to this anthology. It does not adequately capture the effect that Plantinga's advice has had on my life. By the time I arrived at Notre Dame, I had already been impacted by the standard he set when I was a child. Notably, it was not primarily as a *philosopher* that I benefitted from Plantinga's advice, but rather as a *Christian in crisis*. My years as an undergraduate comprised a uniquely difficult period of my life. At that time, I was introduced to works written by those philosophers who had taken up Plantinga's call to pursue autonomous, faithful, integrated Christian philosophy. In the end, in marked contrast to Plantinga's distinction between the *philosophical* and the *pastoral* problem of evil, Christian philosophy became, to me, a pastoral lifeline in a time of suffering. This experience, and the ways that it has shaped me, will form the basis for much of what I say today.

To echo Plantinga, my goal here is to encourage Christian philosophers to boldly pursue holistic intellectual integrity on two fronts: as Christians among philosophers, and as philosophers among Christians. As I read it, Plantinga's advice pertained primarily to the first of these challenges. His life, in contrast, has exemplified a commitment to both. Locally, Plantinga taught Sunday School classes at his church in South Bend, Indiana. More broadly, he worked to transform the rigorous philosophical content of *Warranted Christian Belief* into the more accessible *Knowledge and Christian Belief*. My first piece of advice, then, is this: as Christian philosophers, we should seek to serve the body of Christ *as* philosophers. It is good that we bring careful Christian thinking into academic discourse. It is just as important that we bring careful philosophical thinking into nonacademic Christian settings. The two tasks are mutually beneficial.

Of course, in deigning to give advice, I run the risk of adopting an unearned position of authority. In his address, Plantinga acknowledged the awkwardness of this presumption, writing: "'Who are you,' you say, 'to give the rest of us advice?' That's a good question. I shall deal with it as one properly deals with good questions to which one doesn't know the answer: I shall ignore it."[1] Plantinga was free to ignore the question because his credentials were well and truly established. My professional reputation may not speak for itself. I acknowledge this freely and without reservation, for my advice does not come from my success as an academic philosopher. Instead, my reflections are grounded in a few significant experiences and their effect on my life. For this reason, I want to begin with a brief diversion into the details of my own life story.

I grew up a devout child in a devout family. This is not to say that I was gentle, meek, and mild. I was (and remain) hyperactive, messy, impulsive, and disorganized. I was also very cheerful and, for lack of a better description, *extremely into God*. I clearly recall a post-church conversation about a homily on 1 Thessalonians 5:17. "Of course," someone said, "nobody *really* prays without ceasing!" I remember being puzzled. I remember thinking that I came pretty close. I prayed my way through the day, chatting with God as I went along. To be completely candid, I even believed that I was sort of God's *favorite*. I knew, of course, that he loved everybody, but between me and God, I was pretty sure I held a special place in his heart.

---

1. Alvin Plantinga, "Advice to Christian Philosophers," *Faith and Philosophy* 1, no. 3 (July 1984): 254.

It is a little embarrassing to share these details about my very young self. I am sharing them nonetheless because they set the stage for all that was to come. By college, I would struggle to believe that God loved me at all. I felt almost certain He did not. One thing I clung to in those difficult years was my early childhood assurance and devotion. When I was able to pray at all, I mostly prayed something to the effect of "Look. I'm all that's left of that kid. You have to be faithful to her, so you're stuck being faithful to me." These were not hopeful prayers. They were begrudging, desperate attempts to cling to a God who seemed to have abandoned me completely.

As a teenager, I was enthusiastically involved with my church youth group. I had a Harvard educated pastor, intellectually curious and thoughtful parents, and a church community that was evangelical without being anti-intellectual. It was fantastic. In my freshman year, I began to attend a Christian high school that was rigorous and inspiring. At home, at church, and at school, I was immersed in a loving, intellectually robust, Christian community.

The night before I turned 15, my young cousin drowned. "Paulie" was not yet 4, genuinely hilarious, and a joy to be around. I was a dozen years older than him, but we were close. He was my buddy. My initial reaction to the news was confusion and denial. "He can't be dead because I just saw him last week. He was fine!" To say that losing Paulie was hard would be to understate things significantly. I come from a wonderfully big family. This was not the first death of someone I loved. Still, Paulie's death changed me in a way that those previous losses had not. All at once, I saw what the world was like. My eyes were opened to the reality of our vulnerability, that *nobody* is guaranteed to be here tomorrow. Those whose eyes have been opened in this way will, I think, agree—they stay open. This is a fact of reality that can be suppressed or dampened, but it can't be unlearned.

Paulie's death ended up being the beginning of a season of loss. Over the next four years, my family grieved the death of a number of people whom we loved. I won't go into it all. I will simply note that there were many ungranted prayers for (earthly) healing, and it felt relentless. One day, sometime in high school, my best friend gently cautioned that I had become very angry. Caustic, really. I was getting a little mean. She was sympathetic; she knew why it was happening, but she wanted me to see that it was happening. She was an excellent friend to me in my grief. Our conversation was the push that I needed to acknowledge and address my growing anger. That friend, the friend who had walked with me through so much loss, was murdered at the start of our sophomore year of college. I was unmoored.

In response, I sought isolation. It was difficult to see friendship as anything more than increased vulnerability. I was consumed by anger, sadness, and fear. As for God, He seemed to have gone silent—absolutely, devastatingly silent. But a silent God is not an *absent* God. Even in my pain and anger, I could not shake my belief that God was real, and that He was who Christianity said he was. Fortunately for me, my parents had never affirmed any kind of prosperity gospel—neither for financial wealth nor for health and healing. I imagine most people grow up believing that the worst things won't happen to them. I was not immune to this naïve expectation, but I was spared the damaging theological framework that would have packaged this hope as divine promise. I'm certain that made a difference. In any case, for a long time I believed that Christianity was true but that God, for whatever reason, just didn't want *me*.

Throughout these years, I continued to show up in Christian spaces—church on Sunday, campus Christian fellowship meetings, small group Bible studies. I was fortunate to have friends and family who were not scandalized by my struggles—and I was vocal about those struggles. I was so hurt, and so angry, but I could not walk away. As a philosopher, I would love to say that my reasons for staying were entirely intellectual. They were not. I had a solid theological framework; there was a degree of rational commitment even in the midst of my doubts. Beyond that, the broader truth is that I could not forget the ongoing, consistent, sometimes dramatic and miraculous experiences of God that shaped my childhood and early adolescence. It is difficult to cease believing in a God that you *remember*. I was hurt by God, and angry at God—I wanted answers *from* God.

This is how things stood in my junior year of college when I enrolled in a class called "Reason & Religion." As an English major pursuing a minor in Music, philosophy was not on my radar. I signed up for the class with my roommate simply because we had met the professor (Michael Murray) through our campus Christian fellowship and it sounded interesting. That course altered the trajectory of my life, but not in the way a popular Christian movie about philosophy might depict. I did not get tidy answers to all of my questions about God. I was not rationally persuaded of the existence of God on the basis of philosophical argument. In fact, I was introduced to a number of new challenges to theism. I encountered rigorous arguments for atheism. This was not an apologetics course. It was philosophy, through and through.

My introduction to philosophy did not *end* my struggles. Nevertheless, it offered me a lifeline that would prove invaluable. Here was a new way of thinking about God. Here were all these thoughtful people, writing about

God in a way I had not yet seen. By the time I got to college, Plantinga's advice had taken root and borne fruit in academic philosophy. One of the assigned texts in Murray's class was his edited anthology, *Reason for the Hope Within*. There, serious Christian philosophers gave accessible accounts of their work. I could not get enough. I felt like I had been given the tools to finally work through so much of what consumed me, and to do so in ways that were careful and illuminating. I was especially compelled by the problems of evil and hiddenness. "Yes, the world is rife with suffering, and Christians are not immune. Yes, the presence of God is elusive. Let's examine what that might tell us about God and about ourselves." This was exactly what I needed, and I found it just when I needed it most. One class led to another, and within a few years I was pursuing the PhD at Notre Dame.

These experiences are surely a factor in my belief that Christian philosophers ought to take teaching seriously. They are not the *only* factor. I know that my trajectory was not typical; I had philosophical leanings long before I knew what to call them. I am equally motivated by my experiences as a teacher. If we are honest with ourselves, I suspect that most of us will see that we are likely to make a greater difference in the classroom than we will in our writing. If this is so, we ought to take it seriously. Excellent, meaningful work can be done in the college classroom.

The same is true for our churches. I know that I have been fortunate in this respect. I attend a church that values the strengths of its congregants, proactively prompting individuals to bring what they have to the church. I had only been attending for about a year when they first asked if I would teach a class on Christian philosophy. This class, and the encouragement of my church, ultimately lead me to write an introduction to philosophy for Christians. In a review of that book, Thomas Ward wrote:

> Christian philosophers should take inspiration from *Believing Philosophy* to conduct their own discernment about what comparable sort of outreach work they might undertake, to help nonexperts benefit from our millennia-long tradition of philosophical reflection on divine things.[2]

I wholeheartedly agree. Christian philosophers have a tremendously valuable resource—wisdom and insight on matters of significance. Further, the pedagogical skills we develop in the classroom can, and should, equip us to share these resources. We should do what we can to use our gifts in service to the body of Christ.

---

2. Thomas M. Ward, "Dolores G. Morris, Believing Philosophy: A Guide to Becoming a Christian Philosopher," *Faith and Philosophy* 39 (2022): 654, https://doi.org/10.37977/faithphil.2022.39.4.11.

I want to be clear about this: when I encourage Christian philosophers to bring their gifts to the church, I do not mean that they should all become popular Christian apologists. Even at its best, the apologetic approach is just one way of bringing philosophy into our churches. Instead, I mean that they should consider the implications of their own area of research for more general Christian questions. Crucially, not all Christian philosophers even work in the Philosophy of Religion. Many do not, and they are no less aptly described as Christian philosophers. We may take as our starting point Plantinga's call to a certain kind of holistic integrity: "Integrity in the sense of integral wholeness, or oneness, or unity, being all of one piece."[3] The church does not need an inundation of popular apologetics. The church may very well need help navigating questions about personhood, language, science, technology, aesthetics, and ideology. Philosophers are uniquely situated to be of service in this way.

Even this much can be difficult. Not all churches are interested in what philosophy has to offer. Too many Christians view philosophers with something between suspicion and disdain. What should a person do when her church sees no place for her contributions? This is a difficult question to answer, but the challenge is not unique to philosophers. As believers, we are called to use our gifts in service to the body of Christ. When we find that our contributions are unwelcome, I suppose the best we can do is to keep trying. For some, we may find avenues outside of the church to be a more natural fit. This might be something like a podcast or a substack, but it may also take the form of ordinary friendship and thoughtful conversation. Like me, my husband is a Christian philosopher. He is a part of a few local reading groups, where he serves as both friend and informal guide. Fanfare is not the point. The point is to bring your gifts to the table in Christian service. Philosophers have so much to offer the church. We should do what we can to give what we can to the body of Christ.

Perhaps counterintuitively, there are philosophical benefits to this practice. Inside our narrow academic domains, it can be difficult to see the ubiquity of certain shared attitudes and preconceptions. This isn't unique to philosophy; all disciplines have their framework, all frameworks have their blind spots. We can see this today when we read Plantinga's advice to the Christian philosophers of his day. It took no effort at all for me to escape the grip of logical positivism, despite the hold it seems once to have had. Momentum shifts, attitudes change, and what was once held

---

3. Plantinga, "Advice to Christian Philosophers," 254.

to be nearly inviolable comes to be seen as quaint. One excellent way of coming to see the assumptions into which we have been inculcated is by teaching. How often in the classroom do students ask for a defense of precisely that claim that you took to be incontrovertible? Sometimes, a defense is easy to provide; the truth is clear. Other times, what becomes clear is the tenuousness of the claim. These have become some of my favorite teaching moments. In my experience, it is possible for an untrained student to bring genuine insight to a tired topic. I would even go so far as to say that the insight *depends*, in some way, on the lack of training. Sometimes we need an outside perspective.

This is especially true for Christian philosophers who teach or serve in a nonacademic Christian setting. There are times when philosophical reflections on God reveal theologically important insights. There are times when congregants ask, "Why ever would you say that about God?!"and the answer is straightforward and significant. There are also, I think, times when the answer is less clear. The God of the Philosophers and the God of Christianity may not neatly coincide.

My last piece of advice is more of a hope: that Christian philosophers would be spend more time developing distinctly Christian accounts. Ours is not the God of mere theism, but the God who became man in Christ Jesus. When Plantinga urged us to display more autonomy, integrity, and boldness, he appealed to examples that were largely a matter of theistic commitments. For instance,

> The Christian philosopher quite properly *starts from* the existence of God, and presupposes it in philosophical work, whether or not he can show it to be probably or plausible with respect to premises accepted by all philosophers, or most philosophers at the great contemporary centers of philosophy.[4]

To this I say, "Yes, and we can go further!" It is not merely the God of the philosophers, but the *Christian* God, whose existence we affirm. We should take care to ensure that that the God whose existence we defend in our work is reconcilable with the one we encounter in scripture and affirm in our creeds. We should probably also say more about Jesus.

There are those who would say that the God of the philosophers is and must be the standard. A few years ago, I was chastised on social media for suggesting otherwise. I've thought of this moment often and, in retrospect, I wish I had saved the details. What I do remember quite clearly is the core of the accusation: "If the Christian God is not the God

---

4. Plantinga, "Advice to Christian Philosophers," 261.

of the philosophers, then he is just another idol or false god." At the time I stayed silent. With reflection, I remain opposed to the elevation of the omni-God above all else. It is tempting to believe that the philosophical conception of God is a kind of "pure" concept, resulting from reason alone. The older I get, the less confident I am that *any* of our concepts are pure in this way; none are immune from social and historical influence.

By way of example, two recent atheistic arguments come to mind: JL Schellenberg's Hiddenness Argument and Erik Wielenberg's "The Parent-Child Analogy and the Limits of Skeptical Theism."[5] Different though they be, these arguments share two important features: each is deductive, and each purports to show that certain *hiddenness facts* are incompatible with the existence of a loving God. Both Wielenberg and Schellenberg take the necessitating structure of their arguments to be an asset.[6] Neither requires an inference from *how things seem to us* to *how things are*. Instead, *love itself* is the central concept—parental for Wielenberg, personal for Schellenberg. Finally, in both cases, divine love and (their specified manner of) hiddenness are not held to be merely in tension with one another, but to be logically incompatible.[7]

Elsewhere, I have argued that this conception of love is inextricably shaped by our prosperous 21st century Western culture. Here, I will say just this: A Christian response to either of these arguments must contend with a challenge not faced by all theists. Our God *self-describes* as hidden.[8] His son cried out in agony, "Why have you abandoned me?" If Wielenberg and Schellenberg are correct about love, then the God of the Christian scriptures is no God at all. There is no reconciling the Christian God with these conceptions of goodness and love. Thus, the task of responding to these arguments is markedly different for the Christian than it is for the mere theist. One might defend the God of the philosophers without having defended the Christian God. The bar is higher for the latter than it is for the former.

---

5. J. L. Schellenberg, *The Hiddenness Argument: Philosophy's New Challenge to Belief in God* (Oxford University Press, 2015); Erik Wielenberg, "The Parent-Child Analogy and the Limits of Skeptical Theism," *International Journal for Philosophy of Religion* 78, no. 3 (2015): 301–14.

6. See: Schellenberg, *The Hiddenness Argument: Philosophy's New Challenge to Belief in God*, 112–13. And Wielenberg, "The Parent-Child Analogy and the Limits of Skeptical Theism," 309.

7. In fairness to Schellenberg and Wielenberg, neither accuses the theist of logical incoherence. Both authors adopt a position of epistemic humility. Nevertheless, the point remains for the content of their arguments. Each affirms one or more entailment claims that preclude the possibility of a loving God permitting a certain kind of hiddenness.

8. Examples abound but include: Deuteronomy 31:17-18 and Isaiah 57:17. We do not need to adopt a literal understanding of the anthropomorphic language used in passages like this. Even without doing so, the point remains: Biblical prophets, again and again, proclaim the intermittent (apparent) hiddenness of God. Scripture also affirms the preponderance of evidence *for* God. (Romans 1:21) As I see it, the latter does not override the former.

On the positive side, there are resources available to the Christian philosopher that are not available to mere theism. To see this, teach the problem of evil in a church setting. There, congregants are often surprised to learn how little a role Jesus plays in some Christian philosophical responses to suffering. I am convinced that they are right to be surprised. It *matters* that ours is a God who suffered alongside us. If the incarnation, death, and resurrection of the second person of the trinity make no difference to our philosophical response to suffering, in what sense is it a *Christian* response?

I know, of course, that academic philosophers must be wary of begging the important questions. We cannot assume the truth of Christianity in order to defend the existence of God. All the more reason, I say, to *do more than merely defend* the existence of God. We should be saying more about suffering. We can do more than defend the minimal claim that it is compatible with the existence of a loving God. This ought to be the beginning, not the end, of a philosophical treatment of evil and suffering.

This is my hope and my encouragement for Christian philosophers. We are privileged. We have been given opportunities to read, reflect on, and discuss excellent writing about things that matter. It can be easy to lose sight of what a gift this is. We should take seriously the responsibilities that come with having been given so much. We should use our knowledge and our insight for the glory of God and the benefit of his church.

13

RECONSTRUCTING ADVICE TO CHRISTIAN PHILOSOPHERS

Meghan D. Page

Loyola University Maryland

As I reflect on Alvin Plantinga's "Advice to Christian Philosophers" forty years after its publication, I am immediately struck by the difference in these two historical moments. Plantinga writes of "Christianity...on the move," as evidenced by the growing number of Christian schools and churches, Christian victories in political arenas concerning "prayer in public schools," and the "creationism/evolutionism controversy."[1] The current religious landscape in America is quite different. Christian churches and schools are downsizing if not closing, and numerous surveys report a decline in the number of Americans who identify as Christian. According to a report by the Pew Research Center on March 15, 2024, "80% of U.S. adults say religion's role in American life is shrinking—a percentage that's as high as it's ever been."[2] While some Christians still advocate for organized prayer and the teaching of creationism in public schools, they are a minority, and an overwhelming majority of Christians, especially Christian academics, see no conflict between Christianity and the theory of evolution.

Given this drastic change in social context, it's natural to ask whether Plantinga's advice remains relevant. My own answer to that question is complex. In one sense, I wholeheartedly agree with Plantinga's call for

---

1. Alvin Plantinga, "Advice to Christian Philosophers," *Faith and Philosophy* 1 (1984): 253.
2. Pew Research Center. "8 IN 10 AMERICANS SAY RELIGION IS LOSING INFLUENCE IN PUBLIC LIFE." Washington, D.C.: *Pew Research Center*, March 15, 2024. https://www.pewresearch.org/religion/2024/03/15/religions-role-in-public-life/.

autonomy, integrity, and boldness. However, I disagree with many ways he imagines these values might be embodied and the philosophical stances he suggests. This ambivalence should come as no surprise, given that philosophy is—as Plantinga puts it—a social enterprise, in which "our standards and assumptions—the parameters in which we practice our craft" are deeply influenced by social factors, including but not limited to the various communities we are members of, the bodies we inhabit those communities in, and the dynamic ways our social identities intersect with one another throughout our lives.[3] And while Plantinga and I have some sociological overlap as members of the Christian community and the philosophical community (and the Christian philosophical community), we have experienced these communities with different bodies and in very different times and seasons. This combination of relatedness and difference is what Ellen Ott Marshall describes as the basis for one of the most natural and necessary forces in the creation of the world: conflict. She writes,

> As parts of an ecosystem, we are organisms that are both different from and related to each other. Whether on the large scale of shifting tectonic plates or the small scale of worms and waste in compost, the world of which we are part is made and remade through conflict. We live as part of an ecosystem that undergoes constant change as elements strike together. To be is to be in conflict.[4]

Although we often view conflict as problematic, Marshall reminds us it is a natural part of the world's unfolding. "The dynamics of conflict are the stuff of daily life, the movement of history, the making and remaking of community, and the vibrancy of faith…"[5] She encourages Christians to engage conflict constructively, as a catalyst for "something new and good."

My hope for this paper is to do just that. I intend to honor Plantinga's contribution to the Christian philosophical tradition by striking our views together to produce something new and good, sketching a picture of how the Christian philosopher might creatively navigate her conflicts to do the same. Rather than argue against Plantinga, I offer my view alongside his, highlighting where they diverge. My hope is this juxtaposition of perspectives invites the reader into conversation with what Plantinga describes as "a complicated, many-sided dialectical discussion."[6]

---

3. Plantinga, "Advice," 255.
4. Ellen Ott Marshall, *Introduction to Christian Ethics: Conflict, Faith, and Human Life* (Westminster John Knox Press, 2018), 1.
5. Marshall, *Introduction to Christian Ethics*, 2.
6. Plantinga, "Advice," 271.

To accomplish this task, I spell out a core disagreement between Plantinga and I concerning the philosopher's Christian identity and corresponding role in the academy. Next I discuss how these different views of the Christian philosopher align with different visions of the church-world relation as articulated by Natalie Carnes. Finally, I reconsider the values Plantinga claims should guide the Christian philosopher, offering my own slant on how to rethink and rename them.

Plantinga begins his remarks by noting that "Christianity is on the move."[7] I find it striking that he begins—and continues—to speak of the life and work of Christianity rather than the life and work of Christ. This framing illuminates a core difference between Plantinga and I concerning how we, as philosophers, internalize our Christian identity. Plantinga suggests that to the philosopher, Christianity is a set of propositions, and to be a Christian philosopher is to be committed to the truth of those propositions.[8] He bemoans the days of positivism when the "most popular question of philosophical theology was not whether Christianity or theism is *true*; the question instead was whether it even *makes sense* to *say* that there is such a person as God."[9] He asserts the solution to this problem requires "less accommodation of the current fashion and more Christian self-confidence; Christian theism is true...so the verifiability criterion is false." These passages suggest Plantinga views Christianity as the sort of thing that can be true or false; in the school of twentieth Century analytic philosophy which Plantinga was entrenched, the sort of thing that can be true or false is a proposition. From this vantage point, to be a Christian philosopher is to adopt and defend certain propositions and work out the consequences they imply.

This is not how I internalize my Christian identity. For philosophical, theological, and experiential reasons, I find the framework of "propositional knowledge" to be at best limiting if not altogether misguided. Rather than try to convince readers to share this perspective in the space given, I offer a few reasons I occupy it. Interestingly, many of the philosophical reasons I reject the propositional knowledge framework point towards the *success* of the positivist project. While the project failed to accomplish its goal,

---

7. Plantinga, "Advice," 253.
8. Given the personal overtones of this advice, it is important to note that the "Plantinga" I refer to here is my own reconstruction of Plantinga based on this particular letter. Plantinga himself was a complex person, and even Advice contains portions that suggest his view was more nuanced. Kyla Ebels-Duggan considers a very different theme of Plantinga's advice, and I think there is much truth in what she says ["Christian Philosophy and the Christian Life," in *Christian Philosophy: Conceptions, Continuations, and Challenges*, ed. J. Aaron Simmons (Oxford University Press, 2019), 55-72]. I, in no way mean to misrepresent him, but also want to acknowledge that my representation—like any representation of a dynamic person—is limited, and see my contribution as one part of a larger mosaic of understanding.
9. Plantinga, "Advice," 253.

I see this failure, and the unveiling of important technical truths along the way, as significant philosophical progress. The positivists set out to encapsulate "all truth" into a single formal language, and discovered this was impossible even in principle for both logical and philosophical reasons. Moreover, most cases of scientific knowledge cannot be clearly or successfully translated into the formal, proposition-based languages held so dear by many analytic philosophers. The upshot of this, as I see it, is "the sum of all knowledge" is not something representable by a large set of propositions. For Christians, this should come as no surprise, given our tradition equates Truth with a person.

This brings up some theological reasons I resist viewing the propositional picture of knowledge as complete. The form of the argument is a bit like a *reductio*; I cannot construct a cohesive narrative where God's primary desire is for people to "assert the truth" of a particular set of propositions and God accomplishes this goal through the incarnation, death, and resurrection of Jesus. If the ultimate revelation God wants us to have is a list of true sentences *there had to be an easier way*; at the very least, Jesus could have written them all down somewhere. But alas, that is not the tradition we have inherited. The Gospel of Luke reports that Jesus met some of his followers along the road to Emmaus and "interpreted to them in all the scriptures the things concerning himself (Luke 24:26 RSV)," but doesn't bother to include the interpretations.[10]

This points towards my experiential grounds for rejecting the propositional approach to Christianity. The short story is—*I did not so learn Christ*. I did not become (or remain) a Christian because of the ontological, cosmological, or design argument (spoiler alert: I don't think any of them work). I did not sit down and read the two conflicting creation accounts in Genesis and think "yep, this sounds like an ideal manifestation of propositional consistency!" My journey to faith was one that began (and continues) through experience. I came to a point in my life where I was lost, and when I cried out for help, help came to me in the person of Jesus Christ. And from my own vantage point, I continually experience loving guidance from the person of Jesus Christ through scripture, tradition, reason, and the love and wisdom of others.

I recognize there is much to unpack here about what these experiences are like, how one might see them as involving the person of Jesus Christ, the proper hermeneutics for interpreting scripture, and so forth. However, I leave those issues aside for the sake of the task at hand, which is to emphasize I do not understand my Christian identity as an

---

10. I am grateful to John Chrisman for making this point.

intellectual commitment to a set of propositions but as a choice to follow a person. *Of course* this kind of self-narrative will involve the belief in some propositions—I am not trying to make the argument otherwise. But "defending a list of propositions" is not the posture with which I live into and narrate my Christian identity.

To summarize, though we are both philosophers, Plantinga and I understand our Christian philosophical commitments very differently. For Plantinga, to be a Christian philosopher is to accept certain propositions as true and work out what other propositions follow from them. For me, Christianity is a commitment to follow the person of Jesus, and to be a Christian philosopher is to remain in that posture while doing philosophy and navigating my academic career.

These two understandings of Christian identity, together with differences in the disciplinary norms in our respective philosophical generations, result in different approaches to the secular academy. During Plantinga's career, many philosophers understood the primary project of the discipline to be "working out" the story of the world in a formal propositional language—and very few were willing to admit "God exists" into the set of true propositions. For someone like Plantinga, this presents an irreconcilable conflict. To be a Christian is to defend the truth of **p**, to be a philosopher is to remain agnostic if not deny the truth of **p**, and truth is a binary operator. This scenario exemplifies an intellectual stand-off.

This militaristic analogy is consonant with language used by Plantinga. The Christian philosopher is "on the move" but "marching through largely alien territory" in an academic culture that is "profoundly nontheistic and hence non-Christian—more than that it is anti-theistic." This description of the Christian philosopher's relationship to the academy is filled with antagonism; she will likely find herself under serious pressure to betray her Christian identity to fulfill her philosophical one. To this Christian, Plantinga writes:

> My counsel can be summed up on two connected suggestions, along with a codicil. First, Christian philosophers...must display more autonomy—more independence of the rest of the philosophical world. Second, Christian philosophers must display more integrity—integrity in the sense of integral wholeness, or oneness, or unity, or being all of one piece...And necessary to these two is a third: Christian courage, or boldness, or strength, or perhaps Christian self-confidence. We Christian philosophers must display more faith, more trust in the Lord; we must put on the whole armor of God.[11]

---

11. Plantinga, "Advice to Christian Philosophers," 254.

I see great value in this advice, but also worry that, especially when joined with militaristic analogies, it perpetuates an antagonistic conception of the relationship between Christian philosophers and the broader academy. This worry echoes one expressed by Natalie Carnes concerning the church-world relationship more generally. As an exemplar of her "antagonistic church-world model," Carnes points to Rod Dreher's book *The Benedict Option*:

> …in response to what he sees as a worrying trend of secularization coupled with a weakening of the church, Dreher recommends that Christians form communities that withdraw from certain aspects of society to intensify their Christian practices and strengthen their faith commitments. The choice, as he puts it, is stark: 'Make a decisive leap into a truly countercultural way of living Christianity, or . . . doom our children and our children's children to assimilation'.[12]

Dreher's position resonates with Plantinga's, who advises Christians to focus on their commitment to the Christian community and its interests rather than prioritize the fundamentally counter-Christian philosophical projects of the moment. As an alternative to this antagonistic picture, Carnes describes a protagonistic church-world relation, drawing on critiques of the nature-culture binary to elaborate her view, and contrasting the ecclesiology found in Rowan Williams' *Looking East in Winter* to Dreher's:

> Where the two writers majorly diverge is in framing church-world relations, which are not fundamentally antagonistic for Williams but protagonistic. As God sends the Only Begotten into the world to bring to it eternal life, so is the church, for Williams, sent into the world to discover and share that divine life…Williams's approach suggests an intimacy of church and world, where the two terms under consideration form not a binary but a shingled relation of overlapping objects, a relation of dynamism and exchange.[13]

Where the antagonistic picture of the church-world relation implies a zero-sum game, in which wealth is never created or destroyed and so a win for one is a loss for the other, the protagonistic picture depicts a positive sum scenario: dynamic interactions between the church and the world can produce an increased yield for all parties.[14] The spear of the antagonistic

---

12. Natalie Carnes, "Nature, Culture, Church," in *Confessing the Church: Explorations in Constructive Dogmatics*, ed. Oliver D. Crisp and Fred Sanders (Zondervan, 2024), 82.
13. Carnes, "Nature, Culture, Church," 92.
14. Portions of "Advice to Christian Philosophers" suggests a more protagonistic side of Plantinga, e.g., when he remarks that Christian Philosophy "must pay careful attention to other

church is traded for the pruning hook of protagonism. Carnes connects this picture with "a little yeast leavening the whole lump," interpreting the church as the great leavening agent. I favor the parable of the mustard seed, where the church is planted in the field of the world and grows into a large tree that offers shade and sanctuary to all.

Carnes's protagonistic model of the church-world relation resonates deeply with my own sense of vocation as a Christian philosopher. For me, Christianity is a commitment to a person, a person I believe was sent into the world to make all things new through love. Former Congressional representative Elijah Cummings often quoted Neil Postman to remind us "Children are a living message we send to a time we will not see."[15] Similarly, God sent Christ into the world as a *living* message, and I believe that living message is continued through the mystical church. To be a Christian philosopher is to be a living message of love to the philosophical community. And because this message is alive rather than propositionally fossilized, the messenger has plenty of conceptual freedom and flexibility regarding what philosophical projects and frameworks she might choose to engage. In many ways, the Christian philosopher is herself a product of dynamic exchanges between the church and the world, as she is formed by the practices and teachings of both.

A Christian philosopher, then, comes to the table with a different identity: but that difference is not marked by propositional beliefs. Rowan Williams writes:

> [Christians] do not automatically have more information about moral truth in the abstract than anyone else. What is different is the relations in which they are involved, relations that shape a particular kind of reaction to their environment and each other. If you want to say they know more than other people, it can only be true in the sense that they are involved with more than others, with a larger reality, not that they have been given an extra set of instructions.[16]

So to be a Christian is to be formed in a tradition and connected to the resources and perspectives of that tradition rather than take on a commitment to a set of propositions. I take one's philosophical identity to be of a similar ilk. Philosophers are formed inside of disciplinary traditions that also impart a living heritage. I am a sister of Christ *and* a

---

contributions; it must gain a deep understanding of them; it must learn what it can from them and it must take unbelief with profound seriousness" (Plantinga, "Advice," 271).

15. My reference to this comes from a mosaic of Elijah Cummings next to these words in the Baltimore City Courthouse.

16. Rowan Williams, "Making Moral Decisions," in *The Cambridge Companion to Christian Ethics*, ed. Robin Gill (Cambridge University Press, 2011), 6.

great-granddaughter of Hans Reichenbach; both identities are alive when I engage and process the world.[17]

Of course, living within two traditions does not come without conflict. But rather than view that conflict as a call for allegiance in a militaristic standoff, or a zero-sum decision between Christ and philosophy, I tend to see it as Marshall does—as the potential source of something new and good. The conflicts that arise in me are opportunities for transformation in both myself and my communities—including the transformation of the church. As Marshall notes:

> Christ calls his followers into conflict with their most intimate relations, with cultural practices, with religious and political authorities, with their own inclinations, desires, and prejudices, and ultimately with the principalities and powers of life...Christians should be in conflict with one another because the Christian faith is a dynamic, historical development...To be a Christian is to locate oneself in a historical tradition that has developed and is developing through interactions of difference. To be a Christian is to be in conflict. While we tend to emphasize a Christian's conflict with "the world" in a sectarian sense, we must recognize that conflict is an integral part of the historical and ongoing development of the faith tradition itself.[18]

This brings me to the last difference between Plantinga and myself. Plantinga advises the Christian philosopher to "stand firm" in her current Christian beliefs whenever they are in tension with contemporary trends. I view these tensions as invitations to grow in a variety of different ways; the Christian philosopher, after a careful consideration of all her intellectual resources and experiences, may find herself able to prune a philosophical project in a way that makes it more productive; other times that same Christian philosopher may prune the current teachings of the church; occasionally the Christian philosopher may try to forge new intellectual frameworks that allow for peaceful cross pollination between conflicting traditions. I do not take this openness to growth and compromise to be the even the slightest dampening of one's Christian faith. To quote Katharina von Bora, a former nun who escaped her convent to help bring about the Protestant reformation, "I will stick to Christ as a burr to a topcoat,"

---

17. I should be clear that the lineage to Reichenbach I invoke here is academic rather than genetic. I was advised by Robert Batterman and Mark Wilson; Batterman was advised by Lawrence Sklar who was advised by Hilary Putnam; Wilson was also advised by Hilary Putnam who was advised by Reichenbach.

18. Marshall, *Introduction to Christian Ethics*, 8–9.

and Jesus was not hesitant to challenge the political and religious power structures in which he lived.[19]

Let's turn to the values Plantinga names—autonomy and integrity—and the boldness he sees as a crucial additive to this hybrid. Plantinga describes autonomy as "independence of the rest of the philosophical world." The advice Plantinga gives implies this value is lived out by sticking to one's beliefs even if mainstream philosophy departs from them. I agree the Christian philosopher will often find herself in conflict with prevailing philosophical models and may be unable to straightforwardly "take on" the philosophical categories of her time. All the better for her—critical resistance makes for good philosophy. However, I am hesitant to describe this critical resistance as "autonomy" because it suggests the Christian philosopher resists by relying on herself. As I've said before, what grounds the strength of the Christian's critical resistance is her membership in an additional tradition. Moreover, the Christian philosopher is called not only to resist but to remake and rebuild—to transform prevailing conflicts into something novel and beautiful. In place of autonomy, I offer creativity as a core value of the Christian philosopher.

Plantinga construes the second value, integrity, as an intellectual virtue, something like "making one's beliefs consistent." He suggests it is the solution to philosophers mistakenly attempting to hybridize their views with prevailing philosophical projects in ways I've championed here. I resonate with the sentiment that Christians need to take seriously their Christian identity, but in place of Plantinga's integrity I offer accountability—viewing oneself as responsible for one's choices to the communities in which she belongs.[20] Moreover, on my understanding of Christianity, a very important member of the Christian community is the Holy Spirit.

I mention the Spirit here to address a way in which the value of accountability is easily distorted in Western thought. In *Of Water and the Spirit*, Malidoma Patrice Somé recounts his participation in the initiation ceremony for men of the Dagara tribe. He participated in this ceremony at a much later age than is traditional because he spent his formative years (largely against his will) with the Jesuits and studying at a Jesuit seminary. Part of Dagara initiation ceremony involves establishing a connection with a tree. Little instructions were given to participants, and Somé sat

---

19. Some may know Katharina von Bora as Katie Luther, wife of Martin. These are reported to be her last words.

20. I don't take this to imply everyone (or a majority) in the community must in fact agree with her. At times it may not be safe or appropriate for her to share her reasons with the community, even if she takes them to be exemplary. We are a sinful people and unfortunately individuals are not always safe to be their authentic selves. However, it is important to narrate one's inner life in the frame of this sort of accountability.

for hours in frustration, watching other younger participants complete this mysterious task and get on with their training. Deeply frustrated, Somé fabricated an experience with the tree for the observation of the elders watching him. Their response to his attempt at deception was first laughter and then serious worry about the consequences of his Western education:

> 'What did I tell you? This boy is fighting against himself... This falsehood is not his own invention...The white men have initiated him into acting this way. He has lived around them too long, and now he has become a liar too. If his *Vuur* [spirit] were not stained with white, he would know that this life has no room for lies'.[21]

I have reflected a good bit on the implications this passage has for me, a white philosopher of science teaching at a Jesuit university. From it I hear a penetrating truth about the broader social dangers of positivism; if we restrict knowledge to that which can be "observed" from an "objective perspective," we may well fool ourselves into thinking any narrative we construct is true enough if it aligns with what we think other people can observe. The Dagara elder speaks plainly about the reality of the spiritual life; to live in the Spirit is to live with recognition that all things—including hidden intentions—are open and laid bare. Thus, while Christians are called to transformative social compromise, we live this out through honest self-negotiation rather than betrayal of either the self or the community. Rowan Williams describes this process as the "struggle to make sense of my decision in terms of the common language of the faith, to demonstrate why this might be a way of speaking the language of the historic schema of Christian belief."[22]

Finally, the codicil of boldness. Plantinga refers to this as "Christian self-confidence" and "faith...trust in the Lord." This could mean a variety of things. If we interpret it as the belief we've got everything figured out—the propositions we believe come straight from God and we should never doubt our position—I can't sign on. I suspect this codicil requires a further specifying of the nature of the Christian self. Let's call this alternate codicil authenticity rather than boldness.

Williams offers Christians the following self-narrative: "The self I am, the self that I have been made to be, is the self engaged by God in

---

21. Malidoma Patrice Somé, *Of Water and the Spirit: Ritual, Magic and Initiation in the Life of an African Shaman* (Penguin, 1995), 219

22. Williams, "Making Moral Decisions," 13. It's worth noting that the Christian philosopher, when engaging in philosophical discussions, is also accountable to the broader philosophical community, and must demonstrate that whatever contribution she makes to that community is also a continuation of the historic schema of the philosophical tradition.

love and now in process of recreation through the community of Christ and the work of the Holy Spirit."[23] With this perspective, Christian self-confidence and trust in the Lord manifest as authenticity to one's own voice—viewing that voice as belonging to a beloved and complex person who is still in the process of working out how to live in truth. This authenticity requires courage to honestly face inner-conflict and trust such conflict can usher us into deep wholeness. But this authenticity will not just require something from the Christian as an individual—it cannot happen without a community that nourishes this sort of life. And so, my advice to Christian philosophers is that we think hard about how to build spaces that cultivate this growth in our community. We must set tables to which people can bring their whole selves and work out in loving and non-judgmental accountability what it means to carry on the historic Christian faith today.

I began these comments by noting a difference in the cultural moments that situate Plantinga's advice and my own. Plantinga observed Christian philosophers as gaining ground; I see our community mired in deep conflict. But this latter state of affairs is not necessarily bad news given the productive value of conflict. My advice to Christian philosophers is we work together to forge authentic communities that kindle accountability and creativity, and together reconstruct Christian philosophy in ways that serve generations to follow.[24]

---

23. Williams, "Making Moral Decisions," 7.
24. Many thanks to Natalie Carnes, Kyla Ebels-Duggan, Anne Jeffrey, Alison Krile Thornton, and Byron Wratee for the conversations and comments that shaped this piece. I am also gratefully indebted to conversations at the 8am Wednesday Eucharist led by Rev. Beth McNamara at the Cathedral of the Incarnation in Baltimore, Maryland which continue to be a rich and lively part of my Christian formation.

14

AL'S ADVICE, EMPHASIS SHIFTED

Timothy J. Pawl

University of St. Thomas

I first met Alvin Plantinga in 2002, I think, as an undergraduate philosophy major. I, along with some other employees of the Catholic parish where I worked that summer, was visiting Notre Dame for a conference on the sacrament of Confirmation. While there, I worked up my gumption to find his office. I was already by that point in my studies enamored with his work. There he was, some summer afternoon, philosophizing away in his office. I walked by a few times, fighting something like stage fright, triple-checking it was him, girding my loins. I knocked, he invited me in, and there we sat, in growing awkwardness, as we both came to the realization that I hadn't come prepared to discuss anything.

Al is a charming and gentle guy, and he soon took up the conversational burden, asking where I was a student (just down the road an hour at Valparaiso University), how I liked my studies (very much so!) and what areas of philosophy I was most interested in (metaphysics and philosophy of religion). All told, I probably spent fewer than 10 minutes in his office; maybe closer to five. It was enough time for me to form a distinct impression that he was not only a good philosopher, but he was a good person, or at least good enough to treat a bumbling, starstruck kid with kindness.

That judgment, stripped of its disjunctive hedging, was cemented into place later, during the 2005–2006 academic year, when I visited Notre Dame from St. Louis University through the Midwest Consortium of Catholic Graduate Schools. I was Al's research assistant for the year as well as his student in two graduate courses, one entitled Christian Theism and Philosophy, which was something like a practicum in following the advice he gave some 20 years earlier.

In this brief reflection I intend to highlight one main component of Plantinga's advice, changing not his point but his emphasis. I then consider different ways that revised emphasis can play out in our current situation.

1. Plantinga's Advice and a Changed Emphasis

Plantinga's advice has three main components; by this point in the volume, you likely don't need them all reiterated yet again. So, I'll just note the first, which is the one I want to focus on:

> My plea is for the Christian philosopher, the Christian philosophical community, to display, first, more independence and autonomy: we needn't take as our research projects just those projects that currently enjoy widespread popularity; we have our own questions to think about.[1]

I agree with his advice and think it has done a world of good for Christian philosophers. Plantinga's emphasis on autonomy is where I'd like to focus these comments.

When Plantinga calls for autonomy, as he makes clear, he is encouraging autonomy *from our philosophical communities*, not autonomy *full stop*. Indeed, when it comes to our relation to our Christian communities, he is clear that we have an obligation to serve those communities:

> My point is that the Christian philosopher has a right (I should say a duty) to work at his own projects—projects set by the beliefs of the Christian community of which he is a part.[2]

Plantinga wasn't calling for Christian philosophers to be lone cowboys, autonomously gallivanting from town to town, getting into intellectual shootouts with the resident verificationists or atheists. Indeed, the itinerary for the Christian philosopher isn't set autonomously, but rather by the Christian community. Christian philosophers aren't called to rugged individualism by Plantinga; they are called to realign their relations of dependence, to serve a different master:

---

1. Alvin Plantinga, "Advice to Christian Philosophers," *Faith and Philosophy* 1 (1984): 263.
2. Plantinga, "Advice to Christian Philosophers," 263.

> The Christian philosopher does indeed have a responsibility to the philosophical world at large; but his fundamental responsibility is to the Christian community, and finally to God.[3]

Christian philosophers, like all people, have responsibilities to various communities which must be weighed in our concrete circumstances. That said, on Al's view, with which I am sympathetic, the ultimate responsibility of a Christian is to God; to undertake that responsibility as a *philosopher* who is Christian is to serve God using the philosophical gifts one has been given. But neither I nor Plantinga is claiming that serving *qua philosopher* is one's only or even fundamental responsibility.

The Christian community that we serve is bigger than each of us and it has its own preoccupations:

> Christian philosophers, however, are the philosophers of the Christian community; and it is part of their task as *Christian* philosophers to serve the Christian community. But the Christian community has its own questions, its own concerns, its own topics for investigation, its own agenda and its own research program.[4]

Plantinga emphasized the need for *independence from the philosophical community* in our turn toward service to our Christian communities. Here I am changing not the advice, but the clause being emphasized: Christian philosophers, when serving *as Christian philosophers*, ought to focus their service *to their Christian communities*. That is our obligation as Christian philosophers—to serve the Christian community—we are dutybound to investigate the questions and topics of that community. What can we say of this service?

Before I go on to list eight such sorts of service and to conclude with a bit of advice about how to do that service well, allow me, to put it paradoxically, to say what I am not saying. I am not saying that Christian philosophers have a single obligation—to serve the Christian community with our philosophical skills—as if there weren't other communities that have a real claim on our time and talents: our families, our students, our local congregations, etc. As in all areas of life, there are questions of prudence about prioritizing the communities we need to serve.

2. Types of Service

Consider some service types. I don't mean these to be exhaustive, though

---

3. Plantinga, "Advice to Christian Philosophers," 262.
4. Plantinga, "Advice to Christian Philosophers," 255.

I think they are representative of the work Christian philosophers have done for the sake of the Christian community in the last forty years. We might first distinguish between services that have as their intended results intellectual outcomes and those that have as their intended results practical outcomes.

Concerning intellectual outcomes, we can further distinguish between the interlocutor to be addressed—those within the community and those without. A second needful subdistinction concerns whether we are doing what we might call, for lack of a better phrasing, *offensive* or *defensive* work. These two subdistinctions allow for four varieties of intellectual service.

First, there's the work of *defeating defeaters*. I see this as the work of protecting against threats from the outside. We man the walls here. Someone argues that Christianity cannot be true because of *this*. Christian philosophers have served the Christian community by assessing *this* reasoning, arguing that it is unsound. This is defensive work addressing those outside the community.

A second task is again outward facing. If defeating defeaters is defensive, this one, the task of intellectually *supporting the truth claims of the faith*—or at least those capable of non-revelatory support—is offensive.[5] It presents reasons for the hope we carry within.

Third, there's the work of canvassing the space of possibility open to Christians in *resolving internal tensions*. If the previous jobs were facing outward, this task is an internal one. Here we think *along with* other Christians—never merely *for* other Christians, as if the division of labor allows them to check their intellects at the door of the church.

Fourth, one might be addressing the Christian community, not to put out fires, so to speak, but to *delve more deeply* into the revealed truths and their resonance with us. How might we understand the saving work of Christ? What are the relations between works and faith? Here the Christian philosopher tries to understand more deeply some truth of the faith and does so with the aid of philosophical tools.

In these practices, the tools used are typical philosophical tools of argument analysis, counterexample, distinguishing premises, and so on. Such tools are not distinctive to Christianity; attempts to defeat defeaters to utilitarianism or modal realism or epistemic internalism would differ, not in form, but in matter. We don't have access to additional inferential rules—*modus Christians* to add to *modus ponens* and *tollens*.[6]

---

5. Keep the emphasis on the first syllable; if it meanders to the second you've forgotten the second half of the verse most suited to this project: 1 Peter 3:15.

6. Interestingly, some Christian thinkers have thought that we have *fewer* inferential rules at our disposal *as Christians*. Luther wrote, for instance, that "there are syllogisms that are valid in logic,

These are the most common *research related* tasks, but they are not the only tasks. These four tasks are most well aligned with the first and second traditional spiritual works of mercy: instructing the ignorant and counseling the doubtful. Of course, there are 12 other works of mercy. Christian philosophers work toward those ends, too.

Christian philosophers can work, as philosophers, to put forward the best arguments for why we ought, as Christians, to work to feed the hungry, or to visit the sick, or to comfort the afflicted, and so on. We might think of this as works of *encouragement to Christian living*. I take this to be the first of four practical services the Christian philosopher can perform.

Along the same lines, Christian philosophers have worked to *draw forth riches* from Christian moral wisdom. Many in the Christian tradition, for instance, give concrete advice about how to grow in patience or trust—the Christian philosopher can, using the tools of philosophy, extract and distill such wisdom for others.

A final two sorts of invaluable practical service that a Christian philosopher typically does are *teaching students* and *mentoring the next generation*. Indeed, I dare say that most Christian philosophers who find themselves with academic employment today do so because of the sacrificial service of some prior Christian philosophers working for their good, whether in directly teaching them, or in mentoring them while junior members of the academy.

These eight tasks are, to my mind, the most frequent tasks Christian philosophers have taken up *as philosophers* in the last forty years. I say *as philosophers* because I know there are countless ways that philosophers have served the local church in other manners. I have it on firsthand report that Plantinga used to collect graduate students up to help local folks in need. This is the Lord's work, but he and they didn't do it *qua philosopher*.[7]

Which of these eight tasks—(1) defeating defeaters, (2) supporting the truths of the faith, (3) resolving internal tensions, (4) delving more deeply, (5) encouraging to Christian living, (6) drawing forth riches, (7) teaching students, and (8) mentoring the next generation—is the most important? I think that's a trick question. What's most important changes with the context and circumstances. It would be overly simplistic to judge all the work of Christian philosophers against the measure of just one of these

---

but not in theology." See Martin Luther, *Luther's Works: Word and Sacrament*, 4. Edited by Helmut T. Lehmann (Fortress Press, 1971), 256.

7. And thank goodness this is so! I once helped one of these same Notre Dame Philosophy graduate students pack a moving truck for relocation for a new job. The circle of philosophers stood around weighing the pros and cons of rival Tetris schemes—mattresses first?; mattress last on top?; couches along the sides?, etc.—for the better part of an hour. We were only saved when a non-philosopher, or a philosopher in a stroke of insight acting as a non-philosopher, called us out of our *a priori* reverie.

tasks, as if there is no good Christian philosophical work if it doesn't, say, encourage Christian living.

Moreover, it isn't typically for the individual Christian philosopher to decide which task is the most important. The community as a whole, which the Christian philosopher is obligated to serve, faces different questions, has different concerns, opens various investigations, has different agendas and research interests at different times. The most important task for you may well be the one which the church has greatest need of in that moment, and not necessarily the one you find most intrinsically interesting. As Plantinga says:

> The Christian philosophical community ought to get on with the philosophical questions of importance to the Christian community.[8]

The philosophical questions of importance to the Christian community are often not the questions deemed most exciting or intriguing to professional philosophers, even Christian ones.

An analogy: the medical treatments most important for a certain community are often not the treatments most exciting for medical professionals. My buddy, Alex, cleans out a lot of children's ears at the hospital where he works, even if that part of the job is not the most exciting. He does it because, as a matter of contingent fact, more kids are now putting things in their ears, perhaps because they see such behavior more often these days with the ubiquity of wireless earbuds. Had he practiced medicine 50 years ago, his days would likely be filled with another activity, likely one equally unexciting.[9] He does what he does now because it is needful in the present to the people he serves. He takes his skills to the needs of the community and, as their servant in this respect, he does what they need because they need it. You should go and do likewise.

One disanalogy between you and Alex, though, is that, for Alex, it is easy to discern who exactly he is to serve, given his role in the larger (medical) community. If you were to ask him, he'd tell you the contours of the community based on referring doctors, insurance plans, and the like (if you ask, please wait until I'm elsewhere, as this sounds *boooooring*).

Now, I've been following Plantinga in talking of *the* Christian Community. Indeed, and perhaps you've noticed, all but one quotation I've employed from Plantinga so far included that phrase (one uses it thrice!). How do we tell which community of the various rival contenders

---

8. Plantinga, "Advice to Christian Philosophers," 264.
9. Not that one looks for *excitement* when doing medical interventions on children, but you get the point.

is *the* Christian community, the one which we are to serve, the one the research agenda of which we ought to further?

3. The Christian Community

Is there such a thing as the Christian community? Perhaps so. Perhaps it is the community of all Christians. Indeed, the Greek word, *ekklēsia*, often translated into English as "church," can be translated as "community." The term could be understood this way. As a Christian philosopher, on this interpretation of the term, your job is to serve all the Christians.

That might be so. Surely *in some sense* that is so. But notice, it is hard to see what this universal community's "own questions, its own concerns, its own topics for investigation, its own agenda and its own research program" are. How would I tell what that global, historical community's current agenda and research program are? Does it include Marian miracles, such as the apparitions at Lourdes? Does it include the writings of Joseph Smith? My hunch is that no Christian philosopher feels beholden to serve a community that takes its agenda to include resolving the tensions between, say, the Council of Trent, the Heidelberg Catechism, and Joseph Smith's *The Pearl of Great Price*.

Moreover, if we had to ask what the agenda of the whole Christian community is right now, whether we counted by number of members, or by explicitly promulgated agenda, both measures would make the Catholic Church's agenda the agenda of the Christian community. Who else has a formal structure in place and the sheer labor force to take up a community-wide research agenda? For just one example, think of Leo XIII's call for increased research into Thomism in his *Aeterni Patris* encyclical of 1879, and the results it had, both directly in the thought of Catholics, but indirectly in the philosophical focus of other Christian communities. What other leader of a Christian group could do similarly? But I, even as a Catholic, don't think that protestant philosophers should feel beholden to working out the nuances of specifically Catholic doctrine. And I, of course, don't think I have any obligation to resolve tensions in, say, Reformed soteriology or Anglican ecclesiology.[10] My point? The research program of *all Christians* is either undiscoverable or it is determined by a guy in an impressively tall hat.

Perhaps the community in question is the community of *mere Christianity*, that is, the community that affirms certain basic truths. Christian

---

10. That's the King's job, no?

philosophers, on this view, are obligated to serve that community in its agenda insofar as its agenda sticks to the mere beliefs.

This mere Christianity view, too, strikes me, as it did C. S. Lewis, as the wrong level of generality and practicality for being the community we seek to serve as Christian philosophers.[11] For one thing, taking a stand on what the *mere* teachings are is taking a stand with some and against other Christian communities. There isn't agreement about *what counts as* the mere things. It is usually formed by picking a time-honored set of claims—say, the Apostles' Creed—or just one's preferred set of beliefs allegedly central to scripture and purportedly perspicuously taught therein. The Arians or Nestorians or Mormons are then No-True-Scotsmanned out the door of the sanctuary.

Consider, too, the fact that previous important authors who considered the essentials composed lists that would be denied today by the *mere Christianity* group in consideration. A few instances of many would suffice. Recall Luther's position at the Marburg Colloquy that the real bodily presence of Christ in the Eucharist is an essential Christian teaching, and so he could not join in Christian union with Zwingli. Or consider the views of St. John of Damascus, who writes:

> It is surely necessary to defend this…that in the case of God there are three venerated hypostases, and to believe in the Trinity, to be baptized, not to worship the creation, and to defend the harmony of the holy scriptures, both the Old and the New.[12]

Some mere Christians will already be in disagreement here insofar as they might believe that there is a lack of harmony in the holy scriptures. The reader has no doubt noticed the ellipsis in the quotation. The text I left out includes the following: "that the divinity is impassible and unchangeable." St. John is not inventing out of whole cloth this additional teaching; it was taught at Ephesus and Chalcedon as well.[13] My point is not that St. John *has it right* that divine impassibility and immutability

---

11. C. S. Lewis, who popularized Baxter's term, *mere Christianity*, likened it to a hallway, not a room. It is a shared entranceway for multiple communities; it is not the creed of any particular community. See the end of the preface of Lewis's *Mere Christianity*, e.g., "I hope no reader will suppose that 'mere' Christianity is here put forward as an alternative to the creeds of the existing communions—as if a man could adopt it in preference to Congregationalism or Greek Orthodoxy or anything else."

12. See *Christ: Chalcedon and Beyond* vol 4. of *The Cambridge Edition of Early Christian Writings*, ed. Mark DelCogliano, (Cambridge University Press, 2022), https://doi.org/10.1017/9781009057103, 644.

13. See, for instance, Cyril's letter to John of Antioch, included at Ephesus, which says that God "is unchangeable and immutable by nature" and that the Word could not "change or be susceptible to it" and that "we all confess that the Word of God is impassible," and see Chalcedon's telling act when it "expels from the assembly of the priests those who dare say that the divinity of the Only-begotten is passible." Quotations from Norman P. Tanner, *Decrees of the Ecumenical Councils 2 Volume Set* (Georgetown University Press, 1990), 72–73; 84.

are essential to Christianity. Nor is my claim that you should affirm what Ephesus and Chalcedon say (though I think you should).[14] My point here is just that what gets to count as *mere Christianity* follows on an ecclesiological decision we've already made, explicitly or implicitly. It isn't something we come to independently, then use to determine which community is the Christian community; that's got the ordering backwards.

If you say that mere Christianity is not beholden to a prior ecclesiological decision, but rather just a function of denominational greatest common factoring—we all accept *this stuff*, so let's just assume it and move forward from there—I note that this is not so. There *is* a prior ecclesiological decision there, as your "we all" in "we all accept this stuff" doesn't include the Unitarians (who deny that Christ is one in being with the Father), the Coptics (who deny two natures in Christ), or the Assyrian Church of the East (which sides with Nestorius against Cyril concerning the Council of Ephesus). By "we all" you mean "those of us in these particular sets of Christian groups, not those sets" where the sets are predetermined by dogmatic guardrails. But make no mistake: the sociological gather up of the "we all" happens after an ecclesial pruning.

What to do, then, if service to some universal community that can lead our investigation, form its own research agenda, and so on, is impractical? It seems to me that the best service would then be to a particular community.

4. Serve a Particular Community

What I'd like to encourage is that, when one acts to serve *as a Christian philosopher*, one should serve a particular community. I don't herein mean to argue for a particular community that you ought to serve, but I've got a suggestion if you'd like it.

For any community, to serve it well one needs some knowledge of the relevant areas of service. Alex needs to know about ears to serve his community in the way they want him to serve, as a medical provider. He needs to know about them at the expert level, their internal anatomy, the viable treatment options, and so on. To serve your particular Christian community *qua philosopher*, you need to know at an expert level the things relevant to philosophical service. What's that?

---

14. Though I will note that the Creed of Nicaea ends with an anathema, right there in the creed, which says that those "affirming that the Son of God is subject to change or alteration—these the catholic and apostolic church anathematizes" (Tanner 1990, 5). The creed of Nicaea is often referenced as a marker of *mere Christianity*; if it is, then something like divine immutability *is* part of mere Christianity.

Think back to the main ways that philosophers serve: defeating defeaters, supporting the truths of the faith, resolving internal tensions, delving more deeply, encouraging to Christian living, drawing forth riches, teaching, and mentoring. Each requires a deep knowledge of the teachings of the Christian community. It would be no service to the community—it would be a disservice, a harm—for you to attempt to alleviate tension in a manner that, unbeknownst to you, contradicted the teachings of that community. If a Catholic were to offer a resolution to an objection to the doctrine of the incarnation that presupposed Christ wasn't divine, but instead just a pretty fancy fellow, such a move would be counterproductive for her church. Not only that; in doing so, she'd look, to use a technical term, like a total dumbass.[15]

Compare: You are playing a vibrant round of sportball. You are assigned by your team as net protector. You attempt to fulfill your role, but you line up in front of the wrong goal receptacle. In such a situation—and you can trust me, as I know a lot about sporting—you'd likely feel chagrined. There you were, looking like a total dummy, not a lick of help to your team. Now, this is likely hard to pull off in a real sporting event. But it gets easier the less material the markers are, the less difference there is in the uniforms, the more teams begin playing on the same pitch, the more rivals start disguising themselves as your teammates, the more balls are introduced to the sport, the more nets fill the play area, etc. To serve your team well in such a situation, you need to know your teammates, recognize your own goal, etc. Compared to this chaotic sport foray, theology and ecclesial polity looks like over-caffeinated Calvinball. To serve your particular Christian community well, you need to be seeped in its thought.

5. Conclusion

I encourage the reader to follow Al's advice. The Christian philosopher has a duty—one among many—to serve the Christian community. The most practical way to do so, in my estimation, requires that the philosopher delve deeply into the history and theology of the ecclesial community which she seeks to serve. Plantinga calls for autonomy from the academic culture of philosophy. But to practice what he preaches, the Christian must be subservient to, dependent on, formed by, her Christian community. If I were to augment Al's advice, then—not by way of addition, but by way

---

15. It should go without saying—but it won't, and so I'll say it—that my point here is not that those who deny the divinity of Christ are total dumbasses. My point is that those who attempt to serve the Catholic Church by offering a solution to a problem for Catholics that denies a fundamental, central, essential, explicit teaching of the Church—those people are total dumbasses, in the technical sense.

of changed emphasis—I'd encourage Christian philosophers, in order to do their service as Christian philosophers well, to be seeped in the history and theology of their communities.[16]

---

16. I thank Faith Glavey Pawl, Kevin Timpe, and Christopher Woznicki for helpful comments on this contribution.

15

ADVICE FROM A ROAD

Tim Pickavance

Talbot School of Theology

I believe, though I cannot claim to know, that I first encountered Plantinga's "Advice to Christian Philosophers" during the Spring of 2001. I was, at that time, deep in the sea of the master's program in philosophy at Talbot School of Theology. But I was new to philosophy. I took precisely zero philosophy courses as an undergraduate, and had discovered philosophy—as so many Talbot Philosophy students had—through apologetics, which I had in turn stumbled upon in my flailing undergraduate attempts to talk with college students about Jesus. My undergraduate major was economics, with an emphasis on the math-y bits, and it wasn't until my final undergraduate year that I realized people had questions about Jesus that were philosophical questions, or at least philosophy-adjacent. It was too late to switch majors. So I began a serious study of philosophy by enrolling in the MAPhil at Talbot. The transition was abrupt. Perhaps I wasn't just deep in the sea; perhaps I was drowning.

Anyway, I confess that my first read of "Advice" didn't make much of an impression. It seemed *right*. But nothing about it was a surprise.

I know now what I didn't know then: the reason why "Advice" didn't make much of an impression was a testament to the influence Plantinga had exerted in the philosophical community, Christian and otherwise. Unknowingly, I was learning how to be a philosopher under the protective shadows of philosophers like Robert and Marilyn Adams, Bill Alston, Richard Swinburne, and of course Alvin Plantinga. A world where the sort of work they did was unwelcome and without contemporary precedent was not a world I could fathom. Philosophy done by Christians in the spirit of "Advice", for all I knew as a 21-year-old philosophy noob, was commonplace. Logical positivism was a punchline. The free will defense had solved the logical problem of evil. Dualism was the view of every philosophy professor I'd ever had (all three of them!).

In the intervening almost quarter century since that first encounter with "Advice," I've realized something else: I disagree with Plantinga on a vast array of questions of serious philosophical significance. Whether about the nature of propositions and worlds (they're structured), *de re* modality (worlds have nothing to do with it), the possibility of robustly metaphysical forms of explanation (I'm a constituent ontologist for heaven's sake), the free will defense (God's creative act isn't limited by counterfactuals of creaturely freedom), Molinism (because there aren't any true ones prior to the decree), the semantics of names (I don't believe in the right sorts of essences needed to make the Boethian compromise), the nature of knowledge (it probably can't be analyzed), the role of evidence (it matters more than faculties), and much besides, Plantinga and I don't see eye to eye. Indeed, it's tempting to say that we—insofar as he thinks about me at all!—find each other downright *puzzling*.[1]

Yet, as he is for so many in my generation, Plantinga is one of my philosophical heroes.

One of the reasons Plantinga is among my philosophical heroes is the way his distinctively Christian theological commitments shaped his philosophical work. Sometimes this shaping is overt, as in his later work on the Evolutionary Argument Against Naturalism. Sometimes, however, those commitments do their work in more hidden ways. This is what I really love: watching a great mind draw deeply from a rich, stable theological tradition as he reflects on questions that often are taken to have little connection to theology. And it seems to me that Plantinga's oeuvre is full of this sort of thing. I lack space for details here, so I will content myself with a bald-faced assertion masquerading as an illustration: underneath Plantinga's objection to Lewis's views of propositions in "Two Concepts of Modality"—in particular, the claim that we just know that sets can't be true or false, and that therefore Lewis's view is false—is deep engagement with theological reflection on the relationship between propositions and the mind of God.[2]

---

1. I'm being a bit dramatic here. There are, of course, many things about which Plantinga and I agree. Further, some of the disagreements I note may not run particularly deep. But it's difficult for me to say just how deep the disagreements go, and this is because the way I approach philosophy does run counter to Plantinga in some fundamental ways. Which is the point of this paragraph!
2. See pp. 206ff of Plantinga's fabulous "Two Concepts of Modality: Modal Realism and Modal Reductionism," *Philosophical Perspectives*, Vol. 1, ed. James Tomberlin (Ridgeview, 1987), 189-231.

I bring this up because under the surface of "Advice" are core theological convictions applied to Christian philosophy and to Christian philosophers.

Consider Plantinga's first piece of advice: Christian philosophers should "display more autonomy".[3] The thought is that Christian philosophers need to endeavor to be *Christian* philosophers. We are, Plantinga says, "the philosophers of the Christian community; and it is part of [our] task as *Christian* philosophers to serve the Christian community."[4] This is not meant to take away from our commitment to the philosophical world more broadly. We should both learn from it and engage with the questions it deems to be important, on their own terms. In Plantinga's words, "The Christian philosopher does indeed have a responsibility to the philosophical world at large; but his fundamental responsibility is to the Christian community, and finally to God."[5]

Plantinga's reference point here is the philosophical community, broadly construed. He is approaching Christian philosophical distinctiveness on a path that begins within the broader philosophical community and arrives to Christian philosophical autonomy at its terminus. The broader community is the origin. An awareness of this path is vital. No doubt it is true to the psychology and development of many Christian philosophers, and will continue to be.

Anyway, Plantinga's encouragement of autonomy is, I suggest, one way of articulating the idea that philosophers have a role to play in the Body of Christ. Interestingly, however, Plantinga doesn't mention the Body of Christ *as the Body of Christ* at all, despite that the *Christian community* is explicitly motivating his interest in autonomy.

One can, of course, make a case for an autonomous yet engaged presence within the broader philosophical community by developing a path that begins with the Christian community rather than the philosophical community. On this path, an understanding of the Christian philosopher's autonomy emerges from a more fundamental commitment to the Body of Christ, just as Plantinga suggests.

But conceptualizing the starting point of this path as the Body of Christ is fruitful. Instead of spotlighting autonomy relative to the broader philosophical community, we instead spotlight *interdependence* with the Body of Christ. Autonomy relative to the broader philosophical community will no doubt emerge from this sort of interdependence. In this sense, the shift in emphasis would not fundamentally alter Plantinga's point. However, the path that begins with interdependence with the Body

---

[3]. Alvin Plantinga, "Advice to Christian Philosophers," *Faith & Philosophy* 1, no. 3 (July 1984): 254.
[4]. Plantinga, "Advice," 255.
[5]. Plantinga, "Advice," 262.

of Christ takes us past certain points of interest that are tougher to see on the path that begins with autonomy.

For example, *difference* from the broader philosophical community should not be an animating goal. When difference becomes a goal, it threatens to distort *good*. (It's tempting to talk here about indie music or hipster coffee, but I'll resist...) This is because similarities become, just by being similarities, cause for concern. By beginning from interdependence with the Body, we discover a substantive way to discern how we ought to work like our peers in the broader philosophical community, and how we ought to work differently. Similarities needn't all on their own concern us. No doubt certain dissimilarities will always be present when Christian philosophers work interdependently with the Body of Christ. And these will include the forms of autonomy that Plantinga encourages in "Advice." But as the broader community of philosophers changes—hopefully in part because of Christians' presence within it—those similarities and dissimilarities will change as well. Perhaps we might succeed in persuading the philosophical community about some truth that for a time marked out Christians from the rest of the philosophical community. Or perhaps we might learn that Christian philosophers ought to embrace some truth that our secular colleagues had already embraced. Focus on dissimilarity alone will not do. Difference should be a consequence, not a goal.

Organizing our philosophical work as part of participation in Christ's Body also cultivates humility. Interdependence with the Body of Christ reminds us not just that we can be *Christians* as we do philosophy, but that philosophy isn't the only vocation worth pursuing. Our commitments to the Christian community and to God require that we acknowledge not only the strengths of philosophical exploration, but its limits as well. We must recognize our interdependence with our brothers and sisters in other academic disciplines (more on this in a moment), and also with our brothers and sisters outside of academia. This requires us to look for bridges to serve the church with our philosophy, and also invites us to gratefully live into the reality that we need the rest of the Body of Christ to support and champion what we do. As Paul puts it in 1 Corinthians 12:21, 24-25 (NIV), "the eye cannot say to the hand, 'I don't need you!' And the head cannot say to the feet, 'I don't need you!' ... God has put the body together, giving greater honor to the parts that lacked it, so that there should be no division in the body, but that its parts should have equal concern for each other." Academics are, in my experience, particularly prone to forgetting this truth.

Relatedly, Christian philosophers need other members of the Body to inform our work. Plantinga is certainly right that, when we philosophers work as Christians, we will take seriously evidence and arguments that perhaps our non-Christian philosopher friends will not. But equally, our commitment to the Body of Christ reminds us that just as the Body is dependent on us to do our work, so we are dependent on the Body to do ours. Other academics, including Bible scholars, theologians, psychologists, biologists, physicists, literature scholars, sociologists, and others will often have insights that we ought to bring to bear on our own work. Organizing our work around a commitment to the Body of Christ signals this reality.

Further, our interdependence with the Body highlights that our philosophical interests are not *merely* philosophical. We are trying to understand God and the world that he made. As there is no clean line between the different parts of creation, so there are no clean lines between different academic disciplines. Likewise, there is no clean line between academia and the rest of human endeavor. Our philosophical interests are part of, and ought to serve, a much larger vision of Christ's church working in the world. And that work, both inside and outside the church itself, is the work of holding forth the Truth who is Christ, drawing people into communion with the Father, by the power of the Spirit, and by that communion healing and bringing *shalom* to individuals and communities.

So Christian philosophers ought also find ways to deploy our philosophical work outside of academia. Inside the church, we discover a call to consider ways that our philosophical explorations interact and engage with the lives of people with whom we share a pew. Our brothers and sisters in business, industry, primary and secondary education, social work, and perhaps even our pastors and elders and deacons engage philosophical questions whether they mean to or not. The academic philosophical community would do well to engage these audiences insofar as we are able, in order to love and serve them in the ways we are uniquely equipped, and of course to be loved and served by them. Outside the church, we discover a call to deploy our philosophical work to further the Kingdom of God. This includes looking for bridges from philosophy to apologetics, but includes far more than that.

Crucially, these are obligations of the whole Body, not necessarily of any of us individually. That's part of the beauty of the Body. We can encourage and champion those called to interdisciplinary philosophical work, or general-audience philosophy, or whatever without either jealousy or condescension. Each of us should discern his or her own vocation within the Body, recognizing that there will be a plurality of such calls even within the limb composed by philosophers. The Body needs all sorts!

Putting these pieces together, the road from interdependence shows that Christian philosophers ought to seek oneness with the broader Body of Christ, fulfilling our distinctive role in its mission. We seek to fulfill 1 Corinthians 12:25, "that there be no division in the body, but that the members should have the same care for one another." We are, with the rest of the Body, "standing firm in the same spirit, with one mind striving side by side for the faith of the gospel," as Paul encourages the Philippians (Phil 1:27). Paul goes on in 1 Corinthians to argue that all of this is for the sake of love. Therefore, since God is love (1 John 4:16), the members of the Body of Christ individually and collectively reveal God himself.[6]

Christian philosophers therefore endeavor, through our work as Christian philosophers, to hold forth the Triune God of heaven and earth. We strive to *reveal*.

This brings me to one final reflection. On that first reading of "Advice" back in 2001, I thought it odd that Plantinga spent less time giving advice than he does engaged with substantive philosophical issues. Rather than extended advice-giving, Plantinga devoted most of "Advice" to illustrating how autonomy, integrity, and boldness might make a difference to issues in the theory of meaning, epistemology, and philosophical anthropology. I now think it strange that I once thought Plantinga's strategy strange. As is so often the case, Plantinga was many steps ahead of me. He was living into what he was calling people to do. Rather than merely theorizing the idea of importance, he was working on important things. Instead of merely saying, he was doing (though of course his doing involved more saying!). Perhaps this is the most Christian thing about "Advice", and about Plantinga as an academic more generally.

Let me explain.

In Book VII of *De Trinitate*, St. Augustine is trying—and, if we're honest, failing—to see his way through a thicket of issues of Trinitarian logic created by the idea that Christ is "the power of God and wisdom of God" (1 Cor 1:24).[7] The nature of the problem needn't distract us, but Augustine's attempt to solve it causes him to reflect on what it means that Christ is *Word*.

Coming to the climax of these reflections, Augustine says:

> The reason it says *No one knows the Son but the Father, and no one knows the Father but the Son and whoever the Son chooses to reveal him*

---

[6]. 1 John 4 explicitly makes an argument connecting our love for one another, the Incarnation, and the very nature of God.

[7]. Augustine of Hippo, *De Trinitate*, 2nd ed., trans. Edmond Hill, in *The Works of Saint Augustine: A Translation for the 21st Century*, Vol. 5, eds. John E. Rotelle, et al. (New City Press, 1991/2015.)

to (Mt 11:27) is that it is through the Son that the Father makes his revelation, that is through his Word.[8]

In other words, because Christ is Word, Christ knows the Father. And because Christ knows the Father, Christ becomes a revealer. Augustine goes on:

> The Son *was made for us by God wisdom and justice and sanctification* (1 Cor 1:30), because we turn to him in time, that is at a particular moment of time, in order to abide with him for ever. And at a certain moment of time he too, *the Word, was made flesh and dwelt among us* (Jn 1:14).[9]

This entering into time through the Incarnation is, for Augustine, key. It allows the Word to become the Word *for us*. The Image of God as it manifests in the Word-made-flesh in turn gives us a visible life to image:

> Let us copy the example of this divine image, the Son, and not draw away from God. For we too are the image of God, though not the equal one like him; we are made by the Father through the Son, not born of the Father like that image; we are image because we are illuminated with light; that one is so because it is the light that illuminates, and therefore it provides a model for us without have a model itself. ... But we by pressing on imitate him who abides motionless; we follow him who stands still, and by walking in him we move toward him, because for us he became a road or way in time by his humility, while being for us an eternal abode by his divinity.[10]

This is, of course, Augustine's way of unpacking the idea that we ought to imitate Christ. But the image he uses to do so is vivid and compelling: Christ *became a road for us*.

Augustine in this way connects the life of Christ to our path to life with God, to the life *of* God. Christ's life *is* our path to God's life.

This theme emerges for Augustine through the opening gambit of 1 Corinthians, but the Apostle Paul picks it up in chapter 11 of that same letter. "Be imitators of me," Paul says, "as I am of Christ." Paul is telling the Corinthians that he can be a road for them insofar as he is following the Road that is Christ. Through this command, Paul implicitly suggests that we need roads to the Road, as it were. Or even if we don't *need* them, we sure could use them.

---

8. Augustine, *De Trinitate*, 224.
9. Augustine, *De Trinitate*, 224.
10. Augustine, *De Trinitate*, 225.

In the Body of Christ, we find such roads. As Paul offered himself to the Corinthians, other Christians can likewise serve as roads. This is one final way that emphasizing Christian philosophers' interdependence with the Body of Christ might prove fruitful. And it also highlights something important about Plantinga himself: *Plantinga has perhaps also become a road.* For Christian philosophers, Plantinga has served as a guide, a road map, a person to imitate.

I mentioned above that I disagree with Plantinga about so very many things. But what I cannot fault—indeed what I find most admirable in Plantinga—is the *way* he worked, the way he functioned as a *Christian* philosopher. Plantinga worked as "Advice" calls Christian philosophers to work. He worked with autonomy, with integrity, with boldness, on questions that he saw as relevant to the church but with sensitivity to the best of what philosophers, even secular philosophers, have to offer.

And so it seems to me that Plantinga hunted the truth in order to *reveal*—to reveal God and His works, and to help us understand ourselves and our place in God's world. By seeking to reveal, his work took him steps down the Road that is Christ. Philosophy as Plantinga did it is, in this sense, imitation of Christ. And so Plantinga became an example, a model, an image of a *Christian* philosopher.

Even in "Advice", though of course not uniquely there, Plantinga was modeling this sort of imitation. Plantinga shows the way by becoming a way.

If Augustine was right, Plantinga was doing philosophy as an act of devotion. He was endeavoring to imitate Christ in that way particular to members of Christ's body we call philosophers. Christian philosophers—and here I'm speaking as much to myself as to anyone—ought to imitate Plantinga as he imitates Christ.

In other words—and Plantinga would likely disagree with me about this, too—the path Plantinga offers in "Advice" is *himself*. Plantinga can be our road. On this road our work becomes, like Plantinga's did, *devotion*, steps along the Road to life with God.

16

THE MAKINGS OF A GREAT PHILOSOPHER: ADVICE FOR THE NEXT GENERATION OF CHRISTIAN PHILOSOPHERS

Joshua Rasmussen

Baylor University

1. Introduction

When I first encountered Alvin Plantinga's "Advice to Christian Philosophers" twenty years ago, I was intrigued by his vision of the kind of work a philosopher can do. I was a computer science major at the time, but I was exploring the field of philosophy on the side. In my spare time, I would sometimes work on trying to develop a "perfect" argument for God's existence. Plantinga seemed aware of the philosopher's instinct to craft arguments. He warned that the quest to craft an airtight argument could have an unintended effect: a skeptic might maintain their original position by becoming skeptical of *other* premises you take to be true. He also warned against assuming intellectual frames of analysis set by others. Plantinga's essay lifted my eyes to the value of philosophical work, and it helped me consider the greater purposes of the work I might do as a philosopher.

Shortly after reading Plantinga's essay, I started forming my own approach to navigating the field of philosophy, setting my sights on becoming a professional philosopher. Early in my career, I worked with Plantinga as a research fellow at the University of Notre Dame. There Plantinga modelled for me a *person-first* style of philosophy, which is a style of doing philosophy in the service of people (over other things, like personal reputation or tribal reinforcement). This style was displayed by his clarity in communication, pursuit of a deep understanding of topics of wide interest, and his overall kindness toward people in person.

Inspired by Plantinga's model of using philosophy to serve people, I've been asking myself this question: How can philosophical work *add the most value to others*? I see a great need in our time for the kind of work philosophers can do—and *Christian* philosophers in particular. Many people write me with existential questions; they say they feel lost and worried about the meaning of life. A philosopher's work can help orient people to their inner lights and support them on their journeys. *How* do we do that best? Over the course of my career, I've been seeking to understand how to best serve people with my philosophical work, and I've collected some insights along the way.

In this essay, I want to share some strategies for aligning philosophical work with a higher purpose. I call these strategies "pillars of greatness." These pillars support the work of philosophers who scale their impact, and they help me do work that is more meaningful and more fun while meeting the needs of our time. In what follows, I will describe my four strategies for using one's work to add value to others. While I am primarily addressing the next generation of Christian philosophers, the principles I discuss are universally applicable to anyone seeking to elevate their work to a greater purpose.

2. Pillar 1, Vision: Cultivate a Vision of Who You Are

Your vision of yourself is, in my view, the most significant factor determining what you do as a philosopher. Your vision is your compass. It helps you filter all your activities, job choices, and relationships.

My vision has helped me navigate uncertainty in my career path. I've noticed many occasions where I would be presented with a choice of what to work on or what to teach. When faced with this choice, I find it helpful to ask myself two questions. First, does this work align with my personal feeling of meaningful work (work that is fun and interesting to me)? Second, will this work add value to others by meeting needs people have (and that I also have)? If I can say "yes," to both questions, then I have strong reason to do the project. If I say "no" to either one, I have reason to decline or pursue another path. My vision of myself helps me have a sense of which choice is more aligned with my aim to help people have insights about the things that matter most.

Those who cultivate a vision set themselves apart for greater work. Early in graduate school, I discerned a difference between two types of graduate students. The first type is someone who lacks a vision of a greater reason for their work. They are good at working *within* a system created for them. In school, they may attend all their classes, do all their classwork, and get A's as a great student would. Their work tends to be confined by existing systems of understanding. The other type of student, by contrast, is someone who is tapped into a greater vision of *why* they are doing their work. Their vision is not confined to existing trends or systems, and they do not wait until after they finish their degree or land a job only for someone else to define who they are. Instead, they cultivate a sense of who they want to be—and who they are—*before* they make contributions to the field. As their careers unfold, I see their influence and contribution grow. They have a sense of why they are doing their work—whether or not their work is assigned by others. People recognize this type as leaders.

There is a great need in our time for philosophers who have a higher vision of their work. Early in my career as a philosopher, I discovered that my papers were being discussed by others on their blogs. I noticed that the papers people were most interested in were about topics that touch on existential questions, such as about the existence of God or the meaning of life.

Despite this interest, some of my graduate school advisors warned against working on such topics, especially early in one's career. They said it was better to specialize in topics that are more neutral so that red flags won't be raised about your beliefs when you go on the job market. I felt the pressure of their advice. I also felt pressure to seek status, achievement, and approval. Yet, philosophers who focus narrowly on certain pieces of trendy philosophical discussions tend not to meet the needs or interests of the wider culture, at least not directly.

There is a more harmonious way: philosophers who *utilize* their specialization—whatever it is—to address big questions (or to strategically connect with others who address big questions) scale their impact. These philosophers meet the needs of people inside and outside the field.

Vision gives you a sense of *why* you are doing what you are doing, whether in the classroom, on a podcast, or in a coffee shop working on a new article. For me, the question of how my work can serve others has lifted my eyes to see more clearly how to use philosophical work (or any work) to serve others. I have found that I show up differently when I carry a sense of who I am, and others feel the impact.

Christian philosophers, in particular, are uniquely positioned to carry a vision that serves society effectively. Philosophical inquiries are often underpinned by a theological framework that emphasizes hope, purpose, and intrinsic human value. The Christian perspective supports an optimistic vision of who we are and the fundamental nature of reality. The Christian perspective also includes metaphysical and epistemological resources to inspire intellectual virtues, which are essential for productive philosophical inquiry. Christians can model these virtues in ways that elevate the entire field.

In summary, your work flows from you vision of yourself. Are you a servant? Are you a leader? Who are you? Who do you want to be? Answering these questions are prior to answering the more specific questions of which topics you want to think about or what work you want to do. To cultivate your best work, cultivate the best vision of yourself. If you are a Christian philosopher, you have resources of the Christian worldview to support a God-centered vision of yourself. You can use your vision to serve people by treating them according to *their* greater purpose, even as you carry a vision of your greater purpose.

3. Pillar 2, Joy: Enjoy Your Work

Alvin Plantinga modeled for me value of *enjoying* one's philosophy work. He conveyed this value to me in an unexpected response to an email I sent him during my first year teaching at Azusa Pacific University. In my email, I told Plantinga that I was inspired to do all my work for God's kingdom. The purpose of my work, I told him, was to serve society and advance the truth, beauty, and goodness in the world. Plantinga's response surprised me. While he affirmed my noble interest, he questioned my purely instrumental use of philosophy. He wrote this:

> I'm not sure, however, that this means that every piece of work you do needs to display a direct link with God's kingdom. Part of what God expects of us (I think) is that we develop the image of God in which we were created by exploring the structures embedded in the world God has created. I'd say this is Kingdom work, even if it isn't an exploration of themes directly connected with the Kingdom.

I took from this response that Plantinga sees *intrinsic value* in exploring the structures of reality. This response also matched his engagement with students and other philosophers (in print and in person). In the classroom, he would present ideas with a smile on his face, like he was having fun in the moment of revelation and understanding. He was finding the joy in his work by seeing its intrinsic value.

When you lean into the work you enjoy (and you find the joy in your work), you tend to produce better work, and others benefit. The science of happiness supports this. Studies indicate that joy not only enhances life quality but significantly boosts productivity and creativity in professional settings.

Philosophical work can sometimes feel isolating, particularly when developing new viewpoints that might face scrutiny or outright criticism. However, a philosopher's internal joy has the power to infuse their environment with positivity, impacting colleagues and students alike. Cultivating a sense of inner peace while engaging deeply with philosophical content can turn potential solitude into a serene and enriching solitude. This not only benefits the philosopher personally but also makes the philosophical journey more inviting to others, fostering a more collaborative and supportive academic community.

Your internal excitement provides you information about the work that is most aligned to you. People sometimes ask me why I shifted from computer science to philosophy. A follow-up question: doesn't computer science *pay* more? My answer is that you get paid the most in the long-term doing what you love the most out of love for others. What I loved most about my work in computer science was crafting new algorithms to create 3-D graphics rendering engines. But I noticed that I also enjoy crafting new arguments and ideas to seek a greater understanding of reality. To me, philosophy is a larger playground to pursue the work I love the most. By pursuing the work I love the most, I have fuel to continue my work with increasing excellence.

At each stage of one's career, however, there are pressures to do activities you don't love. Some of these activities may be necessary stepping stones to places where you will eventually do the work you love the most. But be careful. If you take too many steps along a path you don't love, you risk stepping along circular paths set by others.

I think perhaps the biggest obstacle for *Christians* to do work they love is the sense of duty to sacrifice one's "selfish" desires. At least for me, I unconsciously associated the value of sacrificial service with giving up what I enjoy. This association blocked me from realizing that what I enjoy can work very well to serve others more. Realizing this has helped me give myself permission to pursue the kind of work I love the most, for this is the work that ends up serving the most people. My advice: if you find yourself on a circular path you don't enjoy for too long, give yourself permission to set your sights on another path—even if you don't see yet how to get there. By doing the work you love the most, you will produce the work that others love the most.

4. Pillar 3, Honesty: Tell the Truth as You See It

Philosophy is the pursuit of wisdom, but how do you get wisdom? In my estimation, the best *method* to get wisdom is to commit oneself to representing one's present views, to oneself and to others, as accurately as one can. Wisdom is the fruit of honesty over time.

It may seem all too obvious that honesty is valuable to philosophy, but there are many pressures not to be honest in subtle ways. For me, I've noticed my temptation is to display myself *less* confidently than I am in certain contexts. It's not that I'm tempted to say the opposite of what I believe, but rather I want to avoid coming across overly confident (even if I *am* confident). But honesty involves conveying yourself accurately, not more nor less confidently than you genuinely feel.

Other temptations not to be entirely honest come from various social pressures. The pressures to conform to a reputable view, to amplify the voices of celebrity philosophers, or to hide unorthodox beliefs can block the path to wisdom. For many Christian philosophers, there are pressures inside their academic world that differ from pressures inside their ecclesiastic world. For example, people at church may be worried that you are compromising your faith by adopting the wisdom of others, while people in the academy may worry that you are biased by your religion. This difference in expectation was epitomized for me recently when I got mixed messages from different people. Someone outside academia suggested to me that my work as a philosopher only has value if it is an apologetic for Christianity. A few days later, a friend within academia suggested to me that my work is only valuable if it is *not* an apologetic for a religion. These different pressures can pull you in different directions.

A commitment to honesty helps anchor you in the midst of many pressures. I find that the *intent* to remain steadfastly honest helps me provide the most long-term value in my communication, even if I'm mistaken in my present view. While intellectual humility is valuable, it is equally important to avoid dishonesty through feigned uncertainty. By expressing your true level of confidence, you provide more accurate information, and you respect the agency of others to engage with your ideas from their own perspective. Philosophers who commit to honesty foster a culture of transparency and integrity within their communities. This commitment empowers us to serve others not just through our ideas, but through the example we set in upholding truth.

There is a great need for Christian philosophers to model honesty by *committing* to honesty. One of the most common complaints against Christian intellectuals I see on social media is that Christians are not intellectually *honest*. Yet many atheists have also expressed to me personally their appreciation for Christians who convey themselves with authentic tones. They often also express to me increased curiosity about the details of my worldview.

The commitment to honesty fits inside the larger aim to serve others. This larger aim protects you from using "honesty" as an excuse to communicate ideas in self-serving or bullying ways. For Christian philosophers, who are entrusted not only with academic but also spiritual leadership, the commitment to an honest representation of one's views is a model for others. This dual commitment can inspire a more courageous exploration of new ideas and foster a more honest dialogue within the philosophical community, ultimately elevating the entire field by demonstrating how intellectual virtue can lead to new insights and discoveries.

5. Pillar 4, Love: Do Each Project Out of Love for Others

Jesus summarized all the commands into two commands: love God and love others. As a philosopher, I like unifying explanations, and I like that we can provide a unifying explanation of Jesus' summary in terms of a single command: *love personal beings*. (This command leaves open, of course, the prospect of value in loving non-personal things, like insects, flowers, or one's work.)

The pillar of love is perhaps the most important of the four pillars (while it works best with the pillars of vision, joy, and honesty). I think we easily underestimate the transformative power of love. A number of people have e-mailed me to tell me that their worldview was transformed by my work (e.g., they are no longer an atheist). When they describe what transformed them, they say it wasn't just my arguments. They almost always point to the *style* of my presentation and the way I interact with others. In so many words, I think they are saying that they felt my love, and this love came through in my considerations.

Despite the value of love, there are challenges to staying aligned to one's higher purpose. Earlier in my career, I noticed that my desires for status, achievement, and approval clouded my vision of why I was doing my work. These clouds became especially apparent to me one morning when I was at my office ready to work at 4:30 AM. I found myself checking my curriculum vita to see how well I was doing in the "game" of philosophy. I wanted to win. To win the game of philosophy, I needed to gain status through publications and associations throughout a long career. But that morning, I noticed that even if I won (whatever that might look like), the reward would be distant, trivial, and arbitrary. I could spend my entire career seeking to win a game that few people are playing, but that did not seem like my highest purpose.

Upon realizing the value of a higher purpose, I made a decision. I stood up from my desk and began walking across a hallway. I began to set a new course in my mind. I told myself that I shall set my aim to use my philosophy work to *serve others*. That moment of decision shifted the focus of my work. The goal is not to win a game for my own gain, but to add value to others. Adding value to others—in the form of life-giving wisdom—is the game. My decision to give my work a higher purpose has helped me stay on the track of my most meaningful work.

I have often seen the transformative power of love to bring to light a greater, mutual understanding. This occurred in my dialogue with Felipe Leon on God's existence (*Is God the Best Explanation of Things?*), where together we uncovered a surprising common ground: reality has a necessarily existent, foundational layer with fundamental mind-like qualities and can be characterized as "natural." What begins as disagreement morphs into a richer, shared understanding. This transformation doesn't happen overnight; it's the fruit of patience and collaborative effort, fueled by love for people and the truth we can illuminate together.

Christian philosophers who use their work out of love for others are salt and light to their colleagues in the field. This salt and light is attractive, not repulsive. Sometimes I hear non-theist philosophers express to me a background worry that Christians are seeking to promote their own view rather than promoting the cause for wisdom and truth. By having a vision of oneself as a servant of your colleagues in the field, a Christian can avoid a certain trap of using their work to point to themselves. While working from a Christian worldview to serve others does not exclude apologetics *for* the Christian worldview, the purpose is different. Christian philosophers can work *from* a Christian worldview to bring value to others.

To illustrate how love can bring value to others, consider the scenario where a philosopher is faced with two potential projects: one is a sharp critique of a popular element in Chalmers' latest theory of consciousness, which could elevate the philosopher's standing through clever argumentation; the other is to develop a theoretical bridge between Chalmers' work and deeper principles that illuminate the understanding of consciousness. While the first may bring quick academic recognition, the second, rooted in a respect for Chalmers' work and a desire to genuinely advance knowledge, may contribute more substantially to the field and its followers. This decision, guided by a love for the audience, ensures that the work not only respects previous contributions but also enriches the audience's comprehension of complex ideas. Working from love exposes the truth while building up people along the way.

6. Conclusion

A great philosopher has a great purpose. This purpose is *not* to merely build one's reputation, discover the greatest truth, or to win the philosopher's game. The purpose of a great philosopher is to bring more wisdom into more places. To achieve this purpose well, in any age, a great philosopher cultivates an inner well of love. This love fills their vision of who they are, their enjoyment of their work, and their honest aim for truth in the service of others. By fulfilling this great purpose, the next generation of philosophers will, I believe, contribute to a new era of discovery and understanding of who we are and our connection to the deepest structures of reality.

17

ADVICE TO PENTECOSTAL PHILOSOPHERS REDUX: A MORE CONFESSIONALLY DETERMINATE PHILOSOPHY

Yoon Shin

BattleCreek Church

1. Introduction

Readers may wonder why this book contains a chapter written by a pentecostal philosopher.[1] What hath Athens to do with Azusa Street?[2] Isn't pentecostalism an anti-intellectual tradition that looks askance on theology? If theology is under suspicion, what hope is there for philosophy? Indeed, pentecostal philosophy has faced challenges against its existence and legitimacy in its short history from within and outside its own traditions. Yet, pentecostal philosophy has much to contribute to the wider philosophical community.

Before giving my advice, I must direct the reader's attention to the history and challenges that pentecostal philosophy has faced, and to the influential advice James K. A. Smith gave to pentecostal philosophers some 20 years earlier, and another advice given recently by J. Aaron Simmons to contextualize my advice to the current state of pentecostal philosophy. Through this, readers will discover the competing advice

---

1. I use the widely used lowercase "p" pentecostalism to refer to the diverse traditions of global pentecostalism.
2. This is the title of James K. A. Smith's introduction in *Thinking in Tongues: Pentecostal Contributions to Christian Philosophy* (Eerdmans, 2010).

between Smith and Simmons, of which I side with Smith's Plantinga-styled advice because I believe it will better maintain the "pentecostal" characteristics of our philosophy.[3] Although written primarily to pentecostal philosophers, this essay may prove useful to non-pentecostal philosophers as an extension of Plantinga's advice.

2. History

Pentecostal scholarship, but especially pentecostal philosophy, is relatively new in the history of Christian scholarship. As Amos Yong explains, pentecostal scholarship came in three waves. The initial wave began in the 1960s by academically trained Pentecostal historians who sought to preserve pentecostal history and identity. The second wave of biblical scholarship came in the 1970s. Like their historical counterparts, pentecostal biblical scholars began questioning the objectivity of historical-critical hermeneutics and interacted with alternative hermeneutical theories. Their efforts led to great advancements in pentecostal hermeneutics and biblical scholarship, such that biblical studies is now the largest interest group in the Society for Pentecostal Studies.[4] Theological scholarship in the 1990s constituted the third wave, and academically trained theologians have reconsidered the various theological loci through the eyes of pentecostal identity and spirituality to great effect.[5]

The humble beginnings of pentecostal academic scholarship has continued to mature beyond the initial waves. Nimi Wariboko and L. William Oliverio cite the rise of pentecostal philosophy and philosophical theology in the last ten years as an example of this maturity.[6] Pentecostal philosophy has, indeed, made qualitatively important contributions, as detailed by J. Aaron Simmons, even if its quality is not matched by its quantity.[7]

The founding of the philosophy interest group in the Society for Pentecostal Studies in 2002 and the publication of James K. A. Smith's article entitled "Advice to Pentecostal Philosophers" in 2003, which

---

3. My disagreement with Simmons is only with his opposition to Plantinga-styled philosophy. I heartedly approve his call for an "affectively engaging, argumentatively rigorous, and existentially relevant" pentecostal philosophy. J. Aaron Simmons, "Prospects for Pentecostal Philosophy: Assessing the Challenges and Envisioning the Opportunities," *Pneuma* 42, no. 2 (2020): 175.
4. Lois E. Olena, Society for Pentecostal Studies (SPS) 50th Anniversary Monograph, April 12, 2021, https://sps-usa.org/download/history/fiftieth-monograph.pdf.
5. Amos Yong, "Pentecostalism and the Theological Academy," *Theology Today* 64, no. 2 (July 2007): 245–48.
6. Nimi Wariboko and Bill Oliverio, "Pentecostal Scholarship: A Shift Has Occurred," *Pneuma* 42, no. 1 (2020): 1. They also cite fourth and fifth waves of pentecostal scholarship.
7. Simmons, "Prospects for Pentecostal Philosophy," 185–92.

was later included in his important work, *Thinking in Tongues*, gave pentecostal philosophy a home for sustained exchange of ideas and its initial methodological direction.[8] Since its inception, the philosophy interest group has hosted significant philosophical voices, such as D. Stephen Long, Merold Westphal, Charles Taylor, and Richard Kearney. As Simmons notes, however, the philosophical activities in the society and in publications have not marked an explosive growth of pentecostal philosophy.[9] Even after more than 20 years, pentecostal philosophy remains in infancy in terms of its output and members. Smith and Simmons identified four challenges that have contributed toward this lack of growth.

3. Challenges

The challenges that Smith and Simmons have identified have not mostly come from the academic guild. While the wider philosophical community might view pentecostal philosophy with incredulity or with amusement, the challenges to pentecostal philosophy have come primarily from the pentecostal church.[10] Smith describes the first challenge as the antithesis between philosophy and Christianity. Taking Colossians 2:8 at face value, pentecostals view philosophy as necessarily opposed to the Christian faith.[11] Simmons frames this concern as a political problem that stems from the conservative evangelicalization of US pentecostals in their theology and politics. With its doctrinal and hermeneutic rigidity, evangelical pentecostalism considers philosophy as an existential threat to its younger generations that seeks to proselytize them away from "orthodox" beliefs.[12]

The second challenge raises disciplinary concerns that questions the role of philosophy since theology is seen to accomplish all that philosophy can do. Simmons contends that behind this supposed elevation of theology is really a deflationary hermeneutics that jettisons any form of interpretation: since the Bible is clear, the Spirit's illumination is the only

---

8. James K. A. Smith, "Advice to Pentecostal Philosophers," *Journal of Pentecostal Theology* 11, no. 2 (2003): 235-47.
9. Simmons, "Prospects for Pentecostal Philosophy," 176.
10. These challenges originate primarily from classical and neo-pentecostal communities. Charismatics, who are part of established historical traditions, have not faced such backlash due to their philosophical history and historic commitment to robust education. This intellectual cultural difference has proven true in my own experience spent between the Assemblies of God (USA) as a licensed minister and professor in one of its largest universities and the Anglican Mission International as a priest. For an explanation of the differences between classical Pentecostals, Charismatics, and neo-pentecostals, see Allan Anderson, "Varieties, Taxonomies, and Definitions," in *Studying Global Pentecostalism: Theories and Methods*, ed. Allan Anderson et al. (University of California Press, 2010), 16-20.
11. Smith, *Thinking in Tongues*, 2.
12. Simmons, "Prospects for Pentecostal Philosophy," 181.

necessary hermeneutic. In this light, philosophy is a dangerous tool that taints the simplicity of the gospel. However, Simmons correctly notes that this naive hermeneutic makes theology and biblical studies unnecessary since they rely on more than mere pneumatological illumination.[13]

Third, despite the data on the high earnings potential and high scores on law and medical school entrance exams by philosophy majors,[14] the economic challenge purports that philosophy is financially useless. Many pentecostals would agree with the sentiment of Marco Rubio that society needs more welders and less philosophers.[15] Even universities have followed suit. Imagining students as primarily consumers, many executives have prioritized non-academic amenities at the expense of academics. Humanities has been its most frequent victim, one of the most egregious cases in recent memory being that of the Dianoia Institute of Philosophy's dissolution by the Australian Catholic University.[16] Ministerial and theological education have not been immune either. Notably, the reduction of the MDiv has hit a crescendo. With the help of the Kern Foundation, many institutions are even creating 5th year MDiv programs, perhaps with much chagrin from their faculty, that do not *currently* meet military chaplaincy requirements.

Fourth, Simmons locates the epistemic challenge in the Christian philosophical guild that views pentecostalism and its anti-intellectualism with an eye of suspicion.[17] Given that Christian philosophy had to struggle against the legacies of positivism with philosophical rigor, its suspicion of pentecostal philosophy's location within an anti-intellectualist tradition is understandable.

The first three challenges have led to recruitment problems for pentecostal philosophy. I was happy to find four classical pentecostal universities offering some form of philosophy major or minor. However, they are all housed in theology departments. While I think we need healthy blurring between the disciplinary boundaries, I sympathize with Simmons's concern that philosophy's housing in theology departments is

---

13. Simmons, "Prospects for Pentecostal Philosophy," 182.
14. See "Why Major in Philosophy?," accessed May 2, 2024, https://philosophy.unc.edu/undergraduate/the-major/why-major-in-philosophy/; and "Philosophy Majors after College Median Income for Humanities Majors by Career Stage," accessed May 2, 2024. https://cdn.ymaws.com/www.apaonline.org/resource/resmgr/data_on_profession/Philosophy_Majors_After_Coll.pdf.
15. "Republican Candidates Debate in Milwaukee, Wisconsin." The American Presidency Project. University of California, Santa Barbara, November 10, 15. https://www.presidency.ucsb.edu/documents/republican-candidates-debate-milwaukee-wisconsin.
16. "Australian Catholic University Sparks Anger over Scrapping Medieval History and Philosophy Departments," *The Guardian*, September 14, 2023, https://www.theguardian.com/australia-news/2023/sep/14/australian-catholic-university-condemned-over-totally-indefensible-cuts-to-humanities-programs.
17. Simmons, "Prospects for Pentecostal Philosophy," 184.

for the sake of greater surveillance.[18] The last challenge is a professional one that is more within our control. Just as Smith and Simmons have gained respect through their scholarly rigor, pentecostal philosophy must, following Plantinga's (and Smith's) advice, continually and boldly produce quality work and participate in wider conversations without losing its autonomy and integrity.[19]

4. James K. A. Smith's Plantinga-Styled Advice

But let us not dwell on the challenges but look forward to the promises of pentecostal philosophy. Beginnings are often difficult, and some endeavors take longer than others to hit critical mass. However uncertain pentecostal philosophy's future is with the limited number of its participants, its method has broadly followed the trajectory of Plantinga's advice to Christian philosophers, primarily filtered through Smith's Plantinga-styled advice to pentecostal philosophers.

Smith narrows Plantinga's advice to apply to pentecostal philosophy. The primary motivation lies in his criticism that Christian philosophy is too broad to apply to specific Christian traditions and is easily reduced to mere theistic philosophy. To avoid being Christian philosophy in name only, "Christian philosophy must be fundamentally incarnational and cruciform, rooted not simply in theism but in the revelation of the incarnation, the scandal of the cross, and the confession of the resurrection."[20] Smith thus intensifies Plantinga's call for more autonomy, integrity, and boldness.

Pentecostalism has its own distinctiveness, characterized by its spirituality and its embedded worldview. This determinate identity should motivate pentecostals to do philosophy "pentecostally," and Smith echoes Plantinga's advice that pentecostals must exercise their right to philosophize from their pentecostal assumptions.[21] These assumptions do not arise from doctrines. Pentecostalism is primarily a "*spirituality*, an embodied set of practices and disciplines that implicitly 'carry' a worldview or social imaginary,"[22] which is comprised of five worldview commitments: a radical openness to God; an enchanted theology of creation and culture; a nondualistic affirmation of embodiment and materiality; an affective, narrative epistemology; and an eschatological orientation to mission and

---

18. Simmons, "Prospects for Pentecostal Philosophy," 181.
19. Alvin Plantinga, "Advice to Christian Philosophers," *Faith and Philosophy* 1, no. 3 (July 1984): 254.
20. Smith, *Thinking in Tongues*, 11.
21. Smith, *Thinking in Tongues*, 11.
22. Smith, *Thinking in Tongues*, xviii.

justice.²³ This spirituality, with its embodied affections and experiences framed through narratives that form its worldview, should not only act as the pre-philosophical assumptions that direct pentecostal philosophy, but pentecostal philosophy has the right to philosophize from it.

Pentecostal philosophy should exercise more autonomy and integrity from non-Christian *and* Christian philosophy and pursue questions and projects that arise from its pre-philosophical commitments. Smith points to Norman Geisler's mere historical treatment of miracles in *Miracles and the Modern Mind* as a case that contrasts against pentecostalism's continuationist commitment. Pentecostal philosophy, with its radically open worldview and pneumatological ontology, must consider miracles as a contemporary possibility.²⁴ Moreover, the publisher's description of Geisler's book should caution pentecostal philosophers to approach it with a hermeneutics of suspicion, as the publisher promotes the work as a "dispassionate look at the facts and arguments."²⁵ As I have argued elsewhere, affections can be epistemically warranted according to Plantinga's proper functionalism and qualify as knowledge.²⁶ Pentecostal philosophy should be wary of accepting Christian philosophical assumptions that run contrary to its embodied spirituality. It must, therefore, practice more boldness pursuing its agenda "unapologetically informed by the practices of a pentecostal spirituality."²⁷ Given the dearth of pentecostal philosophers, aspiring pentecostal philosophers may be tempted to uncritically adopt the agenda, methods, and pre-philosophical commitments of their non-Christian and non-pentecostal philosophical colleagues and interlocutors. Against this uncritical adoption, pentecostal philosophers must align their philosophy with their worldview.

5. Contra J. Aaron Simmons

Contrary to Smith, Simmons believes that Plantinga-styled philosophy stifles dialogue between interlocutors who do not share similar confessional authority structures. In my exchange with Simmons, I took Smith's Augustinian position of *pistic* methodology for pentecostal philosophy.²⁸ Simmons's Thomistic position recommends greater independence

---

23. Smith, *Thinking in Tongues*, 12.
24. Smith, *Thinking in Tongues*, 14–15.
25. "Miracles and the Modern Mind: A Defense of Biblical Miracles," Wipf and Stock Publishers, accessed May 4, 2024, https://wipfandstock.com/9781592447329/miracles-and-the-modern-mind/.
26. Yoon Shin, *Pentecostalism, Postmodernism, and Reformed Epistemology: James K. A. Smith and the Contours of a Postmodern Christian Epistemology* (Lexington Books, 2022), 181–82.
27. Smith, *Thinking in Tongues*, 16.
28. Yoon Shin, "Confessing at the Altar: A Call and Response," *Pneuma* 42, 2 (2020): 201–19.

between reason and revelation: "the greatest single contribution that pentecostal philosophy can make to Christian philosophy is to challenge the idea that Christian philosophy is something necessarily done within tightly confessional communities."[29] Simmons argues that pentecostalism's radical openness to God should encourage a philosophical methodology that welcomes voices with different pre-philosophical commitments, and this is the only way to ensure that evidence can be shared between interlocutors. *Pistic* commitments, on the other hand, shut down conversations before they can begin by limiting the range of agreeable evidence. A philosophical methodology devoid of special revelation as evidentiary material secures philosophy from spiraling into theology, unlike the Plantinga-inspired analytic theology that blurs the line between philosophy of religion and systematic theology. Who is right? Does the Augustinian position stifle philosophical dialogue and reduce philosophy to theology? Agreeing with Smith, I contend that philosophical dialogue can continue and exhort pentecostal philosophers to blur the hazy line between philosophy and theology.

First, if dialogue is stymied by antithetical authority structures, then pentecostal philosophers can temporarily bracket their pre-philosophical commitments as a possibility rather than actual. This methodological commitment to the hypothetical status of God-talk characterizes Simmons's new phenomenology.[30] While this strategy may seem to question the autonomy and integrity of pentecostal philosophy, it does not *necessarily* oppose them. Simmons is right that radical openness allows for this method. However, this method is available precisely because it is part of a pentecostal worldview. Also, pre-philosophical commitments are not immune to philosophical critique. If an assumed pre-philosophical commitment is discovered in a premise that raises questions of the soundness of an argument, the argument can shift to debate the justification of the commitment.

Second, a strict demarcation between philosophy and theology assumes a Western and even ethnocentric conception of philosophy and insulates rather than broadens philosophical dialogue. Simmons promotes this demarcation because he believes that only shared evidential authority structures, unlike inflexible confessional authority, can accommodate interlocutors of different beliefs. For example, he points to feminist philosophy as a personal, not confessional, approach that promotes dialogue since embodied experiences and affections, even those of

---

29. Simmons, "Prospects for Pentecostal Philosophy," 195.
30. Shin, "Confessing at the Altar," 205.

women, are shareable authority structures with men.[31] However, this view assumes that embodied experiences and affections are religiously neutral. The meaning of one's experiences and affections are shaped by one's linguistic communities that set expectations and interpretations of experiences. A pentecostal's experience of the sublime will be vastly different than that of the naturalist because her community will have set the linguistic expectations to interpret the event confessionally. If this inevitable encroachment of confessional authority structure in pentecostal testimony demarcates her interpretation of the sublime as merely theological and not philosophical, then Simmons's account must be called into account as merely a Western, secularized interpretation of philosophy that insulates rather than broadens philosophical dialogue. Naturalistic philosophy of the West cannot define philosophy for the rest of the world.

As Bryan Van Norden has argued, the West does not have a monopoly on philosophy. Despite Western philosophy's structurally ethnocentric posture toward non-Western thought as other than philosophy, Van Norden, who specializes in Chinese philosophy, has argued that subaltern voices have been carrying on a rich tradition of philosophy as long as the West.[32] The Advaita Vedanta Hinduism is rightfully a philosophical tradition that teaches a way of living that is not devoid of religious elements. Achieving *moksa* or liberation from determinate dualities in life is possible through critical thought, yogic exercises, and an austere life. Even though the ultimate reality of Brahman is impersonal, it is not impersonal in a naturalistic sense. For it is an ultimate reality of *undifferentiated* quality; its quality is the absence of qualities. Moreover, other layers of reality of Brahman imposes differentiations and personalistic religion, even if due to *maya* or illusion.[33] Even if one strains to argue that Hinduism is ultimately atheological, the rest of Hindu philosophy cannot escape more overt religious ideas and practices. If Western philosophy departments will continually ghettoize non-Western thought into world religion or location-specific studies departments, then it should rightfully be labeled as perpetuating an ethnocentric colonial project. For Van Norden, philosophy departments should either become multicultural or rename themselves as departments of Anglo-European philosophy.[34]

---

31. Simmons, "Prospects for Pentecostal Philosophy," 197.
32. Bryan W. Van Norden, *Taking Back Philosophy: A Multicultural Manifesto* (Columbia University Press, 2017).
33. Tyler Dalton McNabb, "Closing Pandora's Box: A Defence of Alvin Plantinga's Epistemology of Religious Belief" (PhD Diss., University of Glasgow, 2016), 82–85.
34. Van Norden, *Taking Back Philosophy*, 35.

The same argument applies for Hebraic thought, as Dru Johnson has argued. Following Yoram Hazony, Johnson states that considering Greco-Roman philosophies as purely secular and without revelatory aspects is myopic, and he argues that Parmenides, Empedocles, Heraclitus, and Socrates attributed their ideas to revelation. Both the Greco-Romans and Hebrews did not assume a reason-revelation dichotomy.[35]

Although Western philosophy considers Greek philosophy as the pinnacle of ancient philosophy, Johnson argues that Hebraic philosophy rightfully belongs in the same category. In *Biblical Philosophy*, Johnson argues for a three-tiered view of rigorous thinking: scholarly, speculative, and philosophical. Scripture demonstrates all these marks. First, it is scholarly, displaying rigorous and logical thought; it is not irrational or arbitrary. Second, it is speculative; it displays second-order thinking about the nature of reality and thinking itself. Third, it reflects on the traditional fields of philosophy, such as metaphysics, epistemology, axiology, and political thought, and advocates the adaptation of a narrative methodology that instructs for the purpose of developing discernment. This advocacy of method is what differentiates philosophical thinking from merely scholarly and speculative thinking. Because it recommends a consistent methodology that should be replicated in others, Hebraic thought, with its confessional authority structure, qualifies as philosophy.[36] If Van Norden and Johnson are right, Western secular philosophy cannot delimit the boundaries of philosophy without being ethnocentric.

No philosophy is perspectiveless. As Roy Clouser argues, the second-order activity of philosophy is guided by religious pre-philosophical commitments. By religion, he means a commitment to some ultimate that has independent existence.[37] On this definition, this ultimate is not dependent on personality or worship.[38] In Hinduism, the worship of Saguna Brahman as *Isvara* or personal deity applies to a lower level of reality that is affected by *maya*. Brahman, as undifferentiated, impersonal absolute reality, however, is not worshipped. Naturalism also does not worship material reality but regards certain aspects of reality as having aseity, such as mathematical laws or laws of logic. They, like the Platonic Forms, have aseity but are not personal and are not worshipped—unless one is a Pythagorean who prays to numbers.[39] Religion, therefore, does

---

35. Dru Johnson, *Biblical Philosophy: A Hebraic Approach to the Old and New Testaments* (Cambridge University Press, 2021) 24-25.
36. Johnson, *Biblical Philosophy*, 35-39.
37. Roy A. Clouser, *The Myth of Religious Neutrality: An Essay on the Hidden Role of Religious Belief in Theories* (University of Notre Dame Press, 2005), 23.
38. Clouser, *The Myth of Religious Neutrality*, 26.
39. Clouser, *The Myth of Religious Neutrality*, 20-21.

not necessitate worship, although it acts as the basic pre-philosophical commitment for reflective activity. Therefore, all philosophy as second-order reflective activity is undergirded by some religious pre-philosophical commitment.

The difference between philosophy and theology is then one of degree. Theology is an explicit reflection on its religious starting point. Philosophy need not reflect on its religious starting point. For example, theological epistemology asks, "What is the knowledge of God?" and philosophical epistemology asks, "What is knowledge?" However, the philosophical question will not, or at least should not, be divorced from its religious worldview. If all philosophy is undergirded by a religious pre-philosophical commitment, then all philosophy is confessional. The quicker we recognize that, the sooner we can free ourselves from the shackles of Western prejudice against non-naturalistic philosophy. With this, I provide my short advice.

6. Advice

Given the stunted growth of pentecostal philosophy, my advice mostly extends Smith's advice that narrows Plantinga's advice about practicing autonomy, integrity, and boldness. Pentecostal philosophers must boldly philosophize from our pentecostal commitments, practicing more autonomy and integrity, even from generic Christian philosophy, while also recognizing that pre-philosophical commitments are open to philosophical critique.[40] But first, we need more pentecostal philosophers. And to become one, students must enroll in philosophy programs. However, the lack of pentecostal philosophy graduate programs lead potential philosophers to be trained in institutions that may cause students to lose their pentecostal commitments.[41] Without a more determinate identity, we can easily fall into a generic mode of the dominant philosophical methodology and style of the day. In history, this is how pentecostalism became identified with evangelicalism. Due to the dearth of pentecostal theological textbooks, early pentecostal educators utilized evangelical literature, leading to the evangelicalization of pentecostalism. The same danger exists with pentecostal philosophy. Without a more self-conscious critical appropriation of styles and methodology that are consonant with pentecostal identity, pentecostal philosophers are in danger of creating a dualism between their pentecostal doxological life

---

40. This advice applies to all Christian philosophical traditions.
41. This example is inspired by the fictitious college student who experiences something similar in Plantinga's "Advice to Christian Philosophers," 254–56.

and their life of the mind. Pentecostal philosophers and theologians must teach our students the importance of theorizing from our identities.

By exercising a more confessionally determinate Planting-styled philosophy, pentecostal philosophers will face dialogues that will prove more difficult due to unshared evidential authority structures. Yet, how is this different from unshared premises? If a premise is under question, then it is just proper to debate its merit. One could also bracket the authority structure to explore ideas for their utility, such as when a Christian philosopher brackets the atheism of Nietzsche to build a "faith-based" epistemology on Nietzsche's perspectivism. Pentecostal philosophers must rely on the Spirit to enliven their imagination to search for areas and methods of investigation that allow for such philosophical dialogue. Pentecostal philosophers must, therefore, be people of prayer to hear and discern the voice of the Spirit.

We must also exercise boldness against Western philosophy's challenge that philosophy and theology have clear boundaries. Against this secular hegemony, we should explore how confessional presuppositions and theological concepts can be utilized for philosophical projects.[42] Part of the initial work, then, requires clarifying the relationship between philosophy and theology.

Such work as appropriating non-pentecostal philosophical education and ideas with our pentecostal identity, discerning the voice of the Spirit, and exercising boldness requires wisdom, humility, curiosity, and other intellectual (and moral) virtues. Finally, then, pentecostal philosophers must be people of virtue. The pursuit of philosophy cannot be divorced from character development in reliance on the Holy Spirit. Remember that pentecostalism is a spirituality. What we do with our bodies matters. A mere life of the mind is not just antithetical to pentecostal spirituality; it cannot even exist without proper intellectual and moral virtues. Development of virtuous character occurs through developing virtuous habits in healthy communities, church, family, and the wider society. Indeed, pursuit of the virtuous life brings us back to the classical definition of philosophy as the love of wisdom. May the Spirit form us in the image of Jesus as we pursue the love of God and love others as we love ourselves.

---

42. This project would differ from analytic theology since I am not calling for mere use of philosophical methods for doing theology.

18

"ADVICE TO CHRISTIAN PHILOSOPHERS" FORTY YEARS ON

Peter van Inwagen

University of Notre Dame

NB: This essay is a revised version of an essay that was written twenty-five years ago.1 The discussion in section 3 of Plantinga's views on how Christian philosophers should think about the problem of free will has been extensively rewritten.

1. Introduction

The following passage from Plantinga's "Advice to Christian Philosophers"[2] is an accurate summary of its central message:

> We come to philosophy with pre-philosophical opinions; we can do no other. And the point is: the Christian has as much right to his pre-philosophical opinions as others have to theirs. He needn't first try to 'prove' them from propositions accepted by, say, the bulk of the non-Christian philosophical community . . . But this means that the Christian philosophical community need not devote all of its efforts to attempting to refute opposing claims and/or to arguing for its own claims, in each case from premises accepted by

---

1. Peter van Inwagen, "Some Remarks on Plantinga's Advice," *Faith and Philosophy* 16 (1999): 164-72.
2. Alvin Plantinga, "Advice to Christian Philosophers," *Faith and Philosophy* 1 (July 1984): 253-71.

the bulk of the philosophical community at large. It ought to do this, indeed, but it ought to do more. For if it does only this, it will neglect a pressing philosophical task: systematizing, deepening, clarifying Christian thought on these topics![3]

"Systematizing, deepening, clarifying Christian thought on these topics"—but what are "these topics"? The paragraphs that precede the quotation demonstrate that this phrase means, near enough, "the problems of philosophy" or "philosophical questions." (I hope that at least the latter phrase is abstract enough that no one will regard it as favoring some parochial view of what philosophy is. I suppose it could be said correctly, if not very informatively, even of Nietzsche and Heidegger that what they did was to think about philosophical questions.) The opposing point of view could be summed up in the following principle:

> No philosopher should presuppose in his or her philosophical work any proposition that is not accepted by the bulk of the non-Christian philosophical community.

When one considers this principle, an important refinement immediately suggests itself. Since Christians are a small minority among philosophers, there cannot be much difference between the set of propositions that is accepted by the bulk of the non-Christian philosophical community and the set of propositions that is accepted by the bulk of the philosophical community *simpliciter*. Let us therefore formulate the "opposing principle" this way:

> No philosopher should presuppose in his or her philosophical work any proposition that is not accepted by the bulk of the philosophical community.

This formulation of the opposing principle has the advantage of not making it appear as if its advocates were concerned to single Christians out, to place restrictions on the presuppositions of Christians but not on the presuppositions of Muslims or Marxists or theosophists or Freudians. The principle does not, it should be noted, forbid the philosopher to question or to attempt to refute propositions that are accepted by the bulk of the philosophical community. Nor does it forbid the philosopher to attempt—like Descartes—to *prove* some of the propositions accepted by the bulk of the philosophical community, provided that in this attempt he or she does not make use of any propositions that are not accepted by the bulk of the philosophical community. The principle does not even say that

---
3. Plantinga, "Advice," 268.

the philosopher *may* presuppose any proposition accepted by the bulk of the philosophical community. It is therefore not a very strong principle. But it is certainly possible to violate it. Here are some simple examples of this. A Christian philosopher argues in one of the following ways—and without significant philosophical preamble:

> God is an immaterial being who has mental states; therefore, it is possible for there to be an immaterial being who has mental states;

> God sometimes performs miracles; therefore not all states of the physical world are consequences of its earlier states or else due simply to chance;

> It would be impossible for any real being to survey the whole of the set-theoretic universe; God knows all truths, but he could not know all the supposed truths of set-theory unless he could survey the whole set-theoretic universe; therefore, the belief of platonist mathematicians and philosophers in the real existence of the set-theoretic universe is an illusion.

But it is not only Christian philosophers who violate the opposing principle. It would, for example, be hard to argue convincingly that the axioms of Spinoza's *Ethic* were even in his day accepted by the bulk of the philosophical community—that the bulk of the late-seventeenth-century philosophical community held that all Spinoza's false conclusions were due to his having made various logical mistakes in course of constructing his demonstrations. More to the point, it is very hard to believe that any philosopher of our own day really subscribes to the opposing principle. It is very hard to believe that there exists a set of propositions that the bulk of the present-day philosophical community accepts and that even one member of the present-day philosophical community presupposes no propositions but those contained in this set. It is very hard to believe even that any present-day philosopher *thinks* this is the way he or she proceeds. For one thing, it is very hard to believe that there is one intellectual community that comprises all those who do profess and call themselves philosophers. But let us waive this point. Let us consider a small, representative group of philosophers who belonged to the same intellectual community if any philosophers ever belonged to the same intellectual community. Let us imagine that John Searle, Daniel Dennett, and David Chalmers were once engaged in a debate about the nature of consciousness. (A good sense of what this debate would be like can be gathered from Searle's reviews of books by Dennett and Chalmers in the *New York Review of Books,* and the subsequent correspondence concerning these reviews. Searle's reviews and some of this correspondence were published in a collection of his writings called *The Mystery of Consciousness*.)[4]

If you try to imagine such a debate, you will see, I hope, that it is simply ludicrous to suppose that there is some set of propositions that is accepted by the bulk of the philosophical community and that Searle, Dennett, and Chalmers are each of them assuming the truth only of propositions that belong to this set. It is ludicrous to suppose even that this is what they *think* they are doing. Each of them does indeed assume certain things that are incompatible with Christianity—that the physical world is a closed causal system, for example—but that's not to the point. Each of them presupposes the truth of propositions that are controversial indeed, controversial within the very intellectual community to which they belong, and this is a feature of all philosophical debates, past, present, and, I daresay, future.

The part of Plantinga's advice I have so far discussed seems to come down to the statement that Christian philosophers need not regard themselves as bound by a certain principle that no philosopher in fact honors or tries to honor. This piece of advice is self-evident, trivial, and very valuable. It is valuable simply because Christian philosophers live in an intellectual atmosphere pervaded by a curious double standard: Christian belief is judged and condemned under an epistemic standard that very little of what anyone believes could satisfy. Let me give an example of this standard at work. A philosopher once told me that he could not accept Christianity or any other religion because there were many religions, each of them logically incompatible with the others, and it was impossible to demonstrate of any particular one that it was correct. This is, when you think about it, a very odd thing for a *philosopher* to say, for, *mutatis mutandis,* it is an exact description of the situation in philosophy. And yet the oddness of what this philosopher was saying was something that had never occurred to him. (The fact that it had never occurred to him—a very intelligent and well-trained philosopher—is itself a very odd fact, one well worth reflecting on.) The double standard works like this: the beliefs of Christians—that the physical world was created by God; that Christ was raised from the dead—are condemned on epistemological grounds because their truth cannot be demonstrated from principles that the bulk of the philosophical community accepts. But this standard is not applied to the philosophical beliefs of non-religious philosophers—beliefs about, say, the reality of universals or the possibility of a private language or the principle of utility. (Nor is a suitably generalized version of this

---

4. John R. Searle, *The Mystery of Consciousness* (New York Review Books, 1997).

standard applied to beliefs about whether literature should be taught on the basis of a canon of time-honored works or about the effectiveness of capital punishment as a deterrent or about whether life is common in the universe.)

2.

It will be noted that, although Plantinga does not forbid Christian philosophers to consider philosophical questions that are, as we might say, entirely secular, he is at pains to insist that if they devote too much of their time to such questions, they will have less time to do something important that they—or at least a significant proportion of them—should be doing: "systematizing, deepening, clarifying Christian thought on [philosophical questions]."

What exactly is this project that Plantinga recommends to Christian philosophers? I have tried to apply these words to myself. I have looked at my own work and I have asked myself whether what he recommends is something I do, and, if it is something I do, when I do it and how much of it I do. If I categorize my work in respect of the ways in which it is related to the Christian religion, I find that it falls into four categories:

1. Apologetic Work. Various philosophers have attacked Christianity on philosophical grounds, and I, naturally enough, believe that their attacks are based on errors and that I know what those errors are. I have attempted, in my apologetic work, to make these errors evident to the reader.

2. Resolving Christian Philosophical problems. I have attempted to suggest solutions to philosophical problems raised by various Christian doctrines—for example, the problems about identity and predication that are raised by the doctrines of the Trinity and the Incarnation.

3. Works for Christians. A little of my work—a few essays—is addressed primarily to my fellow Christians, essays in which I attempt to convince them of things that Christians generally don't believe, but which are, or so I maintain, compatible with Christianity and which should be "live hypotheses" for Christians. (For example, that we are living animals and have no immaterial part.)

4. Religiously neutral works. I have written books and essays that contain nothing of relevance to Christianity or to any religion, books and essays that are as religiously neutral as works on number theory or the history of the bicycle.

Do the first three categories represent cases of "Christian thought about philosophical questions?" I suppose they do, but perhaps not all of them in the same sense. I think one should be suspicious of phrases like "Christian thought," "Christian literature," and "Christian society"—suspicious at least to the extent of making an effort to be absolutely clear about what one means when one uses them. (I believe that the name that was first proposed for this association[5] was "The Society for Christian Philosophy," and that this name was rejected by Bill Alston on the excellent ground that it isn't clear what "Christian philosophy" means.[6])

One might honor these very proper suspicions by playing definition-and-counterexample with the notion of Christian thought. Or one might declare that "Christian thought" is understood in several senses and proceed to enumerate and distinguish them—the various senses of the phrase being illustrated respectively by, say, *The Imitation of Christ, Concluding Unscientific Postscript, A Grammar of Assent, Murder in the Cathedral,* and *Warranted Christian Belief.* You will be relieved to learn that, despite my suspicions about the phrase "Christian thought" being very deep indeed, I am going to do neither of these things. I am not going to do either of them because I want to consider a fact that seems to me to present a more pressing problem: the body of my philosophical work falls in category 4 (above) and thus falls under no definition of "Christian thought" that anyone could conceivably find plausible. If this were a merely autobiographical fact, I would not bother to bring it to your attention. But I think that many (certainly not all) Christian philosophers are in the same situation as I in this respect. And, to revert my own case, not only does the body of my work fall outside the bounds of any reasonable definition of "Christian thought," but all the philosophical work I take the most personal satisfaction in falls in this category—all the work in the doing of which I have felt that my mind was operating at its highest capacity. If you like: all the work I am most proud of. Here, pray God, I am not referring to pride in the theological sense, that perilous state of the soul in which she challenges God's authority and attempts to become her own sole ruler. I

---

5. This paper was originally written to be read at a meeting of the Society of Christian Philosophers.
6. The similarity between the initially proposed name and the eventually adopted name no doubt explains why Plantinga (253) refers to the Society of Christian Philosophers as 'the Society for Christian Philosophers'.

am referring, I hope, to the pride of the artist or craftsman. The pride of the craftsman can, God knows, be the occasion of all manner of sin, but I do not think it is *per se* sinful. It is simply spiritually dangerous—like erotic love or political action or concern for one's physical health. (The point of this list is: What *isn't* spiritually dangerous?)

The proof that the body of my work in philosophy is in no sense "Christian thought" is simple enough: if you read this work in ignorance of its author's biography, you wouldn't be able to tell whether it was written by a Christian. This fact is not a consequence of some deliberate policy of mine; I have not chosen on methodological grounds to exclude my religious views from my work. (With one exception, which I'll mention in a moment.) It's just that I have generally had no opportunity to include or exclude them. Much of philosophy is simply so remote from the concerns of the spiritual life that, like harmonic analysis or condensed-matter physics, it does not interact with one's religious convictions—although, like all honest work, it can be done to the glory of God. In this matter, religion can be usefully compared to politics. W. V. Quine, as most of us know, was politically very conservative. But one could never have inferred this from the writings on which his philosophical reputation rests. And this is not because he had adopted a deliberate policy of keeping his readers in the dark about his politics. It's simply because when one is writing about analyticity or ontic commitment or the problem of radical translation, one doesn't encounter many opportunities to express one's views on Reaganomics or capital punishment or affirmative action. And, of course, if one is writing on these topics one doesn't encounter many opportunities to discuss the Incarnation or the Atonement or the Body of Christ.

I concede that the comparison is not exact. If one is a Christian, one's religious beliefs interact with more philosophical questions than one's political beliefs, whatever they may be, for the beliefs that are *de fide* for Christians fall in very widely separated areas. Christianity is, as we might say, *about* a very wide range of topics. This fact is connected with the "one exception" I mentioned a moment ago—with the one case in which I avoided appealing to my religious beliefs on methodological grounds. My book *Metaphysics*,[7] since it is about metaphysics in general, by the nature of the case contains some discussion of those metaphysical questions that do impinge on theology; for example, the question, "Why is there something rather than nothing?" At the outset of the book, I explicitly confessed my Christian beliefs, and then explicitly stated that I wasn't going to

---

7. First edition, Westview Press, 1993. Fifth edition, Routledge, 2024.

appeal to them, or was going to try not to. But in that book there was a special reason for doing this: namely that, in my view at least, a book that advertises itself as a general introduction to a subject (and one that is not written specifically for the members of some religion or denomination) ought to be as nearly neutral as possible about religious matters.

It is obvious enough that many commonly held philosophical opinions are inconsistent with Christianity. A Christian cannot believe that the physical universe is all that there is or that the world had no beginning in time or that matter is inherently evil. (This last may not be a very popular position nowadays, but times change.) Still, as I say, much of philosophy concerns matters that have no connection with the life of the spirit. In philosophy's house there are many mansions, and it is possible to wander about its corridors for quite a long while without encountering anything that either affirms or contradicts any part of the Christian faith.

Or so I say. But on this point, I think, there is some sort of disagreement between Plantinga and me. He finds much more of philosophy to be of relevance to Christianity than I do. An adequate and fair discussion of this disagreement would have to take into account Plantinga's work on epistemology. I shall have to do the best I can without discussing this work, however, because to do so in any meaningful way would require a paper wholly devoted to that topic, and I am halfway through this one. I will confine my remarks to the philosophy of mind and metaphysics.

Plantinga and many other Christian philosophers see much in the current philosophy of mind that is anti-Christian. And they are right about this if one sees rhetoric and incidental remarks as integral to the works in which they occur. It is undeniable that most current books and essays on the philosophy of mind contain fervent and frequent pledges of allegiance to philosophical naturalism. But to my mind, these pledges of allegiance are mere decorations. If you crossed them out, you would not affect the real philosophical content of the books and essays in which they occur, and, once you had crossed them out, there would be nothing in them that was inconsistent with or even unfriendly to Christianity. The exhortations to philosophical naturalism that one finds in the writings of John Searle or David Chalmers or Paul Churchland remind me of the opening words of an article in a Chinese geological journal that I happened to glance at in the early 1960s: "Applying the thoughts of Chairman Mao to the geology of the Yellow River Basin, we discover . . . ." (The remainder of the article was a perfectly straightforward piece of scientific writing.) Of course, the current philosophy of mind is resolutely anti-dualist, and anti-dualism pertains to the essence and not merely the accidents of its content. And it is true that some forms of dualism are consistent with Christianity; it is in fact true that some form of dualism has been maintained by almost every Christian philosopher and theologian of any importance. Still, there is nothing anti-Christian about anti-dualism (anti-Hindu, yes; anti-Buddhist, yes). It is hard to find any support for dualism in the Bible (I would say it was impossible to find any biblical texts that unambiguously support dualism), easy to find anti-dualist texts (or so I would argue), and it cannot be found in the Creeds.

I have to admit that I am, as a philosopher, not very impressed with most current work in the philosophy of mind, but that is because most of it seems to me to be irremediably infected with metaphysical and logical nonsense, metaphysical and logical nonsense that I claim to have detected by the exercise of natural reason. Rhetorical decoration aside, I find little if anything in it that contradicts God's revelation. (Except, perhaps, in a certain trivial sense: One might take the view that logical nonsense contradicts everything.) If there is much in it that contradicts some of the human constructs that have been built on God's revelation, well, the same could be said of geology. We must never confuse revelation and the human constructs that have been built on revelation.

3.

Having made the general points I have summarized, Plantinga proceeds to give examples of the approach to philosophical problems he recommends for Christian philosophers:

> [The] Christian philosopher has a perfect right to the point of view and pre-philosophical assumptions he brings to philosophic work; the fact that these are not widely shared outside the Christian or theistic community is interesting but fundamentally irrelevant. I can best explain what I mean by way of example; so I shall descend from the level of lofty generality to specific examples.[8]

One of his examples, one of several, is the problem of free will. Of the problems he discusses, this is the only one I can claim to have any special knowledge of, and I will therefore confine my remarks to that one problem. Plantinga begins his discussion of free will by saying,

> There is a fundamental watershed . . . between those who think of human beings as *free*—*free* in the libertarian sense—and those who espouse determinism. According to determinists, every human action is a consequence of initial conditions outside our control by

---

8. Plantinga, "Advice," 256.

way of causal laws that are also outside our control. . . . On this view every action I have in fact performed was such that it wasn't within my power to refrain from performing it . . . If I now raise my arm, then, on the view in question, it wasn't within my power just then not to raise it . . . [The] determinist may reply that freedom and causal determinism are, contrary to initial appearances, in fact compatible. He may argue that my being free with respect to an action I performed at a time *t*, for example, doesn't entail that it was then within my power to refrain from performing it, but only something weaker—perhaps something like *if I had chosen not to perform it, I would not have performed it*.[9]

This is not how I see the problem of free will. This passage in my view goes wrong at the very outset—at the point at which the words "free in the libertarian sense" occur. I maintain that it is a serious error to suppose that libertarians and determinists—hard or soft—use such terms as "free will" and "freedom" in different senses. But I could not defend this view here without a lengthy digression, and this I will not inflict upon the reader.[10] I wish only to point out that Plantinga and I are both Christian philosophers and yet we see the problem of free will in very different terms.

In the text immediately following the quoted passage, Plantinga presents an argument that purports to show that Christian philosophers should believe that human actions are undetermined, and this argument I *will* say something about. The premises of the argument are these:

> God holds us accountable for our actions.
>
> God is just.
>
> If a being holds us accountable for our actions and we are not accountable for our actions, that being is not just.
>
> One is accountable for one's actions only if they are not determined.

From these premises it of course follows that our actions are not determined, and Plantinga concludes that Christian philosophers should believe that our actions are not determined. But it is obvious that God and his justice play no essential role in this argument. Essentially the same

---

9. Plantinga, "Advice," 265.
10. I have discussed the phrase "libertarian free will"—a phrase obviously closely allied with "free in the libertarian sense"—in "How to Think about the Problem of Free Will," *The Journal of Ethics* 12 (2008), 327–341 (reprinted in Peter van Inwagen, *Thinking About Free Will* (Cambridge University Press, 2017), 149–165).

argument could be employed by anyone who believed that *any* being was both just and sometimes held people accountable for their actions. (For example, if Alice believes that she herself is just, and if she sometimes holds people accountable for their actions and believes that she is right in so doing, then essentially the same argument is available to her.) The crucial premise of the argument has nothing to do with God's justice. It is this: One is accountable for one's actions only if those actions are not determined. And whether this premise is true is a purely technical question in philosophy, a question that a Christian and a non-Christian could debate in great depth and at great length without either discovering the religious views of the other. There are Christians who vehemently reject this premise (Jonathan Edwards, for example), and non-Christians who regard it as self-evident (R. M. Chisholm, for example—or Jean-Paul Sartre). I can imagine Edwards's reaction to his fellow Calvinist's assertion that a Christian philosopher should regard human actions as undetermined. In reading Plantinga out from the pulpit, he would probably lay some stress on Romans 9:14-24, and exhort Plantinga to repent his Arminianism. (And what part of the Word of God could Plantinga appeal to in reply—other than the deuterocanonical text Ecclesiasticus 15:14?)

Plantinga also maintains that what is at stake in the debate about free will and determinism is really the concept of agent causation, which, he maintains, is the only possible basis of a properly Christian view of human action. But, as I see it, the question whether agent causation is a coherent concept, and the question whether (granting its coherency) it is of any *use* in making sense of free will, are purely technical questions in philosophy. Again, a Christian and a non-Christian could debate these questions in great depth and at great length without either discovering the religious views of the other. Plantinga argues that theists must believe in agent causation—they must believe that this is the mode of God's action—and that, therefore, Christians know that agent causation is a coherent concept and that they should therefore feel free to appeal to it in their theories of human action. But, for my part, I do not claim to understand how (in a metaphysical sense) God acts. All I know about God's actions are some propositions about the things he has done, propositions that are revealed in Scripture. And the Bible is not a metaphysical text. I grant that the words of Scripture are among the Christian metaphysician's data. In this respect, they stand to philosophical theorizing about God as sensory data stand to scientific theorizing about the natural world: neither biblical texts nor the deliverances of the senses dictate the theoretical uses to which they can be put. Whether the concept of agent causation can help us to arrive at any sort of metaphysical understanding of God is to me an open question. But one thing is obvious: If it is not a coherent concept, it certainly cannot. Since I am not convinced that it is a coherent concept, the question remains open for me. And it remains a purely philosophical question, one I would debate with an unbeliever in much the same terms that I would with a Christian. And I would add that even if I were convinced that God, as agent, can bring about events that have no prior events as their causes, this would not seem to me to be much of an argument for the conclusion that it is possible for human beings to bring about events that have no prior events as their causes. We may be, we are, made in God's image and likeness. Nevertheless, God and creatures are, metaphysically speaking, so vastly different, that any argument of the form "God has F; therefore it is possible for human beings to have F" is bound to be rather weak—even in cases in which F is a property that is not obviously inconsistent with finitude and contingent existence.

4. Conclusion

I am convinced that Plantinga's advice to Christian philosophers contains a severe overestimation of the extent to which the problems of metaphysics and Christian belief are mutually relevant. I concede that this conviction may be parochial. I have discussed only—and all too briefly—a few problems having to do with free will. (I have not, for example, talked about the possibility of arguing against philosophical naturalism.) And, perhaps if I had examined ethics or epistemology, I should have come to a conclusion more favorable to Plantinga's advice. (By the way, one of the best examples of what is uncontroversially Christian philosophy I know—"best" as an example that shows what "Christian philosophy" could mean and "best" as regards philosophical quality—combines ethics and epistemology: Merold Westphal's "Taking St. Paul Seriously: Sin as an Epistemological Category."[11]) That Plantinga's advice embodies a misleading suggestion about the relation between Christianity and metaphysics should be regarded not as a thesis I claim to have established, but as a thesis I have put forward in an attempt to stimulate discussion. If I myself have any advice for Christian philosophers, it is this. Don't suppose that philosophy is terribly important. (I'm going to except apologetic from this general statement—not because I necessarily think that apologetic *is* terribly important, but because it is a special case that requires separate discussion.) Philosophy is what we philosophers do—in the sense that

---

11. In Thomas P. Flint (ed.), *Christian Philosophy* (Notre Dame University Press, 1990), 200–26. I should say, however, that Westphal's criticisms of Plantinga and "Reformed epistemology" in this essay (211 *et seq.*) are based on—dare I say it?—perverse misreadings of the texts he cites.

farming is what farmers do and cabinet-making is what cabinet-makers do. (Of course people in all three categories—philosophers, farmers, cabinet-makers—do lots of things besides philosophizing and farming and making cabinets, things like having families and resisting temptation and voting in elections.) I think the following thesis is one that we should all take seriously: the earthly works of Augustine and Aquinas that are remembered in heaven are not their writings; they are acts unknown to history, acts the earthly memory of which perished when the last people who knew Augustine and Aquinas in this life died.[12] And—if we join them in heaven—so, *a fortiori*, it will be with us.

---

12. When this paper was read to an audience of Christian philosophers—see note 5—this statement provoked some rather severe negative reactions from several members of the audience. Let me stress that "we should all take *p* seriously" does not mean "we should all accept *p*;" it means "we should all think seriously about whether *p* might be true."

19

STICK TO THE POINT

Thomas M. Ward

Baylor University

1. Philosophy from a Perspective

In his famous essay, "Advice to Christian Philosophers," Alvin Plantinga said that philosophy "is a matter of systematizing, developing, and deepening one's pre-philosophical opinions [...] it is also an arena for the articulation and interplay of commitments and allegiances fundamentally religious in nature; it is an expression of deep and fundamental perspectives, ways of viewing ourselves and the world and God." From this understanding of philosophy Plantinga goes on to advise that the Christian philosophical community "has a right to its perspective" and "is under no obligation first to show that this perspective is plausible with respect to what is taken for granted by all philosophers, or most philosophers, or the leading philosophers of our day."[1]

In many ways Christian philosophers have heeded Plantinga's advice, for the good. The last forty years have seen a flourishing of Christian philosophy unimaginable if Plantinga and other Christian philosophers of his generation had not encouraged Christians in philosophy not to fear to do philosophy from a Christian perspective, or for the sake of avowedly religious ends, such as "to serve the Christian community."[2]

---

1. Alvin Plantinga, "Advice to Christian Philosophers," *Faith and Philosophy* 1:3 (1984), 271.
2. Plantinga, "Advice to Christian Philosophers," 255.

But Plantinga also articulated a conception of philosophy that is amenable not just to Christian philosophers but to philosophical members of any group that has "pre-philosophical" opinions. They, at first glance, anyway, have just as much a right to do philosophy from their own perspective as Christians have the right to do philosophy from theirs. In fact, over the last few decades, there has been a proliferation of philosophy done explicitly from various identities, or perspectives, or standpoints.

This development is concerning, because it makes it harder for philosophers inhabiting different identities to do philosophy together. If we universalize Plantinga's advice to Christian philosophers, must philosophy become a loose collection of siloes or fiefdoms, at times vying with one another for influence and sharing no common ground for a dialectical as opposed to a brutely political confrontation?

I'm sorry to say that I think it must. So what I would like to do in this essay is identify the common ground that I think philosophers qua philosophers are committed to—even if unwittingly. I will argue that philosophy has a point—getting at the truth—and it has this point no matter which perspective we take up—even perspectives that deny that philosophy has the point of getting at the truth. Given the point of philosophy, I'll go on to nuance Plantinga's advice. There is a philosophically wholesome way to do philosophy from a Christian perspective, and this way does not abandon the point all philosophers aim at. Even Christian philosophy is, or should be, accountable to what philosophy is, what it aims at and how it aims, just as Christian welding is accountable to the principles and techniques of good welding.

2. The Point of Philosophy

The point of this essay to argue that (1) philosophy does indeed have a point; that (2) philosophers are in danger of not sticking to the point; and to advise that (3) Christian philosophers stick to the point. I'll discuss these points in order.

The sense of point relevant to (1) is something like the goal or telos of a thing or activity. In this sense something can be pointless in the sense (a) that it is not for the sake of anything else, but still, so to speak, pointed in the sense (b) that it is a thing's telos. Happiness, says Aristotle, is pursued for its own sake and not for the sake of anything else, and so is pointless in sense (a); but it is the end at which all human activity is aimed and so is pointed in sense (b). I'm interested here in the point of philosophy in sense (b).

My suggestion is that the point of philosophy is to get at the truth about things. The characteristic activities of philosophy—making distinctions, clearly defining terms, making arguments—are intelligible as philosophical activities insofar as they are truth-seeking activities. They are worth doing, in philosophy, precisely insofar as they advance or tend to advance the philosophical goal of getting at the truth about things. Apart from this goal, the characteristic activities of philosophy amount to sophistry: word play or showing off or mere persuasion or virtue signaling or propaganda.

"Getting at the truth" is a colloquial expression rich in nuance. It suggests a viable pursuit but does not require success. You could be getting at a thing but not get it, or not fully get it. Still, insofar as you're getting at it, you're in pursuit, on the track, and the track has not grown cold.

Getting at the truth is not something that's good to do all the time. I think it should be obvious that in whatever we do we should want to be *aligned* with the truth. But there are some important types of human activity that, it seems to me, not only do not have the point of getting at the truth, but are in fact marred, done badly, if done simultaneously with pursuing the truth. There are times simply to behold, enjoy, adore, relax, appreciate, and truth-seeking can interfere with these. There are times to undertake chores or hobbies in which the philosophical mind is best turned off. There are times for preaching or protesting where truth-seeking can hinder effectiveness—notwithstanding the obvious fact that these aren't good to do if they aren't aligned with the truth. The point is that, however much our other life activities might be or ought to be informed by our philosophy, not all of them share philosophy's point of getting at the truth. Others do, of course: conducting scientific experiments, for example, or working on math problems, or figuring out what's causing that wheezing sound under the hood of your truck.

Now, why should anyone think that the point of philosophy is getting at the truth? Here I would like to explain why, in the form of a dialogue between Smith and Jones.

> Smith: The point of philosophy is getting at the truth.
>
> Jones: I disagree.
>
> Smith: Do you think it has a different point?
>
> Jones: Yes. It's to critique injustice and promote diversity, equity, and inclusion.

Smith: What reasons do you have for that view?

Jones: If it comes to that, what reasons do you have for your view?

Smith: Touché. But, QED.

Smith and Jones have come to a disagreement about the point of philosophy, and, being philosophers, their disagreement turns philosophical—a philosophical disagreement about the point of philosophy. And this sort of disagreement must involve an exchange of reasons, an exchange that is productive only if the participants *already* share a sense of what it is that we're doing when we're doing philosophy—in this case, trying to arrive at the truth about the point of philosophy.

But let's hear a little more of the disagreement between Smith and Jones.

Jones: I deny that the Q has been D'd. Here are my reasons. The goal of getting at the truth is peculiar only to some philosophy, not all. It's peculiar, for example, to most philosophers in the so-called Western tradition. But not everyone, not even every Western philosopher, has thought philosophy's point was getting at the truth about things. Some think its point is not to get at the truth but one's own truth; some think it's to critique injustice and promote justice; some think it's to advance the interests of marginalized groups; and some think philosophy is best pursued as a sort of therapy. These other voices have something to teach us. Philosophy should be inclusive, and insofar as philosophy as traditionally conceived is exclusive—for example by using the standard of the truth as a way to judge what does and does not count as good philosophy—philosophy should be transformed.

Smith: I don't see how the fact of disagreement about the point of philosophy is supposed to de-center truth-seeking as the point of philosophy. People disagree about things all the time and that fact usually has nothing to do with the fact about which there is disagreement. I grant that not every philosopher, Western or otherwise, has thought that the point of philosophy is to get at the truth. But I wonder if those who think that philosophy has a different point are correct to think so. That is, is what they say about philosophy true?

Jones: Look, when you make that move you're just sliding back into your own perspective about what philosophy is. For us to make progress, you must stop making that move.

Smith: But I keep coming back to this: when you state that other conceptions of the point of philosophy are or can be right, you are either making a philosophical claim about the nature of philosophy or you are making a non-philosophical claim about it. If a philosophical claim then you are taking the same perspective about what philosophy is that you tell me I should abandon. If a non-philosophical claim, then I'm not quite sure what to do. We have lots of other things we could enjoyably discuss, but it's not clear how we can go on doing philosophy about the point of philosophy. But I can't conceive how your statement is not a philosophical claim. Aren't we doing philosophy right now?

Jones: It might not register as a philosophical claim to you, if the only way you can evaluate it is according to the canons of your own way of doing philosophy. But I submit that it is a philosophical claim.

Smith: But is it a philosophical claim that you think is true, or not? If you think it's true, then you're again engaging the same sort of philosophy I do. But if not, why should I believe you?

I do not want to speak for Jones here. It seems to me that Smith has hit on something, that he's getting at the truth about philosophy. Jones' attempts to de-center Smith's way of doing philosophy either fall back into philosophy in the same key, or put a stop to the conversation. But, whether we are on team Smith or team Jones, we should be able to recognize a legitimate question: can we consistently maintain that something besides getting at the truth is or should be the point of philosophy? The dialectic indicates that it cannot be. Team Jones should, then, either concede that philosophy really does have the point of getting at the truth, or abandon the dialectic altogether.

3. The DEI Turn in Philosophy

Abandoning the dialectic is a temptation for many these days, and this brings me to point 2. We might distinguish between the activity of philosophy—the sort of activity the point of which is getting at the truth, as

I tried to show in my dialogue—and the academic-philosophical complex. The academic-philosophical complex is the primary institutional setting of philosophical activity, but its aims do not entirely overlap with philosophy as such. The complex is a place of social and professional activity that sometimes includes philosophy but includes a lot of other things besides: recruiting, admissions, retention, some aspects of teaching, applying for jobs, hiring, the process of tenure and promotion, annual reports, work on committees, peer review, conferencing, making and receiving invitations, grant writing and awarding, the academic philosophy blogosphere and social media, and so on. Considered as a social institution of an academic sort, the complex shares a great deal in common not only with other academic complexes but other professional complexes, and indeed with the social world at large. It is no surprise, then, that the sorts of priorities, constraints, values, and pressures of the academic philosophical complex turn out to be very similar to those of many other complexes.

There remains, for some, the philosophical ideal of pure ratiocination, or pure philosophical conversation. But to be in the complex is also to be, sometimes to be forced to be, engaged in other types of practices, whether or not they fit well with the activity of philosophy simpliciter. In our own time, we have seen the professed objectives of colleges and universities pivot away from learning for its own sake and the discovery of truth and toward career preparation and the promotion of social ideals usually gathered under the umbrella of DEI: diversity, equity, and inclusion.

DEI initiatives serve, in principle, several goals that philosophers qua philosophers should endorse. Any philosopher should be able to recognize that one's own background can both heighten in some respects and degrade in others one's ability to do philosophy well. Being an active part of a community of philosophers from diverse backgrounds is therefore, in principle, liable to make everyone in the group better philosophers. Moreover, a philosopher should be able to recognize that merely espousing the ideal of the pursuit of truth does not on its own free one from bias or prejudice against those different from oneself. A philosopher should recognize that we all fall short and do not live up to the ideal of the pure philosopher—even Socrates was not without sin. When we engage the complex, then, are there ways in which we do not operate qua philosophers but instead as men, or women, or as people belonging to various national or ethnic groups, or with various sexual inclinations, and so on? Are there ways in which our interactions with students or colleagues, or our decisions about admissions and hiring, are influenced by extra-philosophical preferences, biases, and prejudices? The DEI regime compels us to ask these and many other similar questions, and the questions, if not the compulsion, are partly to the good of philosophy, even qua philosophy.

But my concern is that many philosophers, even some who would probably come out on team Smith, are in danger of prioritizing or mistaking the academic philosophical complex over, or for, philosophy as such. I worry that the hegemony of DEI is poised not just to reshape the social and professional aspects of the complex but the activity at its core that individuates the complex from other social institutions.

My conviction is that DEI has little value to philosophy as such. DEI, placed at the center of philosophical activity, supplants truth as the point of inquiry. And an intellectual activity sharing many features in common with philosophy but having DEI and not truth as its point, is simply not philosophy, or at least it's bad philosophy. It's more like activism or virtue signaling or propaganda or worse.

Jones might object that the ideals of DEI get at the truth about how the social world ought to be and are therefore not alien to philosophy as such. And maybe so. But philosophy as such always retains the prerogative to ask whether DEI as understood in contemporary American society really does get at the truth about how the social world ought to be, or whether it actually has anything to do with metaphysics or epistemology or logic. And the legitimacy of the question shows that truth, not DEI or other values, is the point of philosophy. However meta our metaphilosophical questions take us, we can see that we're always in fact in pursuit of the truth of the matter. We give and take reasons in the hope of coming to a reasoned judgment about the point of philosophy. And this activity presupposes truth as the final arbiter, not justice or feelings or a history of philosophers acting badly or giving offense. That it is becoming increasingly controversial, even roguish, to question the DEI movement, is good indication that the influence of DEI on the complex is supplanting the activity of philosophy as such—erasing its point with another and so erasing the thing itself.

Whether this sort of argument "lands" with DEI focused philosophers depends in part on how much they retain a conception of philosophy as truth-oriented. Team Jones may retort that the argument is yet another example of a philosopher behaving badly under the cloak of dispassionate reasoning. In doing so they exhibit the misology Socrates warned us about in *Phaedo*—a misology apparently justified by a righteous anger against bad guys.

4. More Advice

And here is where Christian philosophy must look in the mirror—point 3. One way for Christian philosophers to be bad philosophers is to join the DEI revolution underway in philosophy. (How Christians should relate to the triumphant DEI revolution in the academic philosophical complex is a prudential matter about which I offer no advice.) But another, subtler, way for us to be bad philosophers is to adopt the very identitarianism or perspectivism that DEI encourages.

The Society of Christian Philosophers was founded, in part, as a way for the small minority of practicing Christians in Anglophone academic analytic philosophy to have a way to discourse with one another about philosophical issues related to their Christian faith and practice. They were, and we are, a severely "marginalized" group, to adopt a favorite term of the DEI-focused.

But doing philosophy solely from the perspective or identity of being a Christian puts one at risk of taking up formally the same anti-philosophical stance as the DEI-focused. The confidence, or pride (remember St. Paul's boast in 2 Cor 10:17), that we rightly have as Christians, does not matter very much in a discipline whose members value, or take pride in, very different things. In fact it's not relevant to our philosophical work—conceived very narrowly as the activity of doing philosophy as such. I myself regularly pray for help to do philosophy better. I'd like my activity as a philosopher to glorify God and help others come to know and love God. But these facts about me do not give me different standards of what ought to count as good philosophy. I could try to play the marginalized card and make moralistic demands on my peers that they take my perspective seriously given how marginalized, I, as a Christian, am in the world of academic philosophy. But I'm obviously not the right kind of marginalized for this to be a prudent course of action, and more importantly I would be acting badly as a philosopher were I to do so. If, exasperated by my own marginalization, I were to reject canons of good philosophy and instead adopt "God-glorifying" or "apologetically useful" as the points of my philosophical work, I'd be at risk of doing bad philosophy and, in so doing, at risk of failing to achieve my new aims.

To be sure, there is great value in the sort of philosophical work that assumes the truth of Christianity and theorizes accordingly. But it's one thing to recognize, say, that agent causation is a better fit with Christianity than event causation—to pick one of Plantinga's own examples[3]—and go on to tackle the causation literature expecting to find good arguments

---

3. Plantinga, "Advice to Christian Philosophers," 266–267.

for agent causation, and quite another thing to recognize this and argue that agent causation is true because it's a better fit with Christianity. The former has Christianity as a target to aim at in philosophical activity—and while this circumscribes inquiry it does not allow for dialectical shortcuts. The latter makes Christianity a grab bag of premises. Christian philosophers who take up the former method can engage the dialectic with philosophers who do not share their Christianity. Those who take up the latter cannot—even if they can proficiently use the techniques of philosophy. To be sure, Christian philosophers can argue amongst themselves whether agent causation really does have the better fit with Christianity, and can even argue about what fit means in this context and how we should weigh it in theory adoption—but these are purely internal debates, where philosophical methods are so closely interwoven with religious and theological convictions and methods that it is difficult if not wrongheaded to try to unweave them.

Here is a view about the relationship between philosophical activity and Christian commitment I find attractive. An integrated Christian philosophical life involves, as Plantinga reminded us, careful thought about which philosophical views fit well with Christianity.[4] Many views popular in academic philosophy, then as now, do not fit well. Christians therefore have good religious reasons not to accept these. But it doesn't follow that they have good philosophical reasons either to reject these or to accept those views that do fit well with Christianity. To repeat the target metaphor, Christian articles of faith ought to be targets for Christian philosophers to aim at. The point of philosophy is the truth, and "what the Truth has spoken that for truth I hold." But having a philosophical target doesn't make one a good philosopher, any more than having a target makes my sons good shots with a BB-gun. Hitting the target reliably takes practice, and even a skilled shooter won't hit the bull's eye every time. It remains, then, for the Christian philosopher to become really good at philosophy—like Plantinga.

Non-Christians can become good at philosophy too, even if they don't recognize that the truth they're aiming at is The Truth. It does no good to respond to a powerful objection against agent causation that it's the view that fits best with Christianity. You can't satisfy the philosophical appetite that way. You might not know how to reply to the objection on philosophical grounds. But there's no need to abandon the target; you just need to work harder to hit it.

---

4. Plantinga, "Advice to Christian Philosophers," 256.

When it comes to Christian philosophy there is an important qualification to make here. It is no part of historical Christian belief that each of its articles can be shown by philosophy to be plausible. Some exceed philosophy's grasp except in the sense that philosophy might be used to show that certain articles—e.g., the doctrine of the Trinity—are not incoherent. Christians should not overvalue what philosophy can do. There is, however, some reason within Christian belief that makes sense of philosophy's inability to unveil the full mystery of the Christian religion: the deepest truths about God are revealed by God through special revelation, by means of scripture and/or tradition (the "and/or" used for ecumenical reasons)—a savvy strategy on God's part to make the ordinary means of discovering reality's most important truths dependent on coming into contact with himself through the community of believers he established. Whether philosophers inhabiting alternative perspectives have similar articles of faith they exempt from standing at philosophy's bar, and what reasons internal to the perspective are supposed to explain the exemption, are not for me to say.

A Christian welder might, rightly, hope for his welding business to be a way to evangelize or for expressing Christian charity. But however joyful a countenance he displays to his clients, however earnest his evangelistic conversations, however generous his giving, his witness is undermined if his welding work is shoddy. Qua welder his life as a Christian must include excellent welding. Just so, qua philosophers our lives as Christians must include excellent philosophy. And this means excellence in doing that distinctive thing that is philosophy.

My advice to Christian philosophers, then, is to stick to the point. Christian philosophy unable or unwilling to be subject to philosophy's methods of getting at the truth is bad philosophy. Likewise, DEI philosophy similarly unwilling is bad philosophy. Christian philosophers must avoid each. The point of philosophy is getting at the truth. Given the weighty moral calling of being a Christian, it is unsurprising that many Christian philosophers feel drawn to join the DEI revolution. Being Christ-like in philosophy—the academic philosophical complex—demands a focus not just on the pure activity of philosophy as such but the whole social reality of that complex. The stereotypes of the absent-minded, or cantankerous, or coldly objective philosopher, probably are, in general, antagonistic to a Christ-like approach to teaching or interacting with peers. But charity, humility, and compassion are not at odds with the activity of pure philosophy, just as they are not at odds with the activity of pure welding, or plumbing, or mathematics.

Similarly, given the weighty pastoral and evangelistic callings of being a Christian, it is unsurprising that many Christian philosophers feel drawn to a conception of Christian philosophy according to which evangelism or spiritual formation or therapy are its points. Being Christ-like in philosophy—the academic philosophical complex—demands a focus not just on the pure activity of philosophy as such but on the care and eternal destiny of souls. The stereotypes of the absent-minded, or cantankerous, or coldly objective philosopher, probably are, in general, antagonistic to these ends. But the activity of pure philosophy is not at odds with these ends, just as the activity of welding is not at odds with—indeed, is a requirement for—a truly Christian welding business.

As philosophers there is a distinctive thing that we do, philosophy, the point of which is just built into what this thing is and is not ours to manipulate, even in service to noble goals. It may be that many in philosophy are despairing of the value of philosophy for helping people. Perhaps leaving philosophy and taking up pastoral ministry or counseling or social work is the right thing to do. Philosophy might, after all, have rather less usefulness for the kingdom of God than some of us might have supposed it did when we got into this business. But what use it has will only be achieved if we stick to the point. Philosophy is one of those human activities that has the point of getting at the truth. It makes heavy demands. It is relentless and it takes hardly anything for granted. Honest practice of philosophy regularly puts us up against questions or objections that reach to the core of who we are and threaten to rip up our lives. It's ruthless enough to question both DEI and the Nicene Creed. It is a cruel master. I hope we all have lives outside of philosophy—I am grateful that I do. Welding, too, is pretty dangerous, as well as merciless. But welding, like philosophy, has a point. We don't want welders qua welders to try to supplant that point with one more directly oriented toward either social values or religious evangelism. We shouldn't want philosophers to do so either.

20

THE ACORN AND THE TREE: PLANTINGA'S "ADVICE TO CHRISTIAN PHILOSOPHERS" (OR, HOW TO TAKE YOUR OWN ADVICE)

Greg Welty

Southeastern Baptist Theological Seminary

1. Introduction

My co-contributors have written fine essays that rightly bring out the importance of Plantinga's "Advice to Christian Philosophers" for the contemporary philosophical scene, or for themselves as philosophers. But equally fascinating is the importance of "Advice" *for Plantinga*. Delivered November 4, 1983, as Plantinga's inaugural address as the John A. O'Brien Professor of Philosophy at the University of Notre Dame, "Advice" comes at the halfway point of his teaching career. The previous 25 years had been spent teaching philosophy at Yale University (1957), Wayne State University (1958–63) and Calvin College (1963–82), while the next 28 years would be spent teaching philosophy at Notre Dame (1982–2010). When he transitioned to Notre Dame, he found "the prospect of leaving Calvin disturbing and in fact genuinely painful."[1] What could motivate this heart-wrenching decision? Among other reasons, Plantinga wanted to investigate a question he found increasingly difficult to answer: what does it mean to be a *Christian* philosopher (rather than a philosopher who

---

[1]. Alvin Plantinga, "Self-Profile," in *Alvin Plantinga*, eds. James Tomberlin and Peter van Inwagen (D. Reidel Publishing Company, 1985), 33.

happens to be a Christian)?

Prior to moving to Notre Dame, Plantinga had been largely frustrated in his efforts to answer this question. Among the reasons "most important" to him for choosing to teach at Calvin College in the first place was to work on two topics: "the connection between the Christian faith and philosophy" and "how best to be a Christian in philosophy."[2] But progress on these questions was very hard. By his own confession, during the Calvin years he:

> certainly didn't make nearly as much progress, for example, on the question how in fact to be a Christian philosopher, as could reasonably be hoped. Partly this was due, of course, to the fact that this question of how to be a Christian philosopher, the question of the bearing of one's Christianity on one's philosophy, is extraordinarily difficult, and there isn't much by way of guidance or precedent or (recent) tradition with respect to it.[3]

Plantinga produced several important monographs during the Calvin years.[4] But he "didn't make a lot of progress" on how to define "Christian philosophy," though he was "able at least to figure out some of the right questions."[5] The move to Notre Dame commenced a renewed focus on answering this question, starting with his inaugural lecture, "Advice." In contrast to the Calvin years, after ten years at Notre Dame Plantinga could say "This question has come to assume an increasingly large proportion of my time and attention."[6]

During the Notre Dame years, Plantinga penned five articles on the method and content of Christian philosophy. On method (the "how"), these are "Advice to Christian Philosophers" and "Method in Christian Philosophy: A Reply."[7] On content (the "what"), these are "Augustinian Christian Philosophy," "On Christian Scholarship," and "Christian Philosophy at the end of the 20th Century."[8] These present his vision for how Christian philosophers should do their work and what they are

---

2. Alvin Plantinga, "A Christian Life Partly Lived," in *Philosophers Who Believe*, ed. Kelly James Clark (InterVarsity Press, 1993), 66.
3. Plantinga, "A Christian Life," 66.
4. Alvin Plantinga, *God and Other Minds* (Cornell University Press, 1967); Alvin Plantinga, *The Nature of Necessity* (Oxford University Press, 1974); Alvin Plantinga, *God, Freedom and Evil* (Harper Torchbook, 1974); Alvin Plantinga, *Does God Have a Nature?* (Marquette University Press, 1980).
5. Plantinga, "A Christian Life," 77.
6. Plantinga, "A Christian Life," 77.
7. Alvin Plantinga, "Advice to Christian Philosophers," *Faith and Philosophy* 1 (1984): 253-71; Alvin Plantinga, "Method in Christian Philosophy: A Reply," *Faith and Philosophy* 5 (1988): 159-64.
8. Alvin Plantinga, "Augustinian Christian Philosophy," *The Monist* 75 (1992): 291-320; Alvin Plantinga, "On Christian Scholarship," in *The Challenge and Promise of a Catholic University*, ed. Theodore Hesburgh (University of Notre Dame Press, 1994); Alvin Plantinga, "Christian Philosophy at the End of the 20th Century," in *Christian Philosophy at the Close of the Twentieth Century*, eds. Sander Griffioen and Bert Balk (Kok, 1995), 29-53.

to investigate. Of the two methodological articles, "Advice" is the most important, and of the three content articles, "Augustinian" is the most important. Indeed, the two articles are connected: "Augustinian" is explicitly billed as a follow-up to "Advice," outlining "projects to pursue" for those who took his earlier advice.[9]

My thesis in this essay is very simple: "Advice" is a methodological acorn from which a mighty tree's worth of philosophical content would grow, providing a framework that Plantinga would himself fill out with his own work. In "Advice," Plantinga gives three examples of Christian apologetics that are meant to lead us to embrace five principles about *method*, a list of "do's" and "don'ts" for how Christian philosophers are to go about their work. In turn, these principles about method lead us to expand our conception of the *content* of Christian philosophy, from one activity to four. Plantinga would then formalize this vision for the expanded content of Christian philosophy in "Augustinian." Equipped with this vision, Plantinga subsequently did four things: he practiced what he preached, he eventually answered his hardest question, he made good on perhaps the most difficult aspect of his advice, and he bequeathed to later Christian philosophers a good argument they can use to shore up faith in their own calling. In the remainder of this chapter, I make a case for each of these claims.

2. "Advice"

2.1 Five Principles (of Christian Philosophical Method)

"Advice" offers five principles for the "how" of Christian philosophy, filling out Plantinga's central contention that Christian philosophers should display more "autonomy," "integrity," and "courage" in the things they do and don't do as philosophers. These five principles, stated numerous times throughout the article, are:

1. *Don't* restrict your intellectual projects to those pursued by unbelievers.

2. *Don't* take unbelieving assumptions as your starting assumptions.

---

9. Plantinga, "Augustinian," 291. At one time, Plantinga expressed his "hope to write a book on Christian philosophy, if I ever get finished with the books I'm currently writing" (Plantinga, "A Christian Life," 35 fn. 19). It is increasingly likely that these five articles will have to serve as Plantinga's definitive thought on the topic.

3. *Don't* understand or reinterpret Christian belief so that it is palatable to unbelievers.

4. *Do* courageously pursue the questions, concerns, topics, agenda, and research programs of the Christian community.

5. *Do* boldly start with Christian assumptions in your intellectual work (even if these aren't shared outside the Christian community).

Plantinga illustrates how these principles work by offering an implication of each:

> 1 implies: "Don't only develop materialist theories of the human person."
>
> 2 implies: "Don't assume computers provide a good model for the mind."
>
> 3 implies: "Don't reinterpret biblical passages about the soul as really about the body instead."
>
> 4 implies: "Do seek a Christian understanding of human persons that allows for life after death."
>
> 5 implies: "Do assume there is life after death."

2.2 Three Examples (of Christian Apologetics)

Plantinga not only states and illustrates these principles. He thinks they receive a kind of grounding once we reflect on Christian apologetic work in three areas: meaning, knowledge, and persons. At first glance, Plantinga's strategy seems curious. He shows how Christians can do the following:

1. Defend against logical positivism (which implies God-talk is meaningless).

2. Defend against the problem of evil (which implies we don't know God exists).

3. Defend against deterministic free will (which implies God can't hold us responsible).

It's hard to see any connection at all between the workmanlike, bread-and-butter apologetic work listed above, and Plantinga's five principles. In each case, isn't the Christian philosopher taking his cues from the world, pursuing an agenda set by unbelievers? Some outsiders argue against us on the topics of meaning, knowledge, and persons, and we successfully defend ourselves against their arguments. That's what Christian philosophy does: it replies to the critics' charges, and then lays down its pen. How does it display any "autonomy," "independence," and "courage" for the Christian to react to an agenda set for him by outsiders? Don't these examples *undermine* Plantinga's five principles?

But there is more here than meets the eye. Though he rarely flags it for the reader, each apologetic defense (as he presents it in "Advice") is drawn from work Plantinga did prior to writing "Advice." Against logical positivism, Plantinga earlier wrote "Verificationism and Other Atheologica."[10] Accordingly, in "Advice" Plantinga contends that the "Verifiability Criterion of Meaning" has no supporting arguments to speak of, and if the criterion is only meant as a definition of "meaningful," why should that definition be relevant to Christians?

Against the problem of evil, Plantinga earlier wrote "The Free Will Defense," *The Nature of Necessity* ch. 9, *God, Freedom, and Evil* Part Ia, and "The Probabilistic Argument from Evil."[11] Accordingly, in "Advice" Plantinga contends that the logical form of the problem of evil is a failure, since its central conclusion of God-evil contradiction is inadequately supported and can in fact be refuted by considering certain possibilities overlooked by unbelievers. The evidential form of the problem of evil can't be given a cogent form on any extant theory of probability. And even if the argument did work, it wouldn't show that belief in God is irrational given a broader range of evidence (such as that supplied by the *sensus divinitatis*).

Against deterministic conceptions of free will, Plantinga earlier wrote *God and Other Minds* pp. 132-35, and *God, Freedom, and Evil* pp. 31-32.[12] Accordingly, in "Advice" Plantinga contends that the arguments for determinism are "meager and anemic," and there are no "cogent arguments" for analyzing free will in terms of event causation.

It seems evident that Plantinga's own engagement with these three topics earlier in his career revealed something to him: since unbelieving starting points in each area (meaning, knowledge, and persons) have little going for them, why not just *start with* the Christian position and view the problem from that perspective instead? And indeed, this is what Plantinga recommends in each case. Since the verifiability criterion has no basis,

---

10. Plantinga, *God and Other Minds*, ch. 7.
11. Alvin Plantinga, "The Free Will Defense," in *Philosophy in America*, ed. Max Black (Cornell University Press, 1965), 204-20; Plantinga, *The Nature of Necessity*; Plantinga, *God, Freedom and Evil*; Alvin Plantinga, "The Probabilistic Argument from Evil," *Philosophical Studies* 35 (1979): 1-53.
12. Plantinga, *God and Other Minds*; Plantinga, *God, Freedom, and Evil*.

why not just do a Moorean shift against verificationism by starting from Christian theism? "Christian theism is true; if Christian theism is true, then the verifiability criterion is false; so the verifiability criterion is false." Since logical and evidential arguments from evil don't work, why not start from belief in God (via the *sensus divinitatis*)? Since there aren't any good arguments for thinking determinism is true, or that freedom requires determinism, why not start from the fact of divine freedom in creation, and thereby embrace indeterministic, agent causal free will?

This is why, despite initial appearances to the contrary, Plantinga's three apologetic examples undergird his five methodological principles. Superficially, it might look like Plantinga's earlier apologetic work was purely reactive, taking its agenda from the unbelieving community. But he came to see that in each case, the *best* thing to do was to commend a Christian starting point on the matter. It's a bit easier to have "autonomy," "integrity," and "courage," once one sees that unbelieving starting points aren't all they're cracked up to be anyway.

The moral of the story is that the most effective kind of Christian apologetics in the areas of meaning, knowledge, and persons leads you to a Christian starting point for inquiry. God exists; so verificationism is false. We have the *sensus divinitatis*; so the fact of evil doesn't automatically defeat belief in God. Divine freedom in creation defies analysis by deterministic, event-causal free will; so in the absence of good arguments for the latter, we can just start with the former. We have here a series of three discredited unbelieving starting points, and the rise of three Christian starting points in their place. And *this* is what leads to the five principles that Plantinga endorses: don't traffic in unbelieving projects, assumptions, and interpretations; have a bit more boldness in starting with your projects and assumptions instead.

2.3 Four Directions (for the Future)

So careful attention to the activity of Christian apologetics, rightly pursued, encourages Plantinga's five methodological principles. But where do we go from here? Do Christian philosophers exist in a perpetual defensive crouch? Should they do anything more than Christian apologetics, defending the faith from outside attack? In "Advice" (and as we will soon see, in "Augustinian"), Plantinga argues they should do many more things than this. They should embrace a *multitude* of projects, because of the principles he has just defended. That is, the argument of "Advice" transitions from method to content.

Plantinga closes "Advice" by giving several examples of an activity that goes beyond Christian apologetics, an activity he would later call "positive (or constructive) Christian philosophy." This is a second activity Christian philosophers can and should engage in. It involves giving philosophical accounts of various topics from the perspective of Christian claims. Here the goal is not so much to vindicate and support theology in the face of outside attack, but to construct good philosophy from a Christian point of view. Plantinga gives four examples:

1. *Thinking about ethics* "from the theistic perspective" will relate categories of value and obligation to "God and to his will and to his creative activity."

2. *Thinking about epistemology* will see it as the fulfillment of intellectual obligations from God. But why think fulfilling these obligations aims us at truth? "Here the theist has… clear suggestions towards a set of answers."

3. *Thinking about metaphysics* "from a theistic point of view" will end up partly agreeing with 'creative antirealism' in tying the existence and character of the universe to the activity of a person, God himself.

4. *Thinking about philosophy of mathematics* "from a theistic point of view" explains sets as "collections collected by God; they are or result from God's thinking things together."[13]

The similarity between "starting with" a Christian or theistic perspective in these areas, and the earlier "starting with" such a perspective when thinking about meaning, knowledge, and persons, should be obvious. But the goal is different: to develop philosophical theories that are inspired by theology (positive Christian philosophy), rather than defend that theology from criticism (Christian apologetics). The end of "Advice" is Plantinga turning his attention from the "how" to the "what." Plantinga's method for Christian philosophy (via his five principles) argues for a broader conception of the content of Christian philosophy.

Truth be told, this is counterintuitive. We typically start with an activity first, and only then think about the best method. Now that I've decided to bake a cake (my activity), what is the best way to go about it (method)? But interestingly, in "Advice" Plantinga goes in the reverse direction. Careful reflection on method will lead to an expanded conception of the range

---

13. Alvin Plantinga, "Advice," 269–70.

of activities in which Christian philosophers should engage. Because we should start with our own projects and assumptions—those of most importance to the Christian community—Christian philosophy should not be restricted to apologetics, important as that activity is. It should also embrace philosophical theology, Christian philosophical criticism, and positive Christian philosophy. These latter activities are never named in "Advice," though they are in "Augustinian." But they exist in seed form in "Advice," and they find their justification there.

3. "Augustinian"

3.1 The Four Activities

"Augustinian Christian Philosophy," written eight years after "Advice," continues to address the question: "How does Christianity bear on philosophy?" In the opening paragraph Plantinga notes that in "Advice to Christian Philosophers" he said that Christian philosophers have "their own projects to pursue," and now "I want to say more about what these projects... are like."[14]

So "Augustinian" completes what "Advice" started: a wholesale reexamination of what it means to be a Christian philosopher. The presentation is indebted to the conclusion of "Advice": that once we see (by way of method) that Christian teaching can itself be a proper starting point for philosophical inquiry, this has implications (by way of content) for what activities Christian philosophers should engage in. Plantinga is finishing his project of reconceiving the proper activities of Christian philosophy, formally expanding them from one to four. As he puts it in the final paragraph of "Augustinian":

> By way of conclusion, Christian philosophy, so I say, has at least these four major parts or aspects or moments; philosophical theology, apologetics (both positive and negative), Christian philosophical criticism, and positive Christian philosophy.[15]

This position can be summarized in the following chart:

---

14. Plantinga, "Augustinian," 291.
15. Plantinga, "Augustinian," 317.

Activity	Definition	Examples	Result
Christian apologetics	Use philosophy to defend or support Christian claims.	• Refute Problem of Evil • Argue for God	Theology vindicated and supported.
Philosophical theology	Use philosophy to explain or illuminate Christian claims.	Use philosophical distinctions, illustrations, or models to explain: • The Trinity • The incarnation • The atonement	Theology better understood.
Christian philosophical criticism	Use philosophy to refute fundamental worldview alternatives to Christian claims.	Refute: • perennial naturalism • creative antirealism • relativism	Negative evaluation of philosophical alternatives to Christianity.
Constructive (or positive) Christian philosophy	Answer philosophical questions from the perspective of Christian claims.	Develop theistic theories of: • abstract objects • causality • natural laws • knowledge • mind • probability • conditionals • science • freedom • human action • language • duty • human flourishing • love • beauty • play • humor	Good philosophy from a Christian point of view.

Two things should be noted here. First, every example in the third column is supplied by Plantinga himself in "Augustinian." It is quite a to do list! Plantinga thinks that his methodological principles supplied in "Advice" unshackle Christian philosophers to pursue all the projects listed in "Augustinian," and many more, indeed, just about *any* project that takes Christian teaching for granted. These projects are as broad and numerous as the topics composing all of theology and philosophy. Christian philosophers can seek to defeat objections to their faith and provide positive reasons for their faith, use philosophical distinctions to illuminate their faith, wield philosophy to expose the religious roots of alternatives to their faith, and develop philosophical theories by starting with their faith.

Second, any study of "Advice" and its significance will be incomplete if we do not see its fruition, *as advice to Plantinga*, in Plantinga's own career. Reflection on his earlier work in apologetics leads to a method that (in turn) leads us beyond apologetics to other activities, each of which presupposes Christian doctrine as a starting point for serious intellectual inquiry. *And this was the path that Plantinga would follow.*

We see this in his "Christian apologetics," which (on Plantinga's view) sometimes offers argumentative support for Christian claims, sometimes argues for their rational acceptability, and sometimes argues for their coherence with other things we know to be true:

- Christian apologetics as *support*
    - "Two Dozen (or so) Theistic Arguments"[16]
    - Fine-tuning argument[17]
    - Design discourse[18]
    - Theism accounts for assumptions of science[19]

- Christian apologetics as *rational acceptability*
    - Parity argument from God and other minds[20]
    - Modal ontological argument for God's existence[21]

- Christian apologetics as *coherence*
    - Defend the coherence of theism and Platonism, by rejecting simplicity, nominalism, and Cartesian universal possibilism[22]
    - Defend the consistency of God and evil, via the free will defense[23]

---

16. Alvin Plantinga, "Two Dozen (or so) Theistic Arguments," in *Alvin Plantinga*, ed. Deane-Peter Baker (Cambridge University Press, 2007), 203-27. Also reprinted in *Two Dozen (or so) Arguments for God: The Plantinga Project*, eds. Jerry Walls and Trent Dougherty (Oxford University Press, 2018), 461-79.
17. Alvin Plantinga, *Where the Conflict Really Lies* (Oxford University Press, 2011), ch. 7.
18. Plantinga, *Conflict*, ch. 8.
19. Plantinga, *Conflict*, ch. 9.
20. Plantinga, *God and Other Minds*, ch. 10.
21. Plantinga, *The Nature of Necessity*, ch. 10; Plantinga, *God, Freedom, and Evil*, Part IIc.
22. Plantinga, *Does God Have a Nature?*
23. Plantinga, *God, Freedom, and Evil*, Part Ia.

- Defend properly basic belief in God against the evidentialist objection[24]
- Defend divine omniscience from the free will/foreknowledge dilemma[25]
- Defend divine omniscience from Cantorian paradoxes[26]
- Defend the possible warrant of Christian belief against objections from Freud, Marx, postmodernism, and pluralism[27]
- Defend the rationality of belief in God against the evidential problem of evil, by critiquing the theories of probability used in the latter[28]
- Defend the rationality of belief in God against the evidential problem of evil, by deploying skeptical theism[29]
- "Reducing the perplexity surrounding human suffering and evil" by using supralapsarian, "O felix culpa" theodicy[30]
- Refute alleged and superficial conflict between divine creation, divine action (both providential and miraculous), and scriptural inspiration (on the one hand), and biology, physics, evolutionary psychology, and historical Bible criticism (on the other hand)[31]

We see this in his "philosophical theology":

- Use moderate foundationalism to illuminate the natural knowledge of God[32]

---

24. Alvin Plantinga, "The Reformed Objection to Natural Theology," *Christian Scholar's Review* 11 (1982): 187-98. Reprinted in *Philosophy of Religion: Selected Readings, Fifth Edition*, eds. Michael Peterson, William Hasker, Bruce Reichenbach, and David Basinger (Oxford University Press, 2014), 207-15.

25. Alvin Plantinga, "On Ockham's Way Out," *Faith and Philosophy* 3, no. 3 (1986): 235-69.

26. Alvin Plantinga, "Truth, Omniscience, and Cantorian Arguments: An Exchange" (with Patrick Grim), *Philosophical Studies* 71, no. 3 (1993): 267-306.

27. Alvin Plantinga, *Warranted Christian Belief* (Oxford University Press, 2000), chs. 6-13.

28. Alvin Plantinga, "Epistemic Probability and Evil," *Archivio di filosofia* (Italy) 56 (1988): 557-84. Reprinted in *Our Knowledge of God*, ed. Kelly James Clark (Kluwer, 1992), 39-63. Also reprinted in *The Evidential Argument from Evil*, ed. Daniel Howard-Snyder (Indiana University Press, 1996), 69-96.

29. Plantinga, *Warranted Christian Belief*, ch. 14.

30. Alvin Plantinga, "Supralapsarianism, or 'O Felix Culpa'," in *Christian Faith and the Problem of Evil*, ed. Peter van Inwagen (Eerdmans, 2004), 1-25. Reprinted in *The Problem of Evil: Selected Readings (2nd ed.)*, ed. Michael Peterson (University of Notre Dame Press, 2016), 363-89.

31. Plantinga, *Conflict*, chs. 1-6.

32. Alvin Plantinga, "Reason and Belief in God," in *Faith and Rationality: Reason and Belief in God*, eds. Alvin Plantinga and Nicholas Wolterstorff (University of Notre Dame Press, 1983), 16-93.

- Use proper function epistemology to illuminate Christian conversion[33]
- Use possible worlds metaphysics to illuminate God's greatness[34]

We see this in his "Christian philosophical criticism":

- Argue against naturalistic evolution as epistemologically self-defeating[35]
- Argue against theological agnosticism as conceptually incoherent[36]
- Argue against materialist understandings of human beings as metaphysically impossible[37]

Finally, we see this in his "positive Christian philosophy":

- Draw upon theology to model how Christian belief can get its warrant (the *sensus divinitatis* and the internal instigation of the Holy Spirit)[38]
- Draw upon theology to model (most) ordinary causation in the world (divine occasionalism)[39]
- Draw upon theology to model the ontology of sets (a divine activity of "collecting together")[40]
- Draw upon theology to model the laws of nature (the necessity of God's power and the contingency of God's will in creation)[41]
- Draw upon theology to model the efficacy and accessibility of mathematics (God's creating man in the *imago dei*)[42]

---

33. Plantinga, *Warranted Christian Belief*, chs. 8–10.
34. Plantinga, *The Nature of Necessity*, ch. 10.
35. Plantinga, *Conflict*, ch. 10.
36. Plantinga, *Warranted Christian Belief*, chs. 1–2.
37. Alvin Plantinga, "Against Materialism," *Faith and Philosophy* 23, no. 1 (2006): 3–32.
38. Plantinga, *Warranted Christian Belief*, chs. 6–10.
39. Alvin Plantinga, "Law, Cause, and Occasionalism," in *Reason and Faith: Themes from Richard Swinburne*, eds. Michael Bergmann and Jeffrey E. Brower (Oxford University Press, 2016), 126–44.
40. Plantinga, "Two Dozen".
41. Plantinga, *Conflict*, ch. 9.
42. Plantinga, *Conflict*, ch. 9. This list, correlating Plantinga's theoretical conception of the four activities of Christian philosophy with what Plantinga actually did, is adapted from Greg Welty, *Alvin Plantinga* (P&R, 2023), 115–19.

So "Advice" turns out to be a kind of intellectual bridge between the pre-1984 Plantinga, and the Plantinga of University of Notre Dame and beyond. It gave a fundamental rationale for expanding the task of Christian philosophy beyond defensive apologetics, providing a framework that Plantinga would himself fill out with his own work. We can compile an impressively full list of the ways in which Plantinga has pursued the entire range of Christian philosophy as he defines it. His work exemplifies all the methodological principles that he advised other Christian philosophers to follow: not restricting his projects to those pursued by unbelievers, or taking unbelieving assumptions as his starting point, or reinterpreting Christian belief so that it is palatable to unbelievers, instead pursuing questions and topics of central concern to the Christian community.

I make one final point. Plantinga is almost obsessive in using the word "Christian" through his series of five articles on method and content in Christian philosophy (of which "Advice" and "Augustinian" are the most important). For example, in "Advice" he is exceptionally clear that what matters are "the fundamental truths of Christianity," or "Christian doctrine," or "a Christian perspective," "Christian thought," "Christian ways of thinking," and "a Christian and theistic point of view."[43] In "Augustinian," the references to "Christianity," "Christian philosophy," "Christians," "Christian theism," "Christian belief," and so on are legion. Apparently, focusing on or starting with distinctive *Christian* claims is essential to Plantinga's method. But now glance at the above list of Plantinga's contributions. Virtually all of these examples are about defending, arguing, or explaining either the truth of theism, or the coherence of theism, or alternatives to theism, or the coherence of a generic theistic attribute, or basic belief in theism, or reconciling theistic belief with science. Just about the entirety of Plantinga's philosophical work is about theism rather than specific Christian belief.

Is this a problem? Does it reveal that Plantinga didn't practice what he preached? Hardly. First, theism is obviously *included* in Christian belief, and is in fact essential to the latter. Second, there are two times Plantinga goes beyond mere theism to starting with distinctive Christian doctrines, and they are huge. There is Plantinga's (500-page!) account of how belief in "the great things of the gospel" by way of the Holy Spirit's work can satisfy the demands of a defensible, proper function epistemology.[44] And there is Plantinga's appeal to the distinctively Christian doctrines of Incarnation, atonement, and supralapsarianism to reduce the intellectual

---

43. Plantinga, "Advice," 264-70.
44. Plantinga, *Warranted Christian Belief*.

perplexity generated by the evil in the world.[45] To my knowledge, no one else had ever made these particular arguments in the history of philosophy, arguments which map out the consequences of these distinctive Christian doctrines for epistemology and philosophy of religion, respectively.

4. Conclusion

In "Advice," three examples of Christian philosophy as apologetics lead us to embrace five methodological principles, which in turn lead us to expand our conception of the content of Christian philosophy, from one activity to four. Plantinga would then formalize this vision for the expanded content of Christian philosophy in "Augustinian." Equipped with this vision, Plantinga subsequently did four things. First, Plantinga practiced what he preached. The (largely post-1983) examples in each of the four activities of Christian philosophy, listed above, are numerous. Plantinga has offered us a schema for categorizing his own work.

Second, Plantinga eventually answered his hardest question—what does it mean to be a *Christian* philosopher?—thus fulfilling one of the reasons he made the painful transition from Calvin College to the University of Notre Dame. Pursuing these four activities with a Christian starting point enables the Christian philosopher to be, well, *Christian*, with all the "autonomy," "integrity," and "courage" that requires.

Third, Plantinga made good on perhaps the most difficult aspect of his advice: to *start with* a Christian point of view (and not just talk about it). Clearly, Plantinga found this difficult to do. In his impressively broad body of work, he only did it twice: *Warranted Christian Belief* and "Supralapsarianism." But when he did start with distinctive Christian doctrine, the argument was interesting and original. Had anyone ever appealed to the Holy Spirit's work as satisfying the demands of a defensible epistemology? No. Had anyone ever appealed to Incarnation, atonement, and supralapsarianism to reduce the perplexity of the Problem of Evil? No. Plantinga would no doubt urge others to enter into this challenging work to which he has contributed.

Fourth, because Plantinga's argument from method to content is a *good* argument, we Christian philosophers can appeal to it (both now and in the future) as a way of shoring up faith in our calling. Loyalty to God, and a desire to serve our Christian community, matters to how we go about our work, and for which work we do. "The Christian philosopher does indeed have a responsibility to the philosophical world at large;

---

45. Plantinga, "Supralapsarianism".

but his fundamental responsibility is to the Christian community, and finally to God".[46] And Plantinga's method isn't restrictive, but expansive, and liberating. Should I wield philosophy as a tool, in the service of theology? Yes, philosophy can be used to vindicate and support theology (apologetics), help us better understand theology (philosophical theology), and expose bad philosophy as bad theology (Christian philosophical criticism). Should I regard philosophy as an intrinsically valuable subject in its own right? Yes, and theology can be a tool that helps us develop philosophical theories on a range of traditionally philosophical topics (positive Christian philosophy). Plantinga's method gives us a reason to do all these things.

"Advice" provides the theoretical underpinnings for expanding the task of Christian philosophy in the direction later sketched in "Augustinian." It provides a precis of Plantinga's later career. It was clearly crucial for Plantinga's philosophical development, both in theory and in practice. I hope my analysis of it goes some way to making it crucial for our development as well if we are Christian philosophers.

---

46. Plantinga, "Advice," 262.

21

A PLEA TO CHRISTIAN PHILOSOPHERS: FROM ONE WHO CARES ABOUT PHILOSOPHY BUT IS NOT ONE OF YOU

Christopher Woznicki

Fuller Theological Seminary; Jonathan Edwards Center at Gateway Seminary

When I first set foot onto UCLA's campus, with its Romanesque Revival style architecture and green rolling hills, I was in awe. Even as a freshman I knew that at the end of my four years studying physiological science I would be going to medical school (hopefully still at UCLA) so that one day I could serve as a medical missionary. From a young age God had impressed upon my heart a desire to serve and reach those who had not yet heard the gospel. I remember having dreams about being a missionary in places that had not yet heard the good news. The *missio Dei*—God's mission to reconcile humanity to himself—was on my heart, so becoming a medical missionary seemed like a really good way to participate in God's mission. My plan was set! I was going to be a medical doctor! I thought it was a great plan, but I forgot one thing: "A person's heart plans his ways but the Lord determines his steps" (Prov 16:9).

I planned on going to medical school but I quickly found that a weakness that was easy for me to cover up in High School would derail my plans. I was terrible at math. Maybe my brain just wasn't wired for doing math...at least that is what I would tell myself while struggling. Calculus, Physics, and Organic chemistry wrecked me. I received grades in those classes that I had never seen in my entire life. Those letter grades were a matter of knowledge by description and certainly not knowledge by acquaintance for me! At that point, my academic advisor counseled me to try some other classes out. So, I looked through the catalog in search for a general education course that would help me fulfill my graduation requirements. That's when I stumbled upon Phil 7—Philosophy of Mind. I took that class, and I was hooked! It was such a change of pace from my other courses. The next quarter I decided to take a Medieval Philosophy course with Calvin Normore—interestingly enough the TA for that class was none other than fellow contributor to this volume, Tom Ward. My 19-year-old mind was blown. There I was at UCLA studying Augustine, Aquinas, Anslem, and Abelard. I was doing philosophical theology at UCLA—a secular, state university! At that point I decided: I want to be a philosopher.

With the encouragement of some of my pastors (even though some other Christians I knew kept throwing Colossians 2:8 in my face), I changed majors. I spent the rest of my time at UCLA focused on philosophy. In my courses were assigned Geach and van Inwagen on the Trinity, Craig on the Kalam Argument, Robert Adams on Divine Command Theory, and Plantinga on necessity. In other courses we discussed the ontological argument, the implications of the beatific vision for epistemology, how Berkely's idealism affected Christology, and how Anselm's "On the Fall of Satan" sheds light on free will and moral responsibility. I was privileged to have a number of professors who were either committed Christians, or at the very least very sympathetic to Christian intellectual history. I would be remiss to fail to mention John Carriero's influence upon me, especially in regard to early modern philosophical theology.

Although I had resolved to be a philosopher, I had no idea what it meant to be a Christian philosopher. Yes, I was studying philosophy and thinking about theological topics. But what did it mean to be a Christian philosopher? If this was to be my path, I figured that I should at the very least know what it entails. The answer to that question came providentially. Back then I had a habit of wandering the halls of the philosophy floor in Dodd Hall. On the third floor of Dodd, down the hall from the reading room, someone—to this day I don't know who—would dispose of old philosophical journals. They'd be placed on a table, along with other books that were being discarded, with a sign that read: "Free: Take as Many as You Like." As a poor college student I read that sign as an instruction to take *everything* on the table. I'd often find old issues of *Mind*, *Synthese*, *Canadian Journal of Philosophy*, etc. I'd spend time reading articles on topics that I probably would not have come across in my studies. One time however, I found a pile of *Faith and Philosophy*. Eureka! I had hit the jackpot! There were two issues in that pile of *Faith and Philosophy* that shaped my understanding of Christian philosophy.

One of those issues, as you can probably guess, was the issue that contained Plantinga's "Advice to Christian Philosophers." As I read Plantinga's words it was as though I was being given a charge going forward. Display autonomy Plantinga instructed me. Display integrity or "integrality" he advised. Be courageous, be bold, don't be afraid to do philosophy as a Christian. This final piece of advice rang especially loud in my ears. I finished out my time at UCLA unafraid to be the rare Christian student in the department. I knew that as a Christian I didn't have to fear being intellectually inferior. Christianity was a robust intellectual system. Some of the greatest minds in the history of philosophy were devout, Jesus loving, Christians. I didn't have to be apologetic for my faith. Neither did I have to be combative. I could boldly and courageously be a Christian doing philosophy. I would go on to show my classmates that Christians need not be dunces. Christians can be thoughtful. Despite the stereotypes, Christians need not leave their minds at the door when they decide to follow Jesus. I have Plantinga and his advice to thank for this. Finally, regarding Plantinga, I should say that one summer I enrolled to take summer courses at Notre Dame. I had been in communication with Alvin about taking a directed study with him. Unfortunately, summer didn't work well, though he invited me to come visit him as soon as I arrived. Due to a family emergency I had to withdraw that summer and never set foot in South Bend.

The other issue contained Peter van Inwagen's essay, "Some Remarks on Plantinga's Advice." His final piece of advice stood out to me in a far different way than Plantinga's. While Plantinga's advice encouraged me to do Christian philosophy, van Inwagen's tempered my ambitions. He writes, "Don't suppose that philosophy is terribly important."[1] I wish more Christian philosophers would hear that line! Not because philosophy deals with trivialities but because it is a penultimate good. In a line that proved to be controversial he wrote:

> I think the following thesis is one that we should all take seriously: the earthly works of Augustine and Aquinas that are remembered in heaven are not their writings; they are acts unknown to history, acts that the earthly memory of which perished when the last people who knew Augustine and Aquinas in his life died.[2]

While this piece of advice *might* be stated too strongly, the sentiment has always stuck with me through *all* of my writing and research. The

---

1. Peter van Inwagen, "Some Remarks on Plantinga's Advice," *Faith and Philosophy* 16 (1999): 172. See also his chapter in this volume.
2. van Inwagen, "Some Remarks on Plantinga's Advice," 172.

task of loving people well is significantly more important than any mere intellectual exercise. If my intellectual endeavors help me love others well, then they are worthwhile. If not, they are, as Paul would have said, "only a noisy gong or clanging cymbal" (1 Cor 13:1).

With these two pieces of advice in mind I proceeded through my philosophy program. Before I graduated in 2010, I knew I had to make some decisions about what I would do next in my life. I really enjoyed doing philosophy but still had the burden of the *mission Dei* on my heart. So, I figured that I should do philosophy of religion, that way I could be on mission at a secular university. But I knew that in order to do that well I would have to know theology well. This led me to Fuller Seminary. Eventually I took my first systematic theology course with Oliver Crisp. What I remember most about that class was how much my philosophical training fed into our theological discussions. It was almost as though all that I learned—from concepts like identity to mereology to necessity to speech act theory—while doing analytic philosophy served as a resource to draw from when doing theology. Ideas about identity and mereology immediately made their way into Trinitarian discussions. Necessity informed my understanding of perfect being theology. Speech act theory contributed to debates about the nature of Scripture. Analytic philosophy was being used as a tool for doing theology! This was radically different from my encounters with systematic theology, which seemed to take a concordance or proof-text like approach to the task.

Despite providentially stumbling onto a way of doing theology that aligned with my love of philosophy, I still had the burden of the *missio Dei* in the back of my mind. Thankfully I was able to put all the pieces of my journey together. My burden for mission, my love for analytic philosophy, and a call to equip the church all met at Fuller's "Analytic Theology for Theological Formation" project. Analytic theology, rather than philosophy, is where the Lord led me in his providence. Analytic theology proved to be the best way for *me*, Christopher Woznicki, to participate in God's plan to make himself and the gospel known throughout the world. Thus, I am not a philosopher, though I love philosophy. I am a theologian who cares deeply about philosophy. So as someone who cares about philosophy but is not a philosopher, I am making a plea.

1. A Plea to Christian Philosophers

To Christian philosophers: be philosophers! Do not be ersatz theologians. Be genuine philosophers. Be surefooted in theology. But then be philosophers!

Those familiar with the writings of Nicholas Wolterstorff will feel as though these words sound familiar. These words—if you've caught the reference—are actually a riff on his final charge in "To Theologians From One Who Cares About Theology but is Not One of You."[3] In this essay, originally delivered to the Luce Consultation on Theological Scholarship in 2003 Wolterstorff offers some advice to a group of theologians. Wolterstorff begins with an autobiographical account. He actually set out to become a theologian! That was the path that he thought he would be following. Providentially he ended up becoming a philosopher. In some ways his story feels like my story—He felt drawn to one discipline and ended up in another. However, our path has been flipped; I felt drawn to philosophy and ended up doing theology. In both cases there is a genuine admiration and, dare I say love, for the other discipline. There's also a lot of cross disciplinary work involved. Though his list of publications and influence obviously eclipses my own! Still as one who loves philosophy, but is not a philosopher, once again I offer the following plea:

> Be philosophers! Do not be ersatz theologians. Be genuine philosophers. Be surefooted in theology. But then be philosophers.

My plea, from an analytic theologian to Christian philosophers—of the non-theological variety—is to keep pressing forward working on non-theological topics because the analytic theological task depends on your work.

2. The Nature of Analytic Theology

What is analytic theology? If I had a nickel every time someone asked that question... A very simple definition is that "analytic theology is just the activity of approaching theological topics with the ambitions of an analytic philosopher in a style that conforms to the prescriptions of analytic philosophical discourse."[4] To put it even more simply it's theology that engages with analytic philosophical literature and is done in the style of analytic philosophy. I find that even this simple, and intuitive, definition requires some unpacking.

The term has two parts, "analytic" and "theology." Simple enough! The analytic project has a certain style. The style is pretty easy to identify.

---

3. The title, advice, and my general sentiment, is a riff on Nicholas Wolterstorff's essay, "To Theologians: From One Who Cares about Theology But is Not One of You," *Theological Education* 40 (2005), 79-92.

4. Michael C. Rea, "Introduction," in *Analytic Theology: New Essays in the Philosophy of Theology* (Oxford University Press: 2009), 7.

You sort of know it when you see it. If you've read any analytic theology, you'll probably notice a common style. Its style is characterized by logical rigor, clarity, and parsimony of expression. Mike Rea talks about writing philosophical positions and conclusions in sentences that can be formalized and logically manipulated.[5] I don't think that necessarily characterizes analytic theology, though I'd say that in principle much—though not all—of the content should be able to be characterized in such a way. But "analytic" isn't just a style. "Analytic" also refers to its engagement with analytic philosophical literature and the intellectual culture that has formed specifically around analytic philosophy. William Wood, has argued, most convincingly, that it is best to think of the "analytic" aspect of this phrase as referring to an intellectual culture.[6] There's a long history of analytic philosophy's relationship to Christianity—its early stage was not very friendly toward Christianity to say the least—but eventually more and more philosophers like Plantinga, Alston, and Leftow began to make significant contributions to non-theological fields of philosophy as well as to Christian thinking about philosophical questions. These philosophers—among others—paved the way for the mainstreaming of Christians doing philosophical theology. So now, we had a generation of Christians who were not only okay with, but were enthusiastic about engaging with analytic philosophy. It was a small leap from that point to the point where we began to see philosophers engage with questions specific to Christian theology and theologians to engage with philosophical literature. Plantinga's "Advice" played a significant role in that transition!

Yet "analytic theology" isn't just "analytic," it's "theology!" Theology, we're often told is just "God-talk": theo - logos. At least that's what I was told growing up. But that's too simplistic. What are theologians doing and what makes that different from what philosophers of religion are doing? After all, both are addressing questions about God and are thus engaged in "God-talk." That's actually a question that has generated a lot of conversation among analytic theologians like Andrew Torrance, Jonathan Rutledge, and Max-Baker Hytch, just to name a few. I take it that Andrew Chignell is on to something when he writes that philosophy of religion typically constructs arguments in ways that anyone will be able to feel their force on the basis of reason alone but that theology appeals to sources and topics that go beyond merely human cognitive faculties.[7] In other words, I take it that philosophy engages with topics that can be thought about

---

5. Rea, "Introduction," 5–6.
6. William Wood, *Analytic Theology and the Academic Study of Religion* (Oxford University Press, 2021).
7. Andrew Chignell, "'As Kant has Shown…': Analytic Theology and the Critical Philosophy," in *Analytic Theology: New Essays in the Philosophy of Theology* (Oxford University Press, 2009), 119.

using common human resources like reason and experience. Theology engages with sources of reflection that go beyond what is common to all human beings. Still, theology is more than just about which sources of authority are being used. Theology, is in part defined by what it seeks to do and what it's object of study is. William Ames wrote that "theology is the doctrine or teaching of living to God."[8] When analytic theology functions as *Christian* analytic theology—as opposed to mere analytic theology, or even Islamic analytic theology, or Jewish analytic theology, or Wiccan analytic theology (though I am no expert on those other ways of doing analytic theology), or even philosophy of religion—it will draw upon the sources of divine revelation and Christian tradition and it will keep in mind the end of theology which is to live toward God. Finally, I would add one more thing to my understanding of analytic theology. To be truly theological, it must make God the object of its study. Theology, in my opinion, is not merely the study of what humans have written about God. That's a valuable academic discipline, but it's not theology. Theology has God as its proper object of study. Tom McCall hits the nail on the head when he says that "the task of the theologian is not merely to say things about God (or God-and-everything)—it is to speak truly of God (so far as we can) and to do it in a way that celebrates the glory of God's being and actions."[9] This is what John Webster called "theological theology" and T. F. Torrance called "scientific theology." All this to say, I would characterize analytic theology as follows:

> Christian analytic theology is a way of doing systematic theology—which is a discipline that 1) engages with divine revelation and Christian tradition, 2) is directed toward the end of living with and for God, 3) and takes the Triune God and all things in relation to God, as its proper object of study—that utilizes the tools, methods, and resources of analytic philosophy.

Some parts of this definition will prove to be controversial for some analytic theologians. They will have a different understanding of what "theology" is. A Christian theologian will have a different understanding of theology than a Jewish theologians, Muslim theologian, or neo-pagan theologian. Even then Christian theologians will disagree about what theology is! But this is *my* plea to Christian philosophers. So I'll leave it at that…[10]

---

8. William Ames, *The Marrow of Theology*, trans. John Dykstra Eusden (Labyrinth, 1968), 77.
9. Thomas H. McCall, *An Invitation to Analytic Christian Theology* (IVP Academic, 2015), 170.
10. For the bulk of the content in this section see Christopher Woznicki, "Analytic Theology & Jonathan Edwards in a Baptist Context" *Journal for Baptist Theology and Ministry* 20 (2023): 117-120.

3. The Sources Analytic Theologians Use

Christian theologians have always employed philosophical reasoning. I hope that isn't a controversial statement! We assume the law of non-contradiction, we assume the laws of logic like *modus ponens* and *modus tollens*, we think carefully about how conclusions follow from premises, we examine our presuppositions, etc. But there is also substantive content that comes from philosophical engagement. Terms like "person" and "essence" in Trinitarian theology or "nature" in Christology" are loaded with philosophical content. As David Briones has said when thinking about Paul's relationship to philosophy, "We all are necessarily shaped by the social, historical, political, religious, and philosophical factors at work in every day life."[11] That means that philosophical concepts will necessarily work their way into our theological language. Because we're humans living in a historical context we won't be able to avoid that! We ought to consider how philosophical assumptions cohere with theological convictions. But analytic theologians engage with philosophy in more intentional ways. We use analytic philosophy in a systematic way to do theology. We follow in the footsteps of Augustine who famously wrote:

> The Egyptians possessed idols and heavy burdens, which the children of Israel hated and from which they fled; however, they also possessed vessels of gold and silver and clothes which our forebearers, in leaving Egypt took for themselves in secret, intending to use them in a better way… In the same way, pagan learning is not entirely made up of false teachings and superstitions… it contains some excellent teachings, well suited to be used by truth, and excellent moral values… The Christian therefore, can separate these truths from their unfortunate associations, take them away, and put them to their proper use for the proclamation of the gospel.[12]

In many ways analytic theology is just engaged in Augustine's project of "plundering the Egyptians." We do "theological theology" but we pick and choose which vessels of gold and silver we might use fruitfully. As theologians we engage with all the traditional sources of theology: scripture, creeds, confessions, personal experience, etc. but we also make use of analytic philosophy—not just analytic philosophy of religion! Analytic philosophy of religion is extremely useful to the analytic theologian! That should be quite obvious. The work of Richard

---

11. David Briones, "An Introduction," in *Paul and the Giants of Philosophy*, eds. Joseph Dodson and David Briones (IVP Academic, 2019), 1.
12. Augustine, *On Christian Doctrine*, II.xl.60–1.

Swinburne, Paul Helm, Jonathan Kvanvig, and Jerry Walls, has made immense contributions to analytic theology. These Christian philosophers are resourcing analytic theologians. But analytic theology *needs* more than just philosophy of religion to work with. Analytic theology doesn't just plunder the "gold" vessels! It plunders the "silver" vessels as well! We need philosophers who make the "gold" of philosophy of religion and the "silver" of non-religious philosophy! I know how this might sound. It might sound as though I'm saying philosophy of religion is more valuable than non-religious philosophy, after all gold is more expensive than silver! That's far from my intention, though I think many of us who grew up within evangelicalism carry an implicit sacred-secular divide that would rank philosophy of religion as more "godly" or "useful pastorally" than non-religious philosophy. This is unfortunate, but that's a different topic for someone else to write a different essay on advice to Christian philosophers. So let me strengthen my plea to Christian philosophers to be genuine philosophers who work on non-theological philosophy. The analytic task depends on your work!

4. Plundering "Silver Vessels"

By no means are Christian philosophers the "Egyptians" in Augustine's imagery. As Christian philosophers you don't produce philosophical work that simply gets "plundered." As a Christian philosopher I would think that among your various ends is God's glory, even the *mission Dei*. As an analytic theologian I would encourage some of you to intentionally decide what topics to work on with the thought that such topics may be useful to Christians who will pick up your work and think through their theological implications. This is different from thinking that your work must *directly* be theological. It might not. But your work might get picked up by people like me who do analytic theology, and I will be so grateful for it. For example, I can think of several philosophers who work on the topic of forgiveness, though not specifically theologically, just because the theme is important to them as a Christian. For a moment, set aside any thoughts of motivation. Let me provide you a couple of examples of where I've benefited from non-philosophy of religion philosophical work.

One of my areas of research is the doctrine of atonement. I've delved quite a bit into the philosophical literature on the topic, especially, penal substitution. One of the most important questions in this conversation concern's the nature of punishment. What are the necessary and sufficient conditions for punishment? There's quite a bit of debate about whether punishment has expressive function. Some of the most important literature on this specific topic has nothing to do with explicitly theological concerns. Anthony Flew, Stanley Benn, H. L. A. Hart, and especially Joel Feinberg have had significant impact on my own work on the topic. To my knowledge, none of these writers had theological motivations for their work on the nature of punishment. But what if a Christian who is a philosopher did have theological motivations for deciding to work on this topic? She might decide, "I'm going to work on issues related to the nature of punishment as a way to help out the theologians. I won't deal with theories of atonement myself, but maybe I can help theologians who do that!" Personally I would benefit from such work. Careful philosophical work on positive/negative retributivism would be extremely helpful for theologians who work on penal substitution. So often I find theologians being sloppy with their concept of retributive justice. I could provide a long list of topics that are useful to me as a theologian working on the doctrine of atonement. I need the help of non-Christian analytic philosophers to do some of this work! I would also love it if some of my Christian philosopher friends picked up some of this work knowing that it would be useful to theologians, not necessarily because the topics might be trendy in contemporary philosophy, but because they are also useful to the theological task. Such philosophers would be making their own contribution to the larger philosophical community *and* they would be making a contribution that analytic theologians can use.

So, I make my plea: please continue to do work on non-theological philosophy! Keep working on group ontology! I know of analytic theologians working on ecclesiology that need your work! Keep working on action theory. Theologians who do work on atonement have found this field especially fruitful. Work on philosophy of forgiveness, corporate responsibility, group ontology, political pluralism, law, epistemology, non-classical logic. All of these have all figured in to recent discussions in analytic theology. Christians have always needed non-theological philosophy to carry on in their theological work. We can look back to theologians of past eras as examples. In previous work I've highlighted how Jonathan Edwards might even qualify as a proto-analytic theologian. In his theological treatises, and even his sermons, you see the analytic virtues of logical rigor, clarity, and parsimony of expression. And just like analytic theologians he loves definitions! More importantly—for our purposes here—he's thoroughly engaged with the contemporary philosophical literature of his day and that engagement makes its way into how he thinks about theological topics like original sin, creation, and aesthetics. He was influenced by Locke, appears to engage with Malebranche, and is thoroughly familiar with the work of the Cambridge Platonists. It's hard to imagine Edwards without the influence of non-theological philosophy. The situation is no different for analytic theologians today, we need good philosophy to be done on non-theological topics to carry out our task.

5. A Final Plea to Christian Philosophers

Some reader out there might be weighing her options for which kind of philosophy she wants to pursue. Will she follow in the steps of some of her philosophical heroes like J. P. Moreland, Marilyn Adams, William Lane Craig, or Eleonore Stump and do philosophical theology or even philosophy of religion? These figures might have been her gateway into philosophy. There is certainly value in doing philosophical theology or philosophy of religion as a Christian philosopher. The value of this kind of philosophy is probably clear to many, even those outside of the academy. As one who does theology but uses, and cares about philosophy, I would ask her to consider making non-theological philosophy a priority. The theological community needs you. I would ask that you would be sure footed in theology so that you can know what topics might be useful to people like me. I would ask that you would continue to engage in dialogue with theologians so you can be aware of what might be useful for us. Inhabit the spaces of theologians. Theologians ought to do the same for you! As Christians engaged in scholarly study we have a shared task. Together we can join in the shared task of pursuing truthful ways of describing the triune God and the world he has made.

22

BROADENING PLANTINGA'S ADVICE

Eric T. Yang

Santa Clara University

I came upon Alvin Plantinga's "Advice to Christian Philosophers" twenty years after it had been published. The advice he provided has functioned like a trellis for me in my philosophical growth and development over the last twenty years. In short, his advice to Christian philosophers was that we should display more autonomy, display more integrity, and display more courage or self-confidence. I don't disagree with this advice. But in the forty years since his advice was published, the landscape and situation for Christian philosophers in academia has transformed. In light of that, I offer some suggestions of broadening Plantinga's advice to Christian philosophers.

Consider first the advice to display more autonomy. In approaching philosophical inquiry, Plantinga states that what is needed "is more independence, more autonomy with respect to the projects and concerns of the non-theistic philosophical world."[1] The philosophical world at that time was interested in questions regarding what it takes to convert true belief into knowledge, whether necessary truths can be discovered via experience, or whether free will is compatible with determinism (among many other philosophical questions). Of course these questions may be relevant to philosophical issues that concern Christians, but Plantinga's advice allowed us to imagine a world where Christian philosophers can ask and attempt to answer questions that arise from the center of Christian beliefs. Whether his advice was causally efficacious

---

[1] Alvin Plantinga, "Advice to Christian Philosophers," *Faith and Philosophy* 1 (1984): 255.

in bringing about philosophical works on Christian philosophy or not, the fact is that not too long after there was a significant uptick on research done in specifically Christian philosophy of religion, which has led to the prevalence of Christian analytic theology today (enough so that there are academics today who decry such works and wish for its disappearance). And I am a beneficiary of this rise in Christian philosophy of religion and Christian analytic theology, as I have made a career out of writing on Christian doctrines related to the doctrine of the Trinity, the incarnation, the atonement, resurrection, and heaven and hell. Whereas Christian philosophers in the 20th century would have had great difficulty publishing on such topics while being taken seriously for doing so, the landscape for Christian philosophers today is much friendlier to those writing on these Christian topics because of our Christian forebears; and to them all—including Plantinga—I am ever grateful.

The display of autonomy, however, needs to be properly balanced with the display of more reliance and dependence. Intellectual progress would not occur if everyone had to work only on their own projects. Relying on and learning from others is critical for making advances in many areas. Plantinga, of course, was fully aware of this, as he clarified that he did not "mean for a moment to suggest Christian philosophers have nothing to learn from their non-Christian and non-theist colleagues: that would be a piece of foolish arrogance," and he did not "mean to suggest that Christian philosophers should retreat into their own isolated enclave, having as little as possible to do with non-theistic philosophers."[2] So his advice is compatible with learning from others in the larger philosophical community.

However, there seem to be some who identify as Christian philosophers but who have siloed themselves off from the community of non-Christian philosophers. When looking at the bibliography of their works, one will find mostly Christian thinkers, and in some cases, primarily sources produced by Christian publishers. Indeed, some works by Christians who are familiar with philosophy sometimes sound triumphalist, thereby giving apologetics a bad name since it appears as though the aim is to win debates rather than to engage in honest inquiry. The isolation and triumphalism exhibited is not unique to Christians interested in philosophy (as it happens to many others in different groups too), but we Christians should not succumb to these tendencies.

Moreover, a display of autonomy can also be taken too far so as to forget about the wisdom and the insights of the past. It is not uncommon for

---

2. Plantinga, "Advice to Christian Philosophers," 270.

theologians to criticize philosophers for discussing and reflecting on Christian doctrines and ideas while neglecting or ignoring the historical development of these doctrines and ideas. As Eleonore Stump advises, "Christian philosophers should be willing to put some time and effort into learning about the history of Christian philosophy and theology."[3] This advice may be extended to include the contributions from global theology and philosophy, as the diversity of historical thinkers and ideas can only be of benefit to our pursuit of understanding God's revelation to us. It seems that Christian philosophers today are more sensitive to this, but it is good to remind ourselves from time to time.

The second advice Plantinga gave to Christian philosophers is to display more integrity, that is, to be more whole in their philosophical pursuits. The worry generating this advice seems to have been over a kind of fragmentation that may occur in a Christian philosopher, where someone may be pious in their Christian commitments when they are at church or in their individual devotional life, but their approach to philosophical investigation may be such that there is no trace or semblance of being a Christian in their assumptions or their general approach to particular philosophical topics. Rather than pretending that we are atheists or agnostics, Plantinga avers that we have a right to begin our philosophical investigations with a belief in God, just as we have a right to assume the existence of the past or the deliverances of contemporary physics.[4] Accordingly, Plantinga states that Christians need not "assimilate what is current or fashionable or popular by way of philosophical opinion and procedures."[5]

It is worth noting that some of Plantinga's examples in the original article are a bit problematic. For example, he discusses the topic of whether free will is compatible with causal determinism, and he claims that a Christian, given her commitments, should endorse an incompatibilist or libertarian account of human freedom. However, this seems to ignore the Christian philosophers and theologians who endorse the compatibility of causal determinism and human freedom, and this is especially so for those in the Reformed tradition, which is the Christian tradition with which Plantinga most closely associates himself.

No doubt the display of integrity should apply when addressing some questions, such as whether God exists or whether miracles are possible. But similar to Plantinga's poorly chosen example, some Christian philosophers take certain philosophical views as ones that Christians must

---

3. Eleonore Stump, "Orthodoxy and Heresy," *Faith and Philosophy* 16 (1999): 159.
4. Plantinga, "Advice to Christian Philosophers," 260.
5. Plantinga, "Advice to Christian Philosophers," 269.

endorse in order to be Christian, and that rejecting them for alternative views somehow compromises their integrity. For example, I have heard it said (and have read it written) that Christians must be substance dualists about human persons or that they must embrace a classical theistic conception of God in order to avoid falling into atheism. However, there have been in the past and the present Christians who have not sacrificed integrity or capitulated to social pressures in their acceptance of some materialist view about human persons or in their rejection of classical theism for some (so-called) personalist view of God. We should be cautious in how we draw the line in the sand between which views are acceptable as Christians and which views are not.

However, by and large, Plantinga's second advice has made it easier for me to bring my Christian assumptions to bear when working on problems related to Christian doctrines such as the resurrection or the atonement. And in a way, it has allowed me to explore distinctively Christian solutions to metaphysical puzzles related to the composition and persistence of material objects. However, as noted many years ago by Peter van Inwagen, much of philosophical inquiry does not seem to overlap with Christianity (or at least with Christian doctrines) in any significant way.[6] Whether names have their referent as their meaning, whether any plurality of objects compose some further object, whether pragmatic considerations can encroach upon the epistemic status of a belief, or whether exemplars are fundamental to our understanding of other moral concepts can all be addressed without our Christian beliefs and assumptions impacting what view we hold or how we methodologically approach these topics.

Finally, Plantinga advises that Christians display more courage or self-confidence, especially as they put their faith and trust in the Lord. As Plantinga rhetorically asks, "should we be intimidated by what the rest of the philosophical world thinks plausible or implausible?" The answer is supposed to be a resounding *No*. The example that Plantinga provides regarding the need for more courage was in the Christian response to verificationism, which broadly speaking was the view that claimed that a statement is meaningful only if it is analytically true or is empirically verifiable. Christians assert statements such as "God loves us" and "God hears my prayers." But according to verificationism, these statements, and many others used by Christians (and other religious people), turn out to be meaningless since they are neither analytically true nor empirically verifiable. Plantinga notes that Christians should exhibit self-confidence

---

6. Peter van Inwagen, "Some Remarks on Plantinga's Advice," *Faith and Philosophy* 16 (1999): 171.

in the face of verificationism since these statements are clearly meaningful for Christians.[7]

Now I have only heard stories of what it was like for Christians in academia in the early and middle periods of the twentieth century. And I am sometimes baffled by the popularity of verificationism in its heyday, though hindsight is twenty-twenty (as they say). And I do not know if Christian philosophers were actually exhibiting a lack of courage in their failure to criticize verificationism or in their willingness to entertain it. Perhaps it was open-mindedness, or perhaps it was a lack of interest, or a lack of interest in entering or interacting with philosophers in certain areas of specialties that were somewhat hostile to the Christian faith. I don't know; I only know what people have told me about that era.

Regardless, I again agree with Plantinga that Christians should be courageous, though I think that the need to display courage is true for all human beings, no matter what their religious stance is. However, such courage and self-confidence should be tempered by the need for Christian philosophers to display more humility. I of course believe that the need to be (intellectually and morally) humble is true for all human beings, no matter what their religious stance is. However, humility as a virtue is, in many ways, distinctively Christian—or if not, it has at least been heavily emphasized within the Christian tradition. Self-confidence can easily slide into vainglory or problematic forms of pride, whether in one's own individual abilities and achievements or in the merits of the group to which one belongs. While Christians will claim to be in possession of the revelation that is requisite for knowing God in the fullest way available on this side of death, primarily through the knowledge of God through Jesus Christ and his Holy Spirit, this does not entail that Christians do not hold false beliefs, nor does it entail that Christians are intellectually superior to others. We can learn from others, including non-Christian philosophers.

Indeed, we may learn from those with whom we have strong disagreement. Even if we reject certain claims, interaction and sincere dialogue with opposing interlocutors may not only help one become a better philosopher, but it may even help one become a better Christian. We may take atheism to be false, but humbly learning from atheist philosophers has helped me become a better philosopher, a better Christian philosopher, and a better Christian. My self-confidence in the truth of theism should not preclude honest and humble engagement with non-Christians. Humility will help Christian philosophers from being too dismissive and thereby miss out on friendships, associations, and mutually

---

7. Plantinga, "Advice to Christian Philosophers," 258.

beneficial dialogue and learning that happens when people who disagree inquire together.

Plantinga's advice to Christian philosophers focused primarily on the content of what Christian philosophers should consider. The advice, then, helps with regards to what Christian philosophers should present at conferences or publish in journals and in books, or how Christians should respond to certain philosophical views or attitudes held by non-Christian philosophers. However, I believe it is important for Christian philosophers not only to assess the kinds of content and topics that they should focus on in their scholarship but also to reflect on additional ways in which their discipleship to Christ can impact their engagement in other areas of academic life.

Not only should Christian philosophers exhibit humility when they publish but also when they interact with fellow academics at conferences, workshops, speaking opportunities, or any other event in which they interact with people. The desire for recognition is common among academics. We are even advised to network at these events, which requires seeking out and acquainting ourselves with more notable individuals at these venues. When attending someone else's talk, one's motive for raising a criticism may not be for the purpose of entering into mutual dialogue in the pursuit of truth or understanding but for the purpose of showing off one's philosophical abilities to others in the room. When talking to someone in the lobby, some may be partially paying attention to their conversation partner as they subtly scan the room to check if there is anyone more prestigious. But Christian philosophers should be imitating Christ, and he was one who sought after the neglected and the ones of low social status. Christian philosophers should be motivated to love the people with whom they interact, which can be exhibited by asking questions or making criticisms out of the desire to help the speaker improve their work (which is compatible with offering devastating objections that may show that their claims are false or that their arguments fail). As Christians, we ought "in humility to count others as more significant than yourselves" (Phil 2:3), and that includes showing kindness to academics of any rank, and especially those who are exploited, which oftentimes includes graduate students and others who are more vulnerable in academia.

Furthermore, most academic Christian philosophers will spend a considerable time in the classroom (and this is true for most academic philosophers generally). I have been in many conversations with Christian professors who grumble or lament at the state of education and the capabilities and interests of their students in their classrooms. Several times these complaints are justified, as there are many educational situations that not only fail to be ideal but also place undue labor on faculty with no promise of yielding substantive intellectual growth for students. Yet Christian professors may remind themselves that this was the educational situation that Jesus had to endure with his disciples. Jesus' students were not only slow learners, but they were often obstinate and obtuse, failing to learn the repeated lessons that Jesus both spoke and demonstrated during his time with them. One of Jesus' main titles is "rabbi," which means teacher; and he was a teacher that showed love, compassion, and self-sacrifice. This does not mean Jesus never criticized or rebuked his disciples. When we read the Gospels, we find Jesus sometimes being harsh to his students and sometimes expressing frustration that they are not learning what they should be despite the time they spent with him (cf. Matt 17). However, Jesus neither abandoned them nor gave up on them (rather, most of them abandoned him when it became too difficult or when it appeared that they were at the brink of failing as a movement).

I admit sometimes it is hard to love students who appear to be apathetic or antagonistic. In some quarters, education is becoming a consumer product, where students are paying for a satisfying experience.[8] It is not uncommon for professors to look forward to the holidays or the summer to get "real work" done, which often involves academic research and writing. Such talk can make it seem as though students are getting in the way of doing our real work. But Christian work involves loving God and loving others. For most Christian professors, it is part of our vocation to help students cultivate intellectual skills and virtues. No formula can be given with regards to how to best do this, as it will depend on the institution, department, location, culture, and the students themselves. Perhaps we can lament unjust situations or deplorable conditions (which unfortunately some Christian professors find themselves). But love should be the primary (though not only) motivating factor in our decisions and behavior with respect to students.

This will also apply to other areas in academic life, such as demonstrating love and compassion to colleagues or to members of one's department or school. There are many ways to demonstrate love, especially in seeking justice in areas where there is exploitation or marginalization of certain individuals or groups. Again, the details will differ depending on one's situation and context. This can show up by standing alongside those who are in vulnerable situations, or giving space and opportunity with those who often lack a voice to speak up. Or it may involve being quick to confess and apologize when we make mistakes, or by being quick to forgive when

---

8. I write this recognizing that I am at an institution that, for the most part, has excellent students who care and are open to the liberal arts, and therefore open to learning philosophy.

others wrong us. Whatever it may be, Christian philosophers should be sensitive to the ways in which their fidelity to Christ shows up not just in their published work or conference presentations but also in every other aspect of their academic career.

Finally, it behooves Christian philosophers to make contributions to the Christian life outside of academia, and especially in the church. I often hear Christian philosophers express exasperation at sermons they hear at church because the preacher fails to be philosophically or theologically precise or perspicuous. While preachers may present important truths about the good news of Jesus Christ, their sermons may be cluttered with epistemic or intellectual garbage (that is, irrational, superstitious, or false claims that are intertwined with the transmission of true claims).[9] Christian philosophers will be trained to notice logical mistakes, a lack of clarity and precision, and inconsistent remarks; and it may be difficult to tolerate hearing fallacious reasoning for the umpteenth time from the pulpit. Unfortunately, I am familiar with several stories of Christian philosophers who do not regularly attend church because of this. Many pastors may have received some training in Biblical exegesis and theology (and perhaps even philosophy), but most will likely not be experts or specialists in these areas. Yet as long as the Word is preached (and any other sacraments that belong to one's tradition are observed), there is not much more that is requisite for Christian worship. We do not attend church for an insightful and accurate talk. Indeed, Christian philosophers may be able to be of assistance to their church leaders, either by stepping up into various leadership or supporting roles, or perhaps cultivating a friendship with pastors and ministers that may help them grow in these areas. Good church leaders rely on church members for assistance in the areas in which they lack expertise, whether decorating the church, choosing the sound equipment, or deferring to medical professionals. Similarly, good church leaders may rely on the contributions that Christian philosophers can bring to the table. Rather than scoffing at the sermon, perhaps supportive and constructive feedback from a friend can make some way towards helping Christian church leaders.

One way of doing this is writing for non-academics, especially for those that will benefit an ecclesial community or perhaps one's own Christian community, thereby raising the Christian intellectual culture. This is what motivated my friend Stephen T. Davis and me to write *An Introduction to Christian Philosophical Theology*. The book was published through a Christian press (Zondervan), and given the nature of the book, it in no way was going

---

9. For more on the garbage problem in testimony, see John Greco, "The Transmission of Knowledge and Garbage," *Synthese* 7 (2020): 2867–2878.

to help me in advancing towards promotion in my career. But several years ago, many of my friends who were pastors were asking me about some of the logical puzzles related to the doctrine of the Trinity or the doctrine of the Incarnation, and I would share some of the philosophical approaches and views to these issues. They found such material helpful and wished that there was some accessible resource for it. That sparked the idea of the book, and I asked Steve to join me in this endeavor since we both had one foot in academia and one foot in church ministry. And we have heard from several seminary professors and students about the ways in which it has helped them understand the nuance and complexity of some of these philosophical issues associated with Christian doctrines.

Thankfully, several Christian philosophers are writing such books. But I believe there can be and should be more, along with other ways for Christian philosophers to bring their labor to the larger community of professing Christians. We enter such communities not only to contribute but also to learn, as we all bring what we can for the greater glory of God.

23

CHRISTIAN PHILOSOPHERS FACING THE NON-CHRISTIAN WORLD

Linda Zagzebski

University of Oklahoma

If you are anything like me, you dislike unrequested advice. I will not offer my comments here as advice, but rather as personal reflections on the social and professional roles of philosophers who are Christian. As Christians, we have beliefs that shape our world view and the issues in philosophy we find interesting and worth exploring, and some of us think of ourselves as witnesses to a message of redemption. But as philosophers who are already in the profession or are preparing for it, we probably feel that we must adapt to the norms of professional philosophy. We might not do so if we think that professional norms and expectations conflict with our Christian identity, but that choice has costs. If we choose to teach and write for other Christians, we can strengthen the intellectual trajectory of the Christian faith, but we lose our influence over the non-Christian academy. If instead, we write for secular philosophers, that also has costs. To the extent that we spend our time helping to advance work on topics of interest to non-Christian philosophers, we are not using our talents to advance Christian intellectual concerns. There is the danger that our immersion in an academic field that is mostly non-Christian or even anti-Christian can sap our energy and lead our work farther from our core intellectual beliefs and values and into current philosophical fads.

The choice between writing for Christians and writing for mainstream professional philosophers need not be either/or. I am fortunate to be able to write a lot, and I do both. For other philosophers, the choice can be difficult. Life is short and we cannot do everything worthwhile. In professional writing and teaching, I believe that following personal inclination is not the worst way to make professional choices. Often what we are naturally inclined to do is what we do best, and what we do best most fits our unique professional role. The roles we have as individuals are not all the same. I assume that each reader is in a better position to know their own talents, inclinations, and values than I do. I would not presume to say that any Christian philosopher should change their research projects. But sometimes a Christian philosopher wants to concentrate on distinctively Christian philosophy, but feels pressured by the need to get tenure or the mores of their department to avoid teaching and writing Christian work because that will place them in a philosophical side-show in the opinion of their colleagues. Those people may need the confidence to do what they want to do anyway. Alvin Plantinga's "Advice to Christian Philosophers" was an important motivational stimulus to high level work on important issues in Christian philosophy, and the work that resulted partly from his encouragement made it impossible for non-Christian philosophers to ignore Christian philosophy-- which is not to say that they read the work.

Forty years have gone by since Plantinga's advice. The world has changed; the philosophical profession has changed; the students have changed. My reflections now need to be somewhat different from my reflections forty years ago. At that time, I had ideas that I wanted to pursue both in epistemology and in Christian philosophy. My first book was on the dilemma of freedom and foreknowledge (Oxford University Press, 1991), a book I intended to be read by Christian philosophers. My second book was *Virtues of the Mind* (Cambridge University Press, 1996), a book I expected to be read by epistemologists of any stripe. My subsequent personal choices continued to be a mixture of Christian and secular. *Epistemic Authority* (Oxford University Press, 2012), was a general argument for epistemic authority, based on literature that has nothing to do with Christianity, but I intended to show that the authority of the Church can be defended on grounds accepted by most non-Christian intellectuals. I also wrote two books on my exemplarist moral theory. *Divine Motivation Theory* (Cambridge University Press, 2004) came first, and it was distinctively Christian. *Exemplarist Moral Theory* (Oxford University Press, 2017) came later, and it is a theory constructed to compete with the main ethical theories in the contemporary literature. That theory contains the same core idea as in the first book, but it is both broader in scope and broader in the intended audience. My recent book, *Omnisubjectivity* (Oxford University Press, 2023), is a defense of a divine attribute, but I am currently extending it to general work on consciousness and the place of consciousness in reality as a whole. My early book on foreknowledge has developed into a book on time and fatalist arguments.[1] I did not realize until I wrote these words that I tend to write a Christian version of an issue first, and then broaden it to a book for any philosopher. This was not a conscious choice, and it probably does not have relevance to other Christian philosophers.

I worry about modern intellectual trends. We are being pushed into polarized camps even when there is nothing about the ideas that should be polarizing. Anything we write for a general readership, or which gets the attention of the mainstream press will be scrutinized for its perceived political slant, and we will be labeled with words that skew the views we express. For instance, anybody arguing that abortion is morally problematic must be prepared to be labeled a Right-Wing Republican, a Christian nationalist, and a foe of human rights. I wrote *The Two Greatest Ideas* (Princeton University Press, 2021) in the naïve hope that it would be read by intelligent readers of any political persuasion, and that it could help overcome belief polarization. I did not succeed. I cannot tell who reads it, but most of the attention seems to come from Catholic philosophers or people who are following me for other reasons. I hope that other Christian philosophers will do better. I think now that one of the most important social roles a Christian philosopher can have is to influence the culture through writings and podcasts that reach a large number of people. Again, we do not all have the inclination and the skills to do that, but I'm sure that many Christian philosophers do, and it is even more important now than it was forty years ago.

Epistemic bubbles and echo chambers have recently received a lot of attention because of their pernicious effects on the healthy transmission of ideas. The difference between them is described by Thi Nguyen, who defines an epistemic bubble as a social structure in which relevant voices have been inadvertently left out because people tend to obtain their information from like-minded others, but the agent in a bubble is responsive to evidence from outside the bubble if she encounters it.[2] Most of us live in an epistemic bubble. It is the natural outcome of geographical and professional sorting. An echo chamber is more nefarious. It is a social structure that intentionally excludes and discredits voices from the outside, doubling down on pre-existing views. The polarization of beliefs is an unhappy consequence of echo chambers. Studies have shown that beliefs become more extreme when people only converse with and read

---

1. Forthcoming: *Fatalism and the Logic of Time*, (Oxford University Press, 2024).
2. Nguyen, C. Thi. (2020). "Echo Chambers and Epistemic Bubbles," *Episteme* 17:2 (June), 141–161.

the opinions of those who agree with them and disparage the views of those who disagree with them.

Katherine Furman introduces the notion of an *epistemic bunker*, which she believes can explain the exclusionary structure of an echo chamber.[3] The epistemic bunker is often constructed to offer their members emotional and sometimes physical safety. One reason to retreat into a bunker is fear of losing one's job. Academics usually do not fear that their beliefs make them physically unsafe, but it is common to fear that their beliefs will cause them to fail to get tenure or to fail to get a job in the first place. It is interesting that the hostile tone of postings on social media has expanded to the mainstream press and sometimes even to academic meetings. That exacerbates the sense of being in danger among people who feel that they are attacked. There are publications that are Christian bunkers or Christian intellectual bunkers, and if a Christian philosopher teaches at a Christian institution where their beliefs are welcome, they might retreat into a bunker. But a bunker is counterproductive if they teach at a secular institution, and if they perceive danger, it is more common to hide the beliefs their colleagues will attack. Either way, they are prevented from influencing the broader intellectual culture.

It is pretty clear to me that academics are in an epistemic bubble. Like everyone else, we talk to people like us and read and watch news sources that reinforce our own views. Many academics are also in echo chambers. It is curious that people who would vehemently criticize echo chambers in their profession are often in echo chambers about political issues. Christian academics might be in a bubble or a bubble within a bubble, at least part of the time. They might also be in echo chambers, but they are in a better position than I am to recognize it and respond to it.

Plantinga advised Christian philosophers to unashamedly embrace their pre-philosophical beliefs in their philosophical work. Non-Christian philosophers do that, so why can't we? I agree with that. There is no need to apologize for being a Christian. But nobody likes being scorned, and the scorn is much greater now than it was forty years ago. It is understandable that for Christians with a non-confrontational temperament, living in echo chambers or even bunkers may be necessary for self-protection. I would not deny that for some people, the advantages of being in an echo chamber may be greater than the disadvantages. Venturing into hostile territory is not a duty, and it might not even be wise in some circumstances. But the more interesting question for me is what Christians should do who are well-trained in philosophy and who have the temperament

---

3. Katherine Furman, "Epistemic Bunkers," *Social Epistemology* 37:2 (2023): 197–207.

to publicly utter beliefs that some of their hearers abhor. That is tricky because the hearers may be in their own echo chambers and can become even more hostile when they are faced with beliefs contrary to their own. We are not responsible for other people's echo chambers, but we can have the confidence to avoid our own echo chambers and to try to move out of our bubbles.

How much should we let our beliefs be affected by the beliefs of other people who are very unlike ourselves? I believe that open-mindedness is an important virtue, and it is not the same as being wishy-washy in our beliefs and values. I think of open-mindedness as a stance of eager interest in the many ideas the human mind has produced, and a willingness to let these ideas interact with our own. Hostility shuts down open-mindedness, and when we encounter others who shut their minds to us, it is tempting to shut our minds to them. One of us must be mature enough to counter hostility with sympathy and generosity. If we want to influence them, we must be willing to let them influence us. I think that people are naturally attracted to open-minded people and repelled by close-minded people. That gives those who are open-minded an advantage. We cannot individually do much to counter a hostile culture, but we can become less hostile in our own minds. People eventually become tired of hostility and find the friendly openness of ideological adversaries refreshing.

What about philosophers who are culturally Christian but not devout? I think that they have an important role to play in their scholarly work and teaching. They probably have more overlapping beliefs with non-Christians than more traditional Christians do. I think it is obvious that those of us who are self-described Christians do not all believe exactly the same thing about faith and morals, and when we converse with non-Christian academics, we find many areas of agreement. To begin with, all of us, whether we are orthodox Christians or not, have philosophical positions that we often discuss with other philosophers without needing to bring up any issues that bear on distinctively Christian beliefs. Those conversations build camaraderie with members of the philosophical community. We show them that we are smart and have ideas that they can learn from, and that we are happy to learn from them. Once that is established, we can begin conversations on topics of disagreement, which start from an established stance of sympathy and respect. Christian philosophers who have beliefs that are closer to their secular counterparts than other Christians do will be able to go farther in their exchanges with non-Christians before the conversation ceases. That is why I say that Christian philosophers whose beliefs do not align precisely with established Christian teaching have an important social role in the academic world. I think that it is a mistake to view them as second-class Christians. Philosophers who have one foot in the secular academic world and one foot in the Christian world are an important bridge between the two worlds.

There are different ways of teaching and exchanging ideas. We do it in the classroom, and we do it through writing and speaking. We do it through informal discussions. If we can break down the barriers created by bubbles and echo chambers, we can build a healthy philosophical community in which Christians have a respected part. Accomplishing that is not only up to the Christian, of course. Non-Christian philosophers need to take responsibility for their own bubbles and admit when they are in echo chambers. Individually we do not have much power over the profession, but Christianity emphasizes the importance of personal interactions. Our personal roles rarely extend to influencing large numbers of people, and we need not regret that. Our roles are partly determined by our nature and temperament, and partly by our education and the accident of where we end up in the teaching profession. I realize that most Christian philosophers are doing the best they can in their situation, a situation that was not entirely their choice. Rather than to offer them advice, I prefer to express my admiration for them. We are sisters and brothers in the Christian faith, and sisters and brothers in academic philosophy. There is plenty of room for both.

www.ingramcontent.com/pod-product-compliance
Lightning Source LLC
Chambersburg PA
CBHW062017220426
43662CB00010B/1372